D1483845

About Island Press

Island Press is the only nonprofit organization in the United States whose principal purpose is the publication of books on environmental issues and natural resource management. We provide solutions-oriented information to professionals, public officials, business and community leaders, and concerned citizens who are shaping responses to environmental problems.

In 2004, Island Press celebrates its twentieth anniversary as the leading provider of timely and practical books that take a multidisciplinary approach to critical environmental concerns. Our growing list of titles reflects our commitment to bringing the best of an expanding body of literature to the environmental community throughout North America and the world.

Support for Island Press is provided by the Agua Fund, Brainerd Foundation, Geraldine R. Dodge Foundation, Doris Duke Charitable Foundation, Educational Foundation of America, The Ford Foundation, The George Gund Foundation, The William and Flora Hewlett Foundation, Henry Luce Foundation, The John D. and Catherine T. MacArthur Foundation, The Andrew W. Mellon Foundation, The Curtis and Edith Munson Foundation, National Environmental Trust, National Fish and Wildlife Foundation, The New-Land Foundation, Oak Foundation, The Overbrook Foundation, The David and Lucile Packard Foundation, The Pew Charitable Trusts, The Rockefeller Foundation, The Winslow Foundation, and other generous donors.

The opinions expressed in this book are those of the author(s) and do not necessarily reflect the views of these foundations.

POSITIVE
IMPACT
FORESTRY

POSITIVE IMPACT FORESTRY

A Sustainable Approach to Managing Woodlands

Thom J. McEvoy

Foreword by Senator James Jeffords

ISLAND PRESS

Washington   Covelo   London

Copyright © 2004 Thom J. McEvoy. All rights reserved under International and
Pan-American Copyright Conventions. No part of this book may be reproduced in any
form or by any means without permission in writing from the publisher:
Island Press, 1718 Connecticut Avenue, N.W., Suite 300, Washington, DC 20009.
ISLAND PRESS is a trademark of The Center for Resource Economics.

Library of Congress Cataloging-in-Publication Data

McEvoy, Thomas J. (Thomas James), 1953–
  Positive impact forestry : achieving sustainability on family-owned woodlands / Thom J.
McEvoy ; foreword by Senator Jim Jeffords.
       p. cm.
  Includes bibliographical references (p.).
    ISBN 1-55963-788-9 (cloth : alk. paper) — ISBN 1-55963-788-9 (pbk : alk. paper)
1. Sustainable forestry. 2. Forest management. 3. Forest ecology. I. Title.
  SD387.S87M389 2004
    634.9′2—dc22
                        2003022406

British Cataloguing-in-Publication Data available
Book design: Teresa Bonner
Printed on recycled, acid-free paper
Manufactured in the United States of America
09 08 07 06 05 04 03   10 9 8 7 6 5 4 3 2 1

Epigraph

A forest is not, as is often supposed, a simple collection of trees succeeding each other in long perspective, without bond of union, and capable of isolation from each other; it is, on the contrary, a whole, the different parts of which are interdependent upon each other, and it constitutes, so to speak, a true individuality. Every forest has a special character, determined by the form of the surface it grows upon, the kinds of trees that compose it, and the manner in which they are grouped.

—Jules Clave (1862), as translated by George Perkins Marsh in *Man and Nature*

Contents

Contents   xi

Foreword

At least once a year I get a call from a hiker eager and excited to tell me about a discovery of a relatively large American chestnut in my woodlot. My land is open for others to visit and it is always a pleasure to share the excitement of someone who has observed the forest closely enough to recognize the significance of a single tree. Not that long ago chestnut was one of the most important trees east of the Mississippi River. Now it is often a lone tree, no larger than a sapling, sprouting from the stump of a parent that succumbed to blight less than a century ago. Large chestnuts are now rare and the discovery of one tends to rekindle hope for the future of our forests.

My first home was an old farmhouse, situated mid-mountain at about 1,500 feet on the western flank of Vermont's Green Mountains. The cut-over tract of forest that came with the property was of greater interest to me than the house. Composed of young softwoods, the forest, like the house, had far more potential than current value. Here I could work with a young woods and look forward to making a good forest of it. The rest and relaxation of a day spent working in the woods is, for me, always more reward than labor, and the forest is coming along nicely.

My time in the woods is often punctuated by new discoveries of the interactions of man and nature. The lone chestnut is a reminder of human error. A large sugar maple growing from a cellar hole reminds me that I am not the first person to work these woods. A large spruce, somehow spared from successive logging over the generations speaks of the old growth that once was here, and the historic covered bridge just down the road—crafted mostly from chestnut—signifies the importance of timber and healthy forests to our way of life.

At the time of this writing I am working on legislation to designate additional wilderness areas in the Green Mountain National Forest, excluding all mechanized activity and giving nature as full and complete reign as possible. Why? Because human use of forests may obscure the significant, but subtle value of unmanaged ecosystems. Wilderness is needed as a benchmark against which we can measure and understand the scope of what is reasonable use of forests. To understand the impacts of human use we need some areas where nature is left, as completely as possible, to its own devices. Although foresters often disagree (loudly at times), I am convinced that positive impact forestry requires a portion of our forests to be left alone.

Even so, in most cases, management can improve the forest while providing benefits for society as a whole. I think my woodlot is better off for my tinkering, and my forester agrees. The woods give me heat for my home, occasional income to offset property taxes, and great pleasure from working there. My challenge is to return as much value as I get from the forest. "Unmanaged forests are apt to disappear," according to Professor McEvoy, "gradually converted to other uses far less beneficial than forests."

There seems to be a deep gulf between the convictions of forest ecologists and the claims of woodland managers concerning the real value of forests. Some say woodlands are for timber, wildlife, and other tangible benefits. Others say the real value of forests lies in their ecosystems. Professor McEvoy bridges the chasm in *Positive Impact Forestry* by offering many practical ideas on how we can use forests while protecting, and even improving, their mostly intangible values as ecosystems. "Forest management" is taught in terms of ecosystem integrity as well as resource extraction.

Positive Impact Forestry identifies opportunities to restore and enhance one of this country's most valuable natural resources. Foresters may be allowed to leave the position of defending their work as "low impact" and move to the high ground of promoting their work as "positive impact."

The difference must be more than semantic however, and Thom McEvoy provides the tools to ensure that this is so. Beginning at the roots of forestry, he draws on the teachings of Gifford Pinchot, Aldo Leopold, and others. Forest conservation and stewardship means a woodland owner should consider long-term investment over short-term gain. According to McEvoy, "The essence of Positive Impact Forestry is rooted in a commitment to filling society's needs for forest benefits without disrupting the mechanisms by which ecosystems are sustained."

McEvoy has successfully and convincingly interwoven the philosophical, ethical, and theoretical principles of managing forests for human benefits with the practical, technical, and economic realities facing owners and managers. The pages that follow, I discovered, are a comprehensible guide to sustainable forestry that unifies the best thinking of a wide range of forest advocates, from ecosystem ecologists to forest managers, ornithologists to sportsmen, and preservationists to timber buyers. The common interests of all who rely on forests are healthy, sustainable ecosystems and these are fundamental tenets of positive impact forestry.

Senator James Jeffords
February 2004

Preface

Virtually all of the ideas that have meaning for me were the result of startling moments of clarity. Learning has never been a process of mastering the fundamentals of concept A before applying those principles to concept B, patiently building the capacity to master concept C; which is probably why I never learned to play a musical instrument. As a child, new toys rarely lasted longer than a week before I had taken them apart. If a design was simple enough and logical, I could usually reassemble the toy with only a few parts left over. Occasionally I could get the toy to work again. And sometimes I improved a design, or so I thought. Toys with modular components were far more complicated and it took me a while to figure out the designer never intended anyone to disassemble them. I have no idea how many toys I deconstructed before arriving at that "startling moment of clarity."

Today, for lack of time, I am far less inclined to take things apart but also because virtually everything is modular, never intended to be fixed or taken apart, and I learned my lesson years ago. Now the things I remember most are the epiphanies: the startling moments of clarity, especially those that apply to forests. If designs had not gone modular, I might have had a future in toys, but I chose forestry instead.

The really important concepts about forests—some of which I learned years ago but never completely understood at the time—have arrived during my career as a series of epiphanies, for example, when I realized that the forest management planning concept I learned as a student is ridiculously out of sync with "forest time" and that true stewardship is meaningless unless planning crosses generations. Another more recent epiphany involves a subject I have struggled with for years—forest soils—and my illuminating discovery is this: soils, and the enchantingly complex communities of organisms they support, are far more important to the health and function of forest ecosystems—and far more fragile—than most forest managers know or even suspect.

Some other relevant epiphanies about forests: timber management is simply the act of juggling trade-offs between volumes and values that involve periodic reductions in tree densities; trees die because of inefficiencies; extractive practices that predate the arrival of forestry science have caused more harm to forest ecosystems than foresters are willing to admit; motivations and attitudes of those who own, manage, and use forests are far more important to effect positive impact forestry than are knowledge and skills; plantations are not necessarily forests, despite the presence of trees, but with time they can develop into forests; ad valorem tax policies on forests are ridiculous—the ecological equivalent of exsanguination by a thousand cuts; rotations are far too short on good soils; our agriculturally oriented fixation on yields is unwarranted and not sustainable; and periodic thinning will do more harm than good with poor timing and bad practices. Any one or more of these ideas are easily refuted, especially by those who have come to depend on local wood supplies for their livelihood. Nevertheless, the volume increment benefits from periodic thinning, touted by many forestry professionals as the principal reason why owners should manage forests, are wasted when volume is accumulating on trees that harbor decay pockets from earlier logging injuries.

The inspiration for *Positive Impact Forestry* is based on epiphanies about forests and forestry that I have experienced throughout my life, but mostly during the past thirty-two years as a student and professor of forestry, and as an extension forester at the University of Vermont. The book covers a lot of ground—some foresters would say too much ground. As is so often the case when a body of technical information is condensed and interpreted to make it comprehensible and relevant to nontechnical readers, subject depth is the victim of breadth.

Many people are deserving of thanks for their help with this book, not the least of which are my colleagues—too numerous to mention here—who triggered ideas that are the substance of this work. Special thanks go to Dr. Doug Lantange, director of extension at the University of Vermont, for allowing me time to work on the book; to Dr. Paul Sendak, forest economist with the U.S. Forest Service in Durham, N.H., for reading the entire manuscript and offering many excellent suggestions; and to Mr. Ted Gomes, forest owner and manager on the Big Island in Hawaii, who also read the manuscript, offering suggestions and many words of encouragement throughout the project. Other reviewers include Doug Hart, Don Tobi, Bill Hubbard, Chris Schnepf, and John Shane. Also thanks to Bob Montgomery at *Farming: The Journal of Northeast Agriculture* and the *Forest Products Equipment Journal* for granting permission to extract from articles that appeared in their publications. Thanks to Drs. Alan Strong and Jeffrey Hughes for sharing ideas on how to handle some of the subjects, and to Casey Hayes for preparing one of the more complicated tables and to Darrel Pendris for helping to assemble the literature cited section in the final copy. Most of the illustrations are the work of Marna Grove, of Castleton, Vt. I also want to thank ForestryImages.org for allowing me to use a couple of photos from their vast archive of forestry-related digital photography. Thanks to Brian Stone, Vermont Department of Forests, Parks, and Recreation, for use of the water-quality illustrations. Also, thanks to Drs. David Kittredge, Alan Calfee, Gary Sabourin, and to John Deere Inc. for sharing equipment photos. I also want to thank and acknowledge Dr. David Hoge, the only one of thirty forest ecologists in the United States who responded to a question of mine about information included in table 2.1. Also deserving of thanks and praise is the staff at Island Press; especially Barbara Dean, Executive Editor, for many excellent ideas on how best to tell this story, and to many others for their commitment to excellence and professionalism. Thanks also to Hallie McEvoy, my partner and friend, for allowing us to use one of her many excellent photos for the cover.

Finally, I dedicate the book to James Bruce Engle, one of the most distinguished and remarkable people I have ever met. Born the son of a homesteader and raised in a sod house in eastern Montana, Jim excelled in academics, obtaining degrees from the University of Chicago, Harvard, and Oxford. He is further distinguished as the first Rhodes Scholar to also obtain a Fulbright Scholarship. Following his education was a career of 45 years in public service, first in the Navy during World War II then as diplomat representing the United States in 13 countries, four of which were at the rank of Ambassador.

Our mutual interests in forest wildlife brought us together a few years after his retirement and we have become good friends. Jim served as the first president of Vermont Coverts—Woodlands for Wildlife, Inc., successfully ushering an extension education program into a private, nonprofit organization dedicated to furthering the cause of healthy forests. He is a tireless and highly effective advocate for forestry and wildlife, and both he and his family are committed to healthy forest ecosystems that transcend generations.

When I questioned my choice of careers around the time we met, Jim served as mentor and role model helping me through a period during which I could have easily walked away from forestry and academe. More than anyone else, Jim helped me understand the value of my work and the importance of maintaining commitment to a cause. And, he spawned an epiphany that is at least partially responsible for this book: The future of our forests is in the hands of millions of owners, like Jim, empowered by education to do great things.

Thom J. McEvoy
Bolton Valley, Vermont
1 February 2004

CHAPTER 1

Forestry's Past *Is* Prologue

I had the good fortune years ago while studying forestry to meet a farmer during a road-trip over spring break. Still a year shy of graduation, I felt as though I had already mastered the major concepts of my studies. Upon learning I was a student of forestry the farmer insisted I visit his land nearby, to "look at his timber." Since I had no pressing plans and it sounded interesting, I decided to accept his offer. I felt slightly awkward in doing so, but it occurred to me that I might be bound by some forester's equivalent of the Hippocratic Oath to help this man and his forests.

I followed him a few miles up the road, in the same direction I was going, to a beautifully tended farm. We parked our vehicles in front of the barn and jumped into a beat-up old Ford pickup that had seen better days. The tour started almost as fast as the truck, and I learned that the family owned a section of land (640 acres), about a third of which was dedicated to fresh vegetables, corn silage, pasture, and beef cattle. The rest was woodlands that had been in his family since the area was settled, and his great-grandfather was mostly responsible for clearing the lands dedicated to crops (which seemed plausible since this fellow was old enough at the time to be my grandfather). I could see the woodlot beyond the fields.

No more than five minutes after leaving the barn and proceeding on a well-tended trail, we entered the forest, and I was immediately stunned by

The chapter title, "Forestry's Past Is Prologue" is from *The Tempest*, act 2, scene 1, lines 261–263. Antonio to Sebastian: "We all were sea-swallow'd, though some cast again, / And by that destiny to perform an act / Whereof what's **past is prologue**, what to come, / In yours and my discharge." Wm. Shakespeare, 1564–1616, first published in the First Folio, the collected works of Shakespeare, in 1623.

the stature of trees; these were mostly hardwoods with diameters ranging from two to three feet, but there were also widely scattered stems that were significantly larger. Tree heights were well over 100 feet, except in patches where overstory trees had been carefully harvested over the years. I asked if we could stop and walk around a bit and we did.

The forest floor was covered with a litter layer so deep it was like walking on sponge. With my friend's permission, I carefully pulled back the leaf litter and dug down through humus and a mat of roots, more than 12 inches before reaching mineral soil. After realizing I had never seen anything like this, I carefully backfilled the small hole. A few minutes later (or possibly seconds later, because I had lost track of time) while looking straight up through the canopy high overhead, I felt a strong sense of inadequacy. The farmer had been talking all along and I had not heard a word. I realized that this man who had shared his forest would eventually ask what I thought about it. There was nothing I could say except that it was perfect, and I told him so.

Later, he told me that the only tree cutting on the land was done by family members, using a farm tractor and an arch on wheels that lifted the front end of logs. There were only a few rules that originated with his great-grandfather, passed down from one generation to the next. He alluded to an income- and access-sharing arrangement with brothers and sisters, but the specific formula was never made clear and I thought it inappropriate to ask. A general guideline they followed, however, was to harvest only single trees that likely would not survive another cutting cycle, which I understood to be no more frequent than once every ten years and then only during winter months. An extensive and well-maintained trail system was developed by the family, and in one recent cutting cycle they had harvested more than planned due to mortality following a few years of insect defoliations. Nevertheless, a single tree from his forest, the farmer pointed out, usually sold for more money than an entire acre's worth of wood from his neighbor's land. And the only foresters that had ever been on the land came as visitors, just like me.

From a forestry standpoint, the farmer was harvesting only a small fraction of growth potential, but in large, valuable trees, so I could not argue with the result. It was—and still is—one of the most beautiful forests I have ever seen. It was also only the second time I had seen a relatively undisturbed forest soil, one that had never been tilled or burned or seriously disturbed except for the very light harvesting regime the family used. I wondered about the patriarch who had set this plan in motion more than 150 years earlier, what power held sway over his spawn to ensure the forest was never cut any harder than he thought appropriate. As I think back, there are hundreds of questions that come to mind.

Considering that the family had never employed the services of a forester, it was a significant lesson for a young student of forestry full of hubris—a lesson that has stayed with me for many years and is now fundamental to the concept of positive impact forestry: Knowledge about forests is principally a function of care and respect for land. Good practices are second nature to those who learn respect, especially when lessons come from a parent. For those whose families lack these traditions, respect evolves from learning about forests in other ways, which is the purpose of this book.

On the way back to the barn, the farmer seemed to glow with my compliments until I had exhausted all the superlatives that came to mind. After a few moments of quiet, he praised his great-grandfather who laid down the rules, and then he said that good soils and patience probably had more to do with a healthy forest than anything his family had done. Although I did not doubt his word at the time, having witnessed the product of that philosophy, it was years before I could accept this simple wisdom as a fundamental truth about forests; and I have since witnessed the same phenomenon on forest lands of others that have passed down both the land and a legacy from generation to generation, usually without help from professionals. Undisturbed soils and good practices are fundamental to healthy forest ecosystems, and patience is a virtue of forest owners who manage their lands for timber. Knowledge of forests and respect of the land, good practices, healthy soils, and patience are the essence of positive impact forestry, as described in the chapters that follow.

Evolution of Forest Use and Management

Archeological records from areas known to support forests since the time humans arrived on the scene prove that people have always used forests. But there is a significant difference between using resources and managing them. By definition, management is a process of exerting control for the purposes of allocating benefits. Sophistication in methods, in tools, or in the reasoning of those who endeavor to manage is irrelevant. Management implies control, and control means use and allocation.

No one knows when or where forest use shifted from simply accepting what forests are capable of providing to managing them, but one of the earliest indirect records of management is found in North America. Cores extracted from lake bottoms in Florida reveal pollen layers that would indicate a fairly regular, prehistoric pattern of pine ecosystems gradually replaced by oak forests as climatic conditions changed. Following the last glacial period, nearly ten thousand years ago, much of Florida was covered with hardwood forests of oak interspersed with small patches of prairie (Watts 1971). Beginning about seven thousand years ago, a new pattern emerged: well-established oak/prairie communities were abruptly replaced by pine to a much greater extent and faster than earlier transitions, and more so than could be explained by climate changes alone (Myers 1985).

The onset of this new pattern is believed coincidental with the arrival of humans on the Florida Peninsula. Paleo-Indians of that era were well known for using fire to drive game, a forest management practice initiated seven thousand years ago that hastened the conversion of a fire-prone ecosystem into one that is fire dependent.

Despite the fact that burning probably converted relatively game-rich forest habitat into pine communities that supported less game, the people who used these practices were managing forests. And herein lies an important message about management: long-term consequences are not always positive. In fact, the more a management practice focuses on immediate gain—especially when "gain" is solely the product of one value—the more prone management is to fail in time with respect to that value. The practice of using fire to drive game was not exclusive to people of the Florida Peninsula or even North America. Nevertheless, it is one of the only areas where paleobotanical records coincide with human activities that endeavored to "manage" forests for benefits.

It is purely speculative to assume that at some time during the many generations it took to convert oak forests into pine, at least one person—probably many—recognized a pattern; the practice of burning forests to drive game created a different forest that supported less game. But those who were responsible for ensuring people had plenty to eat, seeing no other way to provide food as efficiently as the "old" ways, refused to change. So long as there were plenty of opportunities to manage forests using fire to obtain game, and people were well-fed, there was no reason to change. Herein is another important message about management: When the past is used as sole justification for current practices, it is easy to ignore reasons to change even though failure to change may one day prove fatal. Management practices are a means of achieving desirable futures, but only for those who see the future as far more important than the past.

The failings of prehistoric cultures are forgivable because it is almost impossible to contemplate long-range impacts when immediate needs are so pressing. Unfortunately, there are parallels between the motivations of hungry Paleo-Indians and cash-strapped woodland owners of today who, in times of need, turn to forests. For both, decisions are driven by short-term gain, regardless of long-term impacts on the health and functioning of the ecosystem providing benefits.

In more recent times, but still predating the emergence of forest science, there is evidence of long-range, strategic thinking about forests and management practices capable of providing future benefits. By designating forests and managing them to achieve specific future benefits, decision making transcends generations. One of the most famous true stories of managing forests for future generations comes from the anthropologist and philosopher Gregory Bateson (Brand 1994):

> New College, Oxford, is of rather late foundation, hence the name. It was founded around the late 14th century. It has, like other colleges, a great dining hall with oak beams across the top. These might be two feet square, forty-five feet long.
>
> A century ago, so I am told, some busy entomologist went up into the roof of the dining hall with a penknife and poked at the beams and found that they were full of beetles. This was reported to the College Council, who met in some dismay, because where would they get beams of that caliber nowadays?
>
> One of the Junior Fellows stuck his neck out and suggested that there might be on College lands some oak. These colleges are endowed with pieces of land scattered across the country. So they called in the College Forester, who of course had not been near the college itself for some years, and asked him about oaks.
>
> And he pulled his forelock and said, 'Well sirs, we was wonderin' when you'd be askin.'
>
> Upon further inquiry it was discovered that when the College was founded, a grove of oaks had been planted to replace the beams in the dining hall when they became beetly, because oak beams always become beetly in the end. This plan had been passed down from one

Forester to the next for five hundred years. 'You don't cut them oaks. Them's for the College Hall.'

Providing for the future is an important theme of forestry. The impetus to plant and manage oaks was based on knowledge that the original beams would eventually need to be replaced. It is nothing short of miraculous that the purpose of a planting predating Shakespeare was passed from generation to generation of foresters. The New College, Oxford, story is one of the first examples of people cultivating trees for a specific future use, which is "management" in a context much closer to modern-day interpretations than the game-driving practices of Paleo-Indians.

In the late eighteenth and early nineteenth century, forests of northern Europe were cut hard to support industrial development. A prominent nobleman of that era, Heinrich Cotta, educated in the natural sciences, detected a pattern of forest use that would soon lead to wood shortages. In 1816, Cotta published the first textbook on forestry, *Advice on Silviculture*. In the preface of his book, Cotta postulates an important message about forestry, that it is a science borne of scarcity. This prescient sentiment and other timeless observations about the effects of humans on forests are as true today as they were then. His is one of the few books remembered more for the preface than for the body of the text. "Cotta's preface," as the piece is popularly known today, is a short, but haunting, cautionary note aimed at students of forestry, with a message that will ring true for as long as people depend on forest ecosystems for wood fiber.

I first came across Professor Cotta's words in the epilogue to *Principles of Silviculture* (Daniels et. al. 1979); my choice of textbook for a silviculture course I taught in the late 1970s at the University of Connecticut. The authors obtained a translation by Professor B. E. Fernow—born and educated in Germany, but still a prominent name in American forestry—that was first published in volume 1 of the *Forest Quarterly* in 1902. Most U.S. students of forestry during Fernow's time spent at least a portion of their undergraduate education in Germany, which is arguably the birthplace of forestry as we know it today. When forestry was in its infancy here, German was the second language of many students.

Cotta's grandson, Heinrich von Cotta, is said to have translated the preface in 1865. But this earlier version translates the book title as *Instruction or Course in Afforestation*. Despite a discrepancy in titles (which probably has to do with the emergence of the word *silviculture*, a term Cotta may not have used), the text translations of Fernow and von Cotta agree word for word. A copy of "Cotta's Preface" is available on-line from the Forest History Society's Web site: http://www.lib.duke.edu/forest/Publications/fhtfall00.html.

People who have made careers of forestry, or those who think they know all there is to know about forests but have never seen a translation of Cotta's preface, should prepare to have the foundations of their beliefs challenged like never before. That Cotta made these observations almost two hundred years ago is nothing less than prescient. His message is so important that much of it is discussed below.

"If the inhabitants of Germany should leave their country it would be all grown up with woods within a century," Cotta begins. "Since there would be no one to use them, the soil would be enriched and the woods would not only increase in size, but in productive power. If, however, the people returned again and made just as large drafts as before for wood, litter and pasturage, the woodlands—even with the best forest management—would again not only be reduced in size, but also become less fertile."

In a few sentences, Henrich Cotta has exposed an essential fallacy of forestry; that human intervention improves forests, and that nature is inherently wasteful if humans are not there to monitor and manage things. Yes, management can improve a forest's ability to supply human benefits, but not without costs; and we must be mindful of these costs, says Cotta, lest we make the same mistakes again.

"We have now a forestry science because we have a dearth of wood," says Cotta, yet "forestry does not offer any nostrums and can do nothing against the course of nature." Quoting a celebrated physician of his time, Cotta goes on to say, "The good physician lets people die; the poor one kills them. With the same right one can say the good forester allows the most perfect forest to become less so; the poor one spoils them." Professor Cotta explains his analogy to medicine—which had more than its share of quackery at the time—this way: "just as a good physician cannot hinder that men die because that is the course of nature, so the best forester cannot hinder that the forests, which came to us from past times, become less now they are being utilized. The good forester then [allows] the forest to become less, but only where it cannot be helped; the poor forester, on the other hand, spoils them everywhere."

The condition of forest soils figures prominently in Professor Cotta's commentary about exploitive uses: "Without utilization, the forest soil improves constantly; if used in orderly manner it remains in a natural equilibrium; if used faultily it becomes poorer. The good forester takes the highest yield from the forest without deteriorating the soil, the poor one neither obtains this yield nor preserves the fertility of the soil."

That Heinrich Cotta made these statements about forest soils before much was known about root physiology, mycorrhizal fungi, and the essential complements of soil flora and fauna is remarkable. Given the labor necessary to harvest timber in the early nineteenth century, one can only imagine how Cotta would react to the soil disturbances wrought by some of the harvesting systems we employ today.

As a further caution, Cotta tells readers to avoid the hubris that is peculiar to college graduates. The true student of forestry is rewarded with more questions than answers, and eventually one is "cured of [their] conceit!"

"Forestry," according to Cotta, "is based on the knowledge of nature, the deeper we penetrate its secrets, the deeper the depths before us. What the light of an oil lamp makes visible is easily overlooked; many more things we can see by torch light, but infinitely more in the sunlight. The lighter it grows around us, the more unknown things become apparent, and it is a sure sign of shallowness, if anybody believes he knows it all."

Many of the problems of forestry, according to Professor Cotta, are rooted in the fact that the world of foresters is inevitably divided into two groups: "empiricists" and "scientists." "Rarely are both united," he chides. Empiricists deal in generalities. "Forest management is easily learned [by the empiricists]," says Cotta, "while the systematic teachings of the scientist are soon memorized. But in practice the art of the [empiricist] stands to a thorough forestry science in the same relation as the quack medicine to the true pharmacopeia; and the [scientist] often does not know the forest for the many trees." The message: To practitioners—the forest is far more complicated than you were led to believe, and it is better to err on the side of inaction than to risk irreparable harm for the cause of efficiency. To scientists—learn to know the forest as something far more vast and complex than the sum of its parts. The cause of good science is not to obtain answers, so much as knowing how to ask the right questions.

"Three principal causes exist why forestry is still so backward," says Cotta (remember, his reference to *backward* is from the perspective of 1816); "first, the long time which wood needs for its development; second, the great variety of sites on which it grows; thirdly, the fact that the forester who practices much writes but little, and he who writes much practices but little. The long development period causes that something is considered good and prescribed as such which is good only for a time," (Yes, markets have a way of changing usually on cycles that are far less than even a single rotation) "and later becomes detrimental to the forest management. The second fact (site variation) causes that what many declare good or bad, proves, good or bad only in certain places. The third fact brings it about that the best experiences die with the man who made them, and that many entirely one-sided experiences are copied by the merely literary forester so often that they finally stand as articles of faith which nobody dares to gainsay [contradict, oppose, or deny], no matter how one-sided or in error they may be."

According to the Forest History Society, Heinrich Cotta was born in 1763, so he was 53 years old when he wrote his *Advice on Silviculture.* Most of the documents that describe his background are in German, so it is difficult to develop a vitae. It appears as though he was educated in the physical sciences, and in addition to his book on silviculture, he is also author of at least one other book on plant physiology. In the early 1800s, Cotta is credited with founding the Royal Saxonian Forest Academy, the first school dedicated to forestry. In his time, Cotta was considered a high-ranking officer in the Kingdom of Saxony, and at least one source refers to him as the "founder of forest science."

He is also credited with developing a system of industrial forestry in Germany, and the emergence of his forest academy is said to have coincided with the final conversion of "natural" forests in this region to carefully tended plantations. He died in 1844 at the age of 81, leaving a legacy based on the preface to a book, not on the book itself.

During Cotta's time, eastern forests in the United States were being exploited by an industry that cared little about conservation or the future. The only value of forests was in timber, and when that was gone it was time to move on to other tracts.

In 1847, George Perkins Marsh, a U.S. congressman from Vermont and well-known botanist, called upon Congress to address the "destructive impacts of human activities on forests." At the time, forest industry had moved on to the vast pine forests of the Lake States. In less than thirty years, this entire resource had been expended, leaving an enormous volume of "slash" in tops and other waste wood that fueled some of the most severe fires ever seen in North America, destroying top soil that had formed over the course of millennia.

Forest industry moved from the Lake states to the West, demonstrating no greater wisdom on forest use than that of the Paleo-Indians seven thousand years earlier when, in the waning years of the nineteenth century, B. E. Fernow and Gifford Pinchot came on the scene. These two men are largely credited with bringing European forestry concepts to the United States with help of Theodore Roosevelt.

In 1905, with forest industry firmly established in the Pacific Northwest and already having demonstrated its capacity for ruination, Roosevelt—the first U.S. president to address the destructive practices of forest industry—appointed Gifford Pinchot chief of the newly formed U.S. Forest Service. Considered the father of forestry in the United States, Gifford Pinchot—ever the politician—set the tone for forestry in America with his famous quote on the goals of forest management: "Conservation means the greatest good to the greatest number for the longest time" (1909). He helped stem the tide of deforestation, but his anthropocentric view of forestry was not accepted by all, especially among those who considered forests to be more than trees.

One of the most well-respected foresters of the twentieth century is Aldo Leopold, author of the first textbook on wildlife management in 1933 (Leopold 1933) and of many philosophical essays (for which he is best known) on forests, contemporary forestry, and the dilemma of managers challenged with balancing short-term gains with ecosystem function and health. His perspective on forests was that of an academic, observing the emergence of forestry from shortly after its arrival in North America until his death in 1948, one year before publication of his most famous collection of essays: *A Sand County Almanac* (1949).

Included among these essays is one titled "Land Health and the A-B Cleavage," in which Leopold describes

> a single plane of cleavage common to many specialized fields. One group (A) . . . regards the land as soil, and its function as commodity-production; another group (B) regards the land as a biota, and its function as something broader. How much broader is admittedly in a state of doubt and confusion. Group A is . . . content to grow trees like cabbages; . . . its ideology is agronomic. Group B, on the other hand, sees forestry as fundamentally different from agronomy because it employs natural species, and manages a natural environment rather than creating an artificial one. Group B prefers natural reproduction on princi-

ple. It worries on biotic as well as economic grounds about the loss of species like chestnut, and the threatened loss of the white pines. It worries about a whole series of secondary forest functions: wildlife, recreation, watersheds, and wilderness. To my mind, Group B feels the stirrings of an ecological conscience.

The ideas of Professor Leopold—more so than any other author before or since—capture and eloquently describe the present-day contradictions of forestry: human needs versus those of other forest-dwelling organisms, short-term gain versus long-term investment, dominance versus cooperation, production of benefits versus ecosystem health, tangible versus intangible, the needs of current generations versus those of the future, and the dogma of Group A versus the caution of Group B. Positive impact forestry is prologue based on the tenets of Group B.

What Is Positive Impact Forestry?

Forestry is a science that deals with management and production of human benefits from forests. It is a relatively new science in North America, having arrived coincidental with harvest of the last easily accessible timber in the years following the Civil War and up until the turn of the nineteenth century. Before the advent of forestry in the United States, timber was relatively cheap because of its abundance. Timber barons who made their fortunes converting forest lands into lumber never expected to "grow" timber. Rarely did they hold title to lands for any longer than it took to strip them of logs. And, in some parts of the country, an unscrupulous owner would pass title of cutover lands to the town derelict to avoid property taxes. Less than one hundred years ago, forests were a source of timber, and when the timber was gone, the land—at least to those who exploited it—was worthless.

In some respects, forestry science arrived here too late. Virtually all of the indigenous forests had been cut over for fuel, building materials, and conversion to agricultural land. Forestry arrived amidst a debate about the future of forests and the resources they provide. If not for impending scarcity, it is arguable that forestry science would have arrived in North America when it did.

From its inception, forestry science has emphasized the concept of replacement. When forests are harvested, it is done so with a great deal of thought given to planning the "next" forest. But the emphasis, until very recently, has always been on wood production. Although ecologists who study forests have known for many years that they are far more important for the ecosystems they represent than the wood they are capable of producing, foresters were trained in the Germanic traditions concerned mostly with maintaining wood supply. In fact, the silvicultural systems that students learn—even to this day—are named by the methods used to regenerate forest stands.

In the late 1980s, a new term arrived in the lexicon of U.S. forestry: *low-impact*. It most often appears as an adjective, preceding words like *forestry*, *logging*, and *harvesting*. Ironically, it is one of the only forestry terms that has migrated from third-world countries to the developed world. In equatorial forests, *low-impact* usually means harvesting single trees or small groups so as to maintain ecosystem structure and composition. But felling single trees in excess of 120 feet tall with highly fluted trunks of enormous diameters is not easy. One tree can host more than a dozen vines with basal diameters that rival most hardwoods in the United States. When rainforest trees fall with vines attached, they almost never land where the logger had intended, and vines rake the ground like anchor chains. Felling just one tree can wreak havoc over large areas. Careless logging in tropical rainforests is not only dangerous, it can also have enormous, mostly negative, impacts on sites and soils.

The common practice in tropical forests before low-impact ideas evolved was to cut over an entire area. This may sound like a reasonable alternative; after all *clearcutting* is a highly effective silvicultural method in many forest types in the United States. Unfortunately, clearcutting is not a practical tool in the tropics. Soils there are very highly weathered and virtually all of the mineral nutrient capital is tied up in vegetation. Leaf litter is recycled almost immediately and organic compounds from leaves and other debris help maintain a favorable soil structure. When the source of litter is removed, not only is the site mined of its essential nutrient capital, but the lack of organic compounds causes iron-rich, lateritic clays to harden into a surface that is only slightly more permeable than cured cement.

In the tropics, the purpose of low-impact methods is to keep rainforest crowns intact, maintain soil productivity, and affect species diversity as little as possible. In the United States, these are practices most akin to silvicultural systems we know as *single-tree* and *group-selection* methods (discussed in greater detail below), and have proven to work well protecting sites while allowing indigenous people to harvest valuable trees. It is this primary idea of how to use forests without destroying them, packaged in the term *low-impact*, that we have imported. It is an answer to the question, How can we protect the essential functions of forest ecosystems and use them for wood products and other benefits at the same time?

The *low-impact* concept is perfectly suited to tropical rainforests, but it does not fit as well here in the United States because it suggests impacts—any impacts—are the culprits. The very purpose of forest management is to create impacts that do not exceed the capacity of ecosystems to provide human benefits. This means employing practices that conserve site productivity and protect indigenous species while also achieving objectives.

We have known since forestry was organized into a science that timber extraction has negative impacts on forest ecosystems. Timber removals anywhere in the world also harvest mineral nutrients and disrupt the processes of soil microflora and fauna. But the effect in northern, temperate climates is significantly less than in the tropics. Why? Because the proportion of nutrients stored in forest vegetation, versus in soil, decreases from equatorial regions to boreal forests. In other words, soils in temperate and boreal regions tend to hold a far greater proportion of total site nutrients than held in forest vegetation. The reverse is true in the tropics.

Harvesting bole wood (logs from the main stem) in the United States on rotations exceeding fifty years probably has a negligible effect on total nutrient capital in northern climates (Wenger 1984), but it does have some effect. It is quite likely that forest exploitation is already responsible for major losses of forest nutrients, reducing presettlement productive capacities by an unknown but possibly very significant amount. The advent of forestry has slowed nutrient loss to be sure, but eventually nutrient replacements will be necessary to maintain current productivity. Nevertheless, many forestry experts believe the need for supplemental nutrition in "natural" forests is unwarranted in the near term, except on sites where timber is growing in plantations or on short rotations, or in areas where certain essential nutrients are known lacking. For example, sulfur is commonly lacking in disturbed forest soils of the Pacific Northwest, and even light applications of this element can improve forest growth. In the Northeast, however, sulfur is not lacking due primarily to inputs from the burning of fossil fuels in industrial centers upwind.

In the United States a bigger concern than nutrient loss is the effect of timber extraction methods and equipment on soil flora and fauna, and on fine-root systems of trees. The more we learn about forest soils and tree roots, the more we know it is important to protect the forest floor from skidders, forwarders, and other heavy equipment—even horses. Undisturbed forest soils develop a spongy, leaf-litter layer where organic debris is digested by beneficial organisms that cycle important nutrients back into the soil. Oxygen is abundant in these upper soil layers, which is just as important to the life functions of beneficial organisms as it is to tree roots. Heavy equipment can compress the organic layers greatly reducing oxygen and also the soil's ability to hold water. The negative effect of soil compaction on wet soils, especially those composed of fine-textured clays, is even more dramatic.

Generally, forest managers are aware of these risks and avoid them with good planning. For example, it is standard practice to suspend timber extraction on excessively wet soils. Forestry professionals now know enough about how to lessen the negative impacts of harvesting that in many cases site risks are considered negligible in comparison to the potential benefits of harvesting timber, except in circumstances where financial gain subordinates good practices. For these reasons, this term of tropical origin, *low-impact*, is out of context in the temperate forest; a more suitable term in the United States is *positive impact forestry*.

Positive impact forestry recognizes and accepts the attendant risks of managing forests but also underscores a manager's ability to avoid or mitigate potentially negative impacts. Moreover, the term emphasizes forestry's potential to achieve sustainable benefits—a message that has been lost in recent years. Forestry professionals who use positive impact practices are not only protecting sites, but also looking for opportunities to create or improve habitats, mitigate silvicultural mistakes from the past, enhance investment potential, and conserve productivity for future generations. The difference between activities that merely avoid impacts and those that craft impacts to optimize ecosystem values while providing sustainable benefits is the difference between low-impact and positive impact forestry.

Positive impact forestry encompasses all reasonable, ecologically defensible, and sustainable approaches to managing forests—practices that provide human benefits but within the capacity of forest ecosystems to do so. A positive impact approach raises the integrity of forest ecosystems above all else while also recognizing that humans have the ability to affect the supply of benefits forests can provide. For example, it is possible to create wildlife habitats for complements of species that were not particularly abundant prior to management. Effecting changes in the structure and composition of forest vegetation to favor wildlife where the value of these changes is high for the owner is positive impact forestry. Within the context of this definition, a manager who carefully installs small clearcuts to reproduce early-successional forests favored by game species, like ruffed grouse and deer, is using positive impact practices.

The term conveys an image of forestry with a connotation that makes more sense than *low-impact,* for another reason: Extend the analogy to almost any other profession and from a practical standpoint it is obvious that the services of someone who can create positive impacts are far more desirable than those of someone who simply avoids negative consequences. Who in their right mind would, for instance, hire a low-impact lawyer or accountant?

Arguing the case for the term *positive impact* over the better-known *low-impact* appears at first blush more concept-marketing than new methods. But there is more to it than reshaping forestry's image. Healthy and sustainable ecosystems are the products of positive impact forestry, not more timber. Positive impact practices mimic natural processes to achieve human benefits, but are not intended to remake forests for the sole benefit of humans. Long-term investment supersedes short-term gain, and the needs of families—especially future generations—exceed those of individuals. Finally, the future is a far more important concern of positive impact forestry than the past. If we endeavor to maintain forests in the landscape, we must manage them as such. Unmanaged forests are apt to disappear, gradually converted into other uses far less beneficial than healthy forest ecosystems.

Evolution of Forest Conservation and Stewardship

Positive impact forestry embraces the concept of stewardship, which now—thankfully—permeates the culture of woodland management in the United States. But what does *stewardship* mean and where did it come from? What happened to *green gold* and *sustained yield,* and why is the concept of *renewability* passé? There was a time not too many years ago when the American public gladly accepted the word of foresters on the subject of forest use, and forestry was the greenest of green industries. Now, trust is in short supply, science counts for little, and foresters and forest industry have become apologists. All the while human experience is moving away from forests, and urbanites are challenged—between contemporary education and a sensation-driven media—to make a connection between the wood products they use everyday and the forests they visit for a few days each summer.

The word *steward*, according to *Merriam-Webster's Collegiate Dictionary*, has its origins in Old English. It is defined as a person responsible for managing the domestic affairs of a large estate. *Stewardship* is recognized as the noun form that describes the skills or actions of a steward. Aside from these definitions, before 1990 when the U.S. Forest Service launched its forest stewardship initiative, there were very few references to any—now popular—connotations of stewardship. There are, however, a number of ideas that have evolved from environmental thinking that more accurately characterize the word as it is used today.

Gifford Pinchot, introduced earlier as the father of U.S. forestry, said (of foresters), "[they] must work toward maintaining the balance of nature" (1914). Later, Pinchot identified three principles of conservation, the pillars of modern forestry in America. First, conservation stands for development—it must provide for the current generation before future generations are considered. Second, conservation implies prevention of waste. And, third, conservation must benefit the many and not the few. It was Pinchot's ideas more than those of any other that dominated our approaches to forest management and use in the first half of the twentieth century. But Pinchot was a populist, more concerned with present than future generations. A contemporary interpretation of stewardship implies a debt to the future, but Pinchot might not have agreed.

Thirty years after Pinchot's era of influence, Aldo Leopold (a scholar of biblical proportions among foresters even today) offered a number of ideas that first captured the notion of responsibility to land, encompassed in our modern interpretations of the word *stewardship*. In the quotes that follow, note how easy it is to substitute the word stewardship where Leopold uses the word *conservation*.

According to Leopold, "Conservation is a state of harmony between men and land. By land is meant all of the things on, over or in the earth. Harmony with the land is like harmony with a friend: you cannot cherish his right hand and chop off his left. That is to say, you can not love the game and hate the predators; you cannot conserve the waters and waste the ranges; you cannot build the forest and mine the farm. The land is one organism. Its parts, like our own parts, compete with each other. The competitions are as much a part of the inner workings as the co-operations. You can regulate them—cautiously—but not abolish them" (Leopold 1966).

Leopold goes on to say, "A system of conservation based solely on economic self-interest is hopelessly lopsided. It tends to ignore, and thus to eventually eliminate, many elements in the land community that lack com-

mercial value, but that are (as far as we know) essential to its healthy functioning. An ethical obligation on the part of the private owner is the only
remedy for these situations. A land ethic, then, reflects the existence of an
ecological conscience, and this in turn reflects a conviction of individual responsibility for the health of the land. Health is the capacity of the land for
self-renewal. Conservation is our effort to understand and preserve this capacity." Although Leopold was Pinchot's junior by twenty-two years and
both were trained in the Germanic traditions of forestry, their views about
forests were at opposite ends of a spectrum.

In another, often-quoted, passage Leopold articulates a fundamental
value of stewardship: "It is inconceivable to me that an ethical relation to
the land can exist without love, respect and admiration for the land, and a
high regard for its value. Perhaps the most serious obstacle impeding the
evolution of a land ethic is," according to Leopold, "the fact that our educational and economic system is headed away from rather than toward an
intense consciousness of land. The practice of conservation must spring
from a conviction of what is ethically and esthetically right, as well as what
is economically expedient. A thing is right only when it tends to preserve
the integrity, stability and beauty of a community. The community includes
the soil, waters, fauna and flora, as well as people (1966)." It is significant to
note that Leopold includes people in his concept of community: the idea
that reasonable human use is acceptable just as long as it does not destroy
conditions for other organisms. In Leopold's view, forest diseases and insects (native organisms that occasionally reach populations that can damage timber values or slow its growth) have as much right to use forests as do
humans, and we need to learn how to share forests and to live with these
depredations rather than try to destroy them.

S. H. Ordway said, in his *A Conservation Handbook*, "In an economic
sense, conservation seeks to increase production and productivity, while
avoiding waste and ensuring a continued supply. Ethically, [conservation]
seeks to increase man's understanding that he is one of many living things,
dependent upon living resources of the earth, and that it is his duty to pass
on his resource heritage to succeeding generations in improved condition"
(1949). Ordway was one of the first authors to suggest the responsibility to
make improvements for future generations, which has become a central
tenet of stewardship as we know it today.

In 1969, S. B. Hutchinson suggested in his article "Bringing Conservation into the Mainstream of American Thought" that "only when the abrahamic philosophy toward natural resources ceases to dominate the scene

and the right to ownership is recognized as the right to careful use will completely adequate resource management be (*sic*) possible." His reference to "abrahamic philosophy" comes from Aldo Leopold and probably refers to Abraham's biblical appointment to lead humans as they "replenish the earth and subdue it and have dominion over every living thing" (Genesis 1:28). Hutchinson goes on to assert that

> much has yet to be learned about local planning for resource management. Two "truths" are beyond dispute, however. The first is that the production of raw materials, natural beauty, pollution, land stability, recreation, etc., are not independent considerations but interlocked pieces of a total problem. Before really effective local resource programs can be developed, a master design must be prepared. The second truth is that the future is the most impenetrable of all unknowns. What we don't know about the future is in fact more important in planning than what we do know. For this reason, resource management designs should contain a large factor of safety. Moreover, resource planning should attempt to reserve a maximum choice for future generations by postponing actions that need not be made today. (1969)

President Dwight D. Eisenhower is attributed with a quote that has helped define stewardship. In response to a reporter's question about his goal in life, Eisenhower allegedly said (to the surprise of many): "To leave a piece of land in better condition than I found it," this probably in reference to a farm he retired to in northern Virginia. The idea of improvement is now a common theme implied in stewardship, and it appears as though it is also an idea we inherited from indigenous people. At a treaty signing near the end of the nineteenth century, an Apache is credited with the following quote: "We do not inherit land from our forefathers. We borrow it from future generations."

So what is forest stewardship? It is a process whereby the use of resources does not substantially detract from or degrade the value of forests for use by other organisms and future generations. A good forest steward is someone who makes forest management decisions within the context of a long-term plan of objectives that are at once economically expedient but conserving of resources, and socially, environmentally and ecologically responsible.

Stewardship is the new mantra for some managers, but for others it is just another example of liberalism at its worst; wait until the economy down and forest stewardship is out the window. It is true that our modern interpretation of stewardship has evolved during prosperous times, but most managers agree that regardless of the economy, the days of cut and run are almost over. Those who understand and embrace the tenets of forest stewardship are more apt to survive and prosper than those who do not. And it is the forest stewards, as proponents of positive impact forestry, who will deliver forests and all their benefits to future generations.

Defining Sustainability

Is it possible for communities to grow and be sustainable? And just what does it mean to be sustainable? Does it mean restoring a way of life that has long since passed, or does it mean conserving the landscape as we now know it, encouraging earth-friendly uses but also accepting the dictates of higher authorities on exactly what we sustain and who pays for it? After all, sustainability is, arguably, antithetical to human nature: we conserve only after having provided for ourselves.

For example, in northern New England people come from cities to recreate in forests. They love the landscape and what they perceive to be a special way of life. Some leave the city and buy played-out "hill farms" for grossly inflated prices, build new, state-of-the-art houses and then become staunch defenders of the very landscape they have just altered. The mentality is the following: Once you're here, pull up the ladder so no one else can come. It is truly ironic that the values which attract people to northern New England—or to any forest area—are the values most at risk by their arrival.

Is it possible for people to continue the migration from cities to forests and farm lands, to establish lifestyles similar to those who came before them, especially now that city dwellers feel the presence of an enormous bull's-eye over their heads? Is there a level of immigration that will not impair sustainability? Or is the term *sustainable growth* an oxymoron? Here are some sobering statistics.

According to the Worldwatch Institute, since 1900 world population has increased from one billion to six billion people, and the economy is twenty times larger. In seven years, from 1990 to 1997, world economic growth matched the sum of all growth from the beginning of civilization to 1950. The current rates of population and economic growth, according to the Institute, are not sustainable, in fact—not even close (Brown 1998).

In the past fifty years, according to Worldwatch, the consumption of lumber has tripled, paper use is up by a factor of six, fish catch increased by a factor of five, and fossil fuel consumption increased four-fold. For the first time in many areas of the world, soil erosion is exceeding soil formation, and fisheries once thought inexhaustible are now closed indefinitely.

Water is a resource we have in relative abundance in most of the United States, but it is in very short supply around the world, and the situation is dire. Most of the world's population does not have access to clean water.

How about the atmosphere? Even though there have been gains in controlling air pollution, atmospheric CO_2 has climbed to the highest level in 150,000 years. Consider this: the thirteen warmest years since 1866 have occurred since 1979, and within these thirteen years, the four warmest have occurred since 1990. The last decade of the twentieth century was the warmest on record. A warmer earth means more turbulence, more storms, and more weather extremes.

The once extremely profitable insurance industry is very concerned with these storm trends, and for good reason. During the first seven years of the 1990s, weather-related insurance claims were four times higher than the sum of all claims in the previous decade. The insurance industry's inability to calculate the cost of natural catastrophes is an externality of the excesses and expectations of the industrial world. If this alarming trend continues, either insurance companies—the U.S. government included—will get out of the business of insuring high-risk property or the cost will exceed even a very wealthy person's ability to pay. The good news is this: areas that should never have been developed in the first place, such as barrier islands, chaparral forests and other fire-driven ecosystems, estuaries, and floodplains—all important wildlife habitats—will revert back to their natural state because humans cannot afford to live there and society will no longer bail them out or pay to rebuild.

The situation with wildlife, according to Worldwatch, is especially dire. Of nearly ten thousand species of birds still on earth, more than one thousand are threatened with extinction. Of the 4,400 mammalian species, 1,100 are threatened with extinction. Among mammals, the 232 primates are most at risk. Survival of nearly half are in question; half of our closest relatives are struggling to survive.

The state of the world, according to Worldwatch authors, is summed up as follows: "Humanity now faces a challenge that rivals any in its history—restoring balance with nature while expanding economic opportunities for billions of people whose basic needs—for food and clean water, for example—are still not being met. The challenge facing the entire world is to design an economy that can satisfy basic needs of people everywhere without self-destructing. The enormity of this task is matched only by it urgency." The authors go on to say "In effect, we are behaving as though we have no children. . . . As a species, we seem to have an infinite capacity to postpone difficult decisions (Brown et al. 1998)."

Biologists worldwide see the current state of affairs as so dire to have labeled it "The Sixth Extinction." According to biologist Niles Eldredge, "The mounting loss of species threatens to rival the five great mass extinctions of the geological past. It is the first mass extinction in 65 million years, and the only one attributable to humans" (2001). This same article quotes Harvard biologist, Professor E. O. Wilson, who has calculated that the earth is currently losing species at a rate in excess of thirty thousand per year—more than three species every hour due to human-induced "ecosystem stresses" caused by landscape changes, pollution, overexploitation of species, and introductions of alien species. Although no one knows for sure, it is almost certain that extinctions have included species of microflora and fauna in forests soils, diminishing ecosystems, but in unknown ways.

Changing demographics are affecting local economies in forest areas around the United States—economies that once depended on forest industry. Rural people are still trying to fathom the influx of relatively wealthy, mostly urban telecommuters—men and women who have discovered they can make just as much money with phones, fax, e-mail, and Web sites as going to the office each day. Who wants to live in the city anymore? To a family living in an apartment thirty floors up, a neglected farm house and couple of hundred acres look like a fantastic bargain. But it is questionable if telecommuters bring anything to local economies other than more kids in schools increasing the need for revenue, higher property values and taxes, more pressure to convert forests into housing, and more voices when it comes time to make tough decisions.

Changing communities leads to polarization, and highly polarized communities do not make good decisions. It becomes increasingly difficult to find good people who want to work in the woods, in the log yard, or on the green-chain at the local sawmill for minimum wage. Those who live in forest areas tend to delay tough decisions because it is almost impossible to envision roles their children might play, and their children's children.

Creating communities in forest areas that are sustainable *and* affordable by future generations seems next to impossible.

Compared to many other countries, the United States is rich with forests and, due to fantastic resiliency, these areas will probably remain in forests even with climatic changes and exploitive practices. Much of the forest, however, is within an easy driving distance for an enormous urban population in the United States and Canada. High demand for real estate is apt to continue and more and more forests will be dedicated to homesteads. With the exception of houses creeping up hillsides ever more evident each year when the leaves fall, from a distance—and to the untrained eye—the forest will appear much as it does today. But, as forest holdings become parcelized the viability of managing them declines. If traditional uses of forests, such as for wood, clean water, wildlife, recreation, scenic vistas, and a sense of place are important, how do we sustain them? Eventually, parcelized land is taken out of production and our ability to sustain forests for traditional values declines, until the tree-covered landscape we now know as "forests" gradually transforms into one big backyard, and the working forest becomes a facade.

So far, forest science is reasonably sure we can extract continuous flows of wood from most forests, assuming long-term ecosystem function and health is always held to a higher level of importance than timber yields. Yes, we can replace trees with more trees, but it is not the same thing as saying "forests are renewable." There is a sustainable level of production at which forest-grown fiber is indeed renewable. But if ecosystems take precedence over production, as they should (a fundamental concept of positive impact forestry), that level is considerably less than we expect of forests today.

An Ecosystem Approach to Managing Forests

Few terms in forestry have caused so much confusion, angst, and rancor among foresters in the United States than that of *ecosystem management*. Many managers are taking the position, "If you can't define it, then it does not exist!" Others argue the term is implicit in the work foresters do, that forest management necessitates manipulation of forest ecosystems and, therefore, foresters are already practicing ecosystem management. Still others, uncomfortable with an emphasis on wood production in forestry practice, feel that there may be something to this new terminology. Forests are more than wood factories, home for wildlife, filters for water, places to recreate, and inspiring vistas. Forests, enlightened managers realize, are enchantingly complex, and the elements we see—trees, shrubs and animals—are but a small part of the total. It is likely, in fact, that one day a forest will be defined more on the basis of what you don't see in soils than on trees.

Even after much debate, many forestry professionals remain unconvinced that the actions of a forest ecosystem manager differ significantly from those of a careful forest manager. Some are even offended because embracing the new concept is tantamount to admitting they were doing something wrong before. And the debate goes on.

"They hear *ecosystem* and I hear *management*," one industry pundit said some years ago, which underscores the undeniable fact that the term is politically charged, and that rankles some managers. Is the term simply a palliative for both camps, allowing environmental interests to say, "We've won, forest ecosystems are protected," while foresters counter, "Yeah, but we're still managing them"? Is ecosystem management an attempt, as some have speculated, to justify a no-cut policy on public lands? Or is it a new way of looking at forests, a rethinking of silvicultural practices that, up until now, have worked pretty well—or have they?

What do proponents mean when they use the term *ecosystem management*? Part of the problem with the concept is the term itself. A more appropriate and meaningful term might be *ecosystem approaches to management*, since ecosystems—by definition—are self-sustaining and do not need management. Humans need forests, not the other way around.

An ecosystem approach to forest management employs positive impact practices that place the long-term health and functioning of the system above all else. Yet it is, by definition, an attempt to meet society's needs for forest benefits without disrupting the mechanisms by which the system itself is sustained; a catch-22 if one assumes that humans are not part of the system. But humans are very much a part of forests and will remain so indefinitely. The difference between humans and other organisms is our ability to reason and to use forests regardless of the needs of other living creatures, and herein is the conflict.

Proponents of ecosystem approaches believe that traditional forest management practices are too anthropocentric, that nature is not a gift to humankind. In a sense, humans are just one more organism at the table and we must share. But how much should society forfeit to protect some obscure soil fungi or wildlife species or any other organism that relies on forests? And who decides what is important? Who speaks for the forest?

A significant part of the problem is we do not understand forest ecosystems very well. Foresters know a lot about growing trees and about protecting or creating habitats for wildlife. But when it comes to understanding the impacts of harvesting on, say, populations of beneficial bacteria, we're all guessing. There are so few examples of unmanaged forests to offer comparisons that we have no idea if past practices have been detrimental or beneficial. And we have no way of knowing if practices that increase wood production in the short term—which is good for humans—are, in the long-term, detrimental to the site. Among the concerns of ecologists are nutrient exports in harvested wood fiber, extirpation of native species, effects of heavy equipment on soil structure, pollution impacts, habitat loss and degradation, invasion by exotic species—and these are just some of the more obvious (Bormann and Likens 1981).

There is also a question of scale that recognizes ecosystems are hierarchical and nested one inside the other. An ecosystem is definable at almost any level, from the interactions of mycorrhizal fungi on tree roots to the entire earth; the larger the level, the slightly better our understanding. But at global levels and for some systems, our understanding is the mathematic equivalent of knowing the numbers but not the equation. In other words, we understand the processes, but not how they interact. Why? Because ecosystems are both predictable and chaotic. For example, notice how smokes rises off a cigarette the next time you are in a room with a smoker. No sooner is a pattern detected than it changes. But the further away smoke moves from the source (and the longer you stay in the room), the more uniform it becomes. It is a chaotic process that eventually produces a uniform result. Most sciences are based on predictability; how then does one study a system that is both chaotic and predictable?

We are only just beginning to understand the interactions and synergies of forest ecosystems, and science is catching up. But based on what we already know there is reason for caution, which is a basic tenet of positive impact forestry.

A physician and biologist by the name of Lewis Thomas in his book, *The Lives of a Cell* (1974), postulates that plants and animals are a conspiracy of cells; that the evolution of higher organisms is the result of cooperative behavior between different cell types. We are, Thomas argues, the product of our cells, and complexity is the result of synergism, not the other way around. Literally, we are told by our cells to organize in such a way that allows them to procreate and continue, the messages carried by DNA.

Ecosystem organization, some ecologists argue, is exactly analogous to that of the cells of Lewis Thomas. Also known as the *Gaia hypothesis* (and probably first adapted from the science fiction of Isaac Asimov), "the conspiracy of the parts" suggests that the earth is an organism unto itself and, like cells, the parts are assembled for a larger purpose. If this is true, it is more than enough justification for putting sustainability of forest ecosystems above human use, and reason enough to manage forests for positive impacts.

As the old saying goes, the devil is in the details. Ecosystem approaches to managing forests will redefine our concept of private property rights, which has many woodland owners concerned. This issue alone will feed the debate to clearly establish society's values regarding forests and help define, more specifically, what we are willing to pay for and what we are willing to give up. If the expectation of ecosystem approaches to using forests prevails, expect to see changes in silviculture—toward the direction of positive impact practices outlined here—especially in the timing and methods of timber extraction on some sites. Also, look for longer rotations and higher management expenses but tempered with a public willing to pay more for earth-friendly products. Finally, we must contemplate a day when wood fiber production is relegated to "farms," or even to processes that don't involve trees, because society will have decided that forests are too valuable to log. Notwithstanding, wood has characteristics that are irreplaceable and it is possible to harvest trees without harming forest ecosystems. This is one of the primary tenets of positive impact forestry.

The goal of this book is to help readers understand the impacts of deliberate human activities on forests and to effect changes that are capable of providing benefits without damaging ecosystems. Chapter 2 lays the groundwork for understanding the disturbance processes managers use to bring about change in forests. Essential to understanding planned disturbances are the effects of tolerance to competitive conditions on species succession. By their actions, forest managers can speed up, suspend, or reverse succession and thereby control the complement of species in any given stand. But as trees change so does the complement of wildlife that uses forests. Although managing woodlands for wildlife is not presented until much later, chapter 2 helps explain why owners who want to manage for wildlife can use their properties to serve as the missing link in a larger landscape.

Knowing how trees grow is absolutely fundamental to managing forests, especially for those owners who are looking to maximize timber values.

Trees are fairly simple organisms, but they have developed fascinating strategies to deal with competitive conditions, and managers will often take advantage of these strategies to fulfill management objectives. Managing forests is really nothing more than controlling the timing and severity of disturbances, but it is essential to understand that compounding disturbances or stresses can be detrimental.

Also presented in chapter 2 is a discussion of the unique features of forest soils within which live flora and fauna that are essential to trees. This section explains the need for caution during timber extraction since soil structure and habitat are easily damaged by heavy equipment. Tree roots, especially fine root systems that account for only a small portion of tree weight but a disproportionately large amount of surface area, are also easily injured by the use of harvesting equipment, particularly at certain times of the year. Readers will understand why it is important to plan harvests when soils are frozen, if at all possible, or at least when trees are dormant and soils are dry. Finally, some of the most important concepts of forest site are discussed in chapter 2, from which follow the application of silvicultural practices.

The fundamentals of forestry science, from the effects of tree spacing on diameter growth to the timing and design of disturbances used to reproduce forests are discussed in chapter 3. There are many different methods that allow managers to utilize the natural reproductive capacity of trees to get a new stand started. In many forest types, tree planting is not necessary with proper silviculture and careful timing of practices. In addition, the chapter describes how mangers can focus limited resources on selected trees, how to evaluate timber investments, and how to make use of a relatively new method of growing timber that cultivates individual trees for the future crop. Finally, because of the many misconceptions about forests and forestry—some promulgated by those who know virtually nothing about forests, some spawned by those who think they know about forests, and some by those who know better—an entire section is devoted to common silvicultural misconceptions and myths.

Effecting change in forests is most often accomplished by changing the structure and composition of trees. In premature and early-mature forests, periodic timber sales are the most practical tools to create favorable changes. But a timber sale is a business transaction, so it is essential that owners recognize the skills and motivations of different service providers, from consulting foresters to logging contractors. In chapter 4, readers will learn how trees are evaluated for the market place, how to determine the correct time to harvest, and how to negotiate with foresters and loggers, and they will learn about some of the more important aspects of a timber sale contract. In addition to learning how to work with people that can create positive impacts in forests, readers will also discover how to evaluate the ethics of their decisions, recognizing that harvesting is a double-edged sword.

Positive impact forestry is the product of understanding the impacts of various traditional forestry methods and crafting those methods to achieve results that promote sustainable forests. Low-impact logging methods aimed at protecting forest ecosystems is the subject of chapter 5. Readers will learn the fundamentals of protecting soils laid bare on timber extraction trails and how to protect streams from soil sediments and petroleum-based fuels, fluids, and lubricants. This chapter also describes revolutionary tree-felling techniques that can provide far more protection to forest stands than traditional methods. It sounds almost too good to be true, but these tree-felling methods also greatly increase worker productivity and safety. Finally, we'll take a "systems" look at timber harvesting and extraction, and review the advantages and disadvantages of different equipment configurations. New harvesting technologies notwithstanding, the most important factor in choosing an equipment configuration that best fits the circumstances has nothing to do with equipment or innovations. The skills, attitudes, and motivations of equipment operators are far more important to a successful harvest than equipment, and, thus, learning how to evaluate forest contractors is essential to a successful timber harvest.

With only a little extra planning and almost no sacrifice of timber-oriented objectives, woodland owners can have a tremendously positive impact on wildlife. Chapter 6 describes the fundamentals of managing woodlands for wildlife and the organizations that have emerged in recent years for the cause of using forestry practices to provide for wildlife. In addition, readers will learn about nontimber products, such as medicinal plants and mushrooms, that have become highly valuable—but controversial—resources in some areas. There is a positive impact approach to managing the nontimber resources of forests, and it is far easier to implement than most readers would guess. Finally, we will explore one of the greatest threats to forests, not just in the United States but around the world: invasive species in the form of plants, insects, fungi, and bacteria. What are they? How do they colonize forests? And what are best strategies for excluding pernicious exotic species from woodlands?

In chapter 7, readers will glimpse some alternative futures for forests, including changes in industry, the effects of climate-induced changes on forest ecosystems, and regulation of forestry practices. Relatively recent innovations in aviation, communications, electronics, and other fields are compared to the potential for innovation in our methods of using forests. Positive impact forestry methods advocate long rotations using practices that manage for high values over large volumes.

Finally, readers will learn of an insidious threat to forests that is at least as significant—if not more so—to the future of forests than the threat of exotic species: the continual division of land into smaller and smaller parcels as families pass wealth to heirs. This process is known as *parcelization* and the effect causes a fragmentation of purpose, so that forest lands are converted from a working landscape into everyone's backyard.

There are many methods to pass forest lands and management legacies intact, and these are the subject of chapter 8. Readers will learn the importance of intergenerational planning for forests, and the advantages and disadvantages of different methods, from the formation of limited liability companies to land trusts. The goal of positive impact forestry is to keep lands intact, maintaining long rotations that promote healthy ecosystems and valuable products. But it requires a commitment of families to forego short-term gain in favor of long-term investment. This, more than anything else, is one of the best reasons to keep land within the family and to use positive impact forestry methods.

CHAPTER 2

Understanding
Forest Ecosystems

An ecosystem is defined by the interaction of living organisms and the environment that supports them. Ecosystems exist regardless of scale: they range from coexistence of alga and fungi that form communities we know as *lichens,* to the entire earth. Understanding the significance of scale is one of the difficulties associated with making decisions that have impacts on ecosystems. Recognizing the significance of interactions between organisms and the physical environment in which they coexist also adds complexity to the picture. The concept of *ecosystem* is easy to understand, but the significance of scale and interactions is daunting.

Forest ecosystems are defined by the types of trees they support within a hierarchy at the top of which are *forest regions* or *biomes.* A biome is further subdivided into *forest types.* A forest type, as the term is used here, defines the associations of forest species that are apt to occur together.

Biomes, or forest regions, are mostly determined by broad climatic patterns, while forest types are defined by a local expression of climate and other site-related factors (Braun 1950) (fig. 2.1). For example, in the Northeast the boreal forest region extends southward from the very northern limits of tree growth in Quebec, into northern New England where it occurs as a red spruce–balsam fir forest type. This type quickly grades into a northern hardwood forest type (sugar maple, American beech, and yellow birch) at lower elevations in the north, but it extends as far south as northern Georgia only at higher elevations.

With all forest species, elevation is a proxy for climate. In the case of spruce-fir, the proxy is primarily temperature and, more specifically, temperature extremes on the low end that define extent of the type. In some

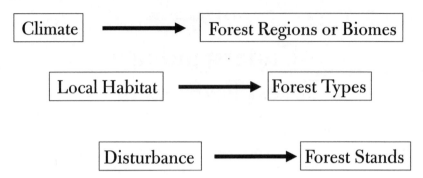

FIGURE 2.1   Forest regions, or biomes, are defined by broad climate patterns and are local expressions of climate—mostly influenced by geographic features. A forest stand is a very local forest type, usually one that has been disturbed.

cases, elevation is a primary determinate of rainfall patterns, and so it might be a combination of moisture and temperature that defines a type. Of all the climatic factors that determine what grows where, annual precipitation is probably the most important factor affecting forest growth and the location of types. In areas where annual rainfall changes over short distances, usually due to the effects of elevation, a closed-canopy forest will open up as conditions become dryer. The ponderosa pine forest type in the intermountain areas of the western United States is a good example of a moisture-dependent type. At an elevation where precipitation is adequate, ponderosa pine grows in dense stands, but at lower elevations stands grow in open, park-like conditions and eventually as widely scattered single trees on open range lands.

A very local expression of any given forest type is called a *stand*. A stand is the primary management unit in forestry and is usually defined as an area that is "sufficiently uniform in species composition and/or structure as to make it distinguishable from surrounding areas" (Smith 1997). In other words, the concept of *forest type* is really an abstraction, but a forest stand is a local expression of a type. The stand is what you see at any point in time and it is usually also the product of disturbances that have occurred in the past. For example, a stand of northern red oak composed of trees averaging 120 years of age is a local expression of the oak hickory type in the central hardwood region. If it is distinguishable from surrounding forests of the same species because of age and size, it is treated as a stand. In this case, age or structure is the factor that determines delineation. In other instances,

species composition, soils, wildlife habitats, the owner's management objectives, or a combination of factors delineate one stand from another.
Foresters do not manage forest types, but rather they manage stands, and
the term *forest management*—in a traditional sense—means the collective
management of stands within a defined geographic area, often a single ownership. Delineation of stands is not always as obvious as separating pines
from hardwoods, and in many areas stands are actually a cacophony of
species representing a convergence of two or more forest types.

There are three generalizations about where forests grow that are important to keep in mind. The first is that topography has a significant influence on climate, from the effects of elevation on temperature and rainfall
to the orientation of valleys and other land forms and their effects on pre-
vailing storm winds. Many excellent forest soils reside in areas that are
threatened by storm winds. The risk of attempting to grow trees on long
rotations on dangerously exposed sites is a significant management consideration.

The second generalization is that soil is the primary determinate of productivity in forests. European families that settled North America quickly
figured out how to judge land by species composition and structure of
forests, and these lands were cleared for agriculture. Today, more than half
of the land area of the United States is capable of supporting forest vegetation, but less than one-third is now forested. The balance is used for agriculture or has been developed.

The third generalization about forest sites is that plant and animal communities change when site conditions change. In other words, if a forest
manager removes a portion of the canopy to let in more light, perhaps to
begin regenerating the forest, the changes brought about by these actions
influence factors like temperature, wind speed, and relative humidity. Such
conditions may change the complement of birds that use the canopy for
nesting or for other purposes. Warmer soils brought about by more sunlight hitting the ground will have an effect on the population of organisms
that live in the soil. Even a forest that has been severely disturbed—by fire,
disease or insect depredations, wind, or when a manger prescribes a
clearcut—is still a forest, but with an entirely new complement of species
that will use the site. Most forest ecosystems, except those that developed
in highly protected areas, are well adapted to dealing with catastrophic
conditions. Disturbance is the rule in most forests, not the exception. Positive impact forestry mimics the effects of natural disturbances to keep

ecosystems intact while also providing timber for human use. Only ecosystems capable of maintaining their essential integrity while also providing timber and other human benefits are suitable for positive impact forestry. Those ecosystems at risk from timber extraction—for whatever reason—are not suitable for timber production and thus are used only passively or not at all.

Species Succession and Tolerance

A thorough understanding of local patterns of forest succession is fundamental to the practice of positive impact forestry. Succession is the orderly and predictable replacement of plant and animal communities as conditions change over time. The key phrase is "orderly and predictable." If not for a manager's ability to predict changes in successional patterns brought about by disturbances—especially those caused by human interventions—there would be no scientific basis for managing forest ecosystems to obtain benefits.

The patterns and processes of forest succession have been the subject of many studies, and much has been written to describe how it plays out in different forest types. But for every answer that science uncovers, new questions emerge, generating many different theories about how forests change, and why. In western forests there are ecosystems that have never seen human disturbances, and studies of these areas are enormously valuable in our quest to understand succession elsewhere. In eastern forests, such is not the case; virtually every acre has suffered the impacts of human exploitation. So much so that we can only speculate about pattern and process absent human interventions. Unfortunately, forest science arrived on the scene well after most presettlement forests had been cut hard for products or cleared for agriculture, and so in the eastern forest we lack critical baseline information about how forests change when humans are not around.

The engine of forest succession is fueled by the relative tolerance of trees to competitive conditions. Complements of species are adapted to changing forest environments, but the growth and maintenance of these species lead to further changes (Horn 1971). Each succeeding complement tends to persist longer than the species it replaced until the site is occupied by a complement of species that will persist in the absence of disturbance. Trees that are capable of fulfilling their life cycle—reproduction, establishment, growth, and maintenance—in extremely competitive circumstances are said to be *tolerant*. These species are often found in the understory of older stands where timber has been lightly harvested in the past, or in the overstory as old-growth sentinels—and in the understory—of very mature stands that have avoided disturbances for many, many years. Only species that are capable of establishing offspring in their own shade will persist when a successional pattern reaches a *climax*. Environmental change in an undisturbed climax association is very slow and mostly associated with replacement of old-growth trees that succumb to a combination of stresses, causing them to relinquish their positions in the canopy usually to offspring (or close relatives).

Tolerance is a relative indication of a species' ability to survive competition for light, nutrients, moisture, and space. On most sites, the one environmental factor that is more determinative than others is a species' *relative tolerance* to low light. Tolerant species are capable of growing in shaded conditions. The more shaded the conditions under which a species can reproduce, establish, grow, and maintain itself, the more tolerant the tree, and the more likely it is to persist in a climax forest. It is this ability more than anything else that allows tolerant species to dominate sites when severe disturbances are lacking. In most forests, however, experiencing the effects of a severe disturbance is not a question of if; rather, it is question of when. In these areas, a climax forest is a temporal phenomenon; given time, even the most stable forest will experience a disturbance severe enough to set succession back, creating an environment favorable to species that are less tolerant.

An *intolerant* species, as the name implies, is the opposite of tolerant. In other words, tree species that are intolerant of highly competitive and low-light conditions are incapable of reproducing, establishing, growing, and maintaining themselves under their own canopies. The intolerants, or *pioneers*, since they are the first species to invade severely disturbed sites, have developed strategies that allow them to take advantage of catastrophic conditions. For example, aspen—or popple—reproduces with prolific quantities of light, wind-borne seed that can easily germinate on bare soil, exactly the sort of reproduction strategy one would expect of a species that is incapable of germinating in its own shade (fig. 2.2). But this same species will also sprout from dormant buds on the root system that are triggered to develop when the tree detects that the top is missing and soils are warmed by sunlight.

FIGURE 2.2   A young aspen seedling on an exposed shale cobble.

In northern areas, from Maine to Washington where aspen stands are extensive, managers mostly rely on this spouting ability to reproduce stands of aspen. The hitch is that the disturbance must be severe and properly timed. Clearcutting is the only method that will successfully reproduce aspen. In other words, species that are adapted to catastrophic events require catastrophic conditions to reproduce successfully.

Other examples of intolerant reproduction strategies:

The jack pine of northern Michigan is adapted to fire. It produces a cone sealed with pitch that must be softened by bright, hot sunlight, or fire. Cones open explosively, ejecting seeds usually onto a recently burned surface where seed will geminate even in extremely harsh conditions. Jack pine is the principal species of one of a few forest types in the United States that are adapted to fire. Also known as *fire-dependent* communities, some other examples are chaparral forests of the southwestern United States and lodgepole pine in the intermountain areas of the West, where aspen is also considered a fire-dependent community.

Pin cherry, a noncommercial species of the northeastern United States, is attractive to birds and other animals for the pulp of its fruit. When the seed passes, it is capable of living in the soil for periods in excess of 120 years, waiting for a catastrophe to remove the overstory and allow the warmth of sunlight to trigger germination. Although not really considered a fire-dependent community, when pin cherry seed is in the soil, a fire will promote conditions that favor germination.

The Ohia tree, native to the Hawaiian Islands, has a wind-borne seed that germinates on relatively recent, grainy lava flows. It is a very slow-growing tree, which is uncharacteristic of intolerant species as a whole, but it also develops into pure stands with a very dense canopy. Although the Ohia is intolerant of shaded conditions, and thus qualifies as a pioneer species, it also forms a climax type on sites where it grows. This is known as an *edaphic climax* because soil conditions are the primary controlling factor.

Douglas-fir is considered a midtolerant species of the northwestern forest that is adapted to periodic catastrophic fires, which prepare an ideal seed bed for Douglas-fir seed. Once established, it is fairly resistant to fire (except when fire gets into tree crowns), and it is a relatively long-lived species. In the absence of disturbance, Douglas-fir stands are gradually replaced by more tolerant trees like western hemlock, noble, silver, and grand fir, and western red cedar, depending on elevation and latitude. Although clearcutting extensive areas of Douglas-fir has been highly controversial, some form of disturbance that exposes mineral soil is necessary to reproduce this species by natural means. Harvesting single trees or small groups will mimic a pattern that causes succession to move forward. More tolerant understory species will fill in the gaps and eventually reach the main canopy.

Forest succession is usually represented as a unidirectional process that proceeds from a stand composed of pioneer species—which require open,

TABLE 2.1

The Most Common U.S. Tree Species Associated with Successional Patterns of Growth, Described in Figure 2.3

Region	Pioneer	Early-Successional	Subclimax	Climax
Southeast	loblolly pine	sweetgum	oaks	
Mid-Atlantic	tulip poplar	black locust/ash	oak/hickory	maple/beech
Mid-southcentral	red cedar/black cherry	black walnut	oak/hickory	maple/beech
Upper Mid-west	aspen/pine	gray/white birch	red/black oak	maple/beech
Northeast	aspen	w. birch/sweet birch	yellow birch	maple/beech
Southwest	aspen/ponderosa pine	Douglas-fir	white pine	cedar/fir
Northwest	red alder/aspen	Douglas-fir	spruce/hemlock/cedar	true firs

Source: Fowells 1965.

There are many exceptions to these sequences that are related to site conditions, such as time since last disturbance, silvicultural practices, and other factors. Note: This is a greatly simplified representation intended only to give readers an idea of the different species associated with different stages of succession in different regions.

bare-soil conditions for seeds to germinate and which are often short lived (at least in a relative sense), fast growing, sexually precocious, and somewhat smaller in proportion at maturity—to a stand composed of climax trees—which are generally long lived and slow growing but highly tolerant of competitive conditions and which will prevail in the absence of disturbance (table 2.1 and fig. 2.3). Between the two extremes are those that sometimes act like pioneer species and sometimes like climax species. *Midsuccessional species*, also known as *subclimax species*, are the schizophrenics of forest trees because, depending on the circumstances, they can assume the characteristics of either pioneer or climax species. Propagating midsuccessional species requires careful site interpretation in order to ascertain the role they have assumed. This topic is discussed in greater detail in chapter three.

Generally, as succession progresses from pioneer to climax species, ecosystem complexity tends to increase, as does biodiversity and tolerance. With each step of succession, stability tends to increase so that each succeeding change will last longer then the preceding stand, but the ability of the stand to recover from disturbance decreases. For example, if an aspen stand is clearcut or burned or blown down by a hurricane, it comes back as aspen. But if a climax sugar maple forest is clearcut (and the soils disturbed), succession is set back to an earlier stage, although how much earlier depends on the severity of the disturbance. Slight disturbances tend to move succession forward.

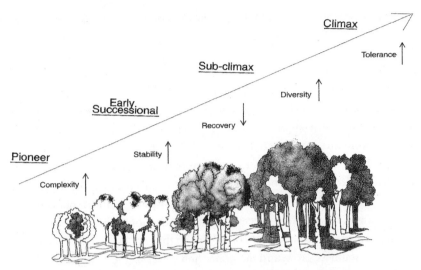

FIGURE 2.3 Forest succession is often portrayed as a unidirectional process that progresses—in the absence of disturbance—from pioneer species that are adapted to catastrophic disturbances to climax species that will remain in the stand until a disturbance that favors pioneers. Complexity, stability, diversity, and tolerance all increase as succession proceeds from pioneer to climax species, but a community's ability to recover from disturbance decreases—the more severe the disturbance, the less chances are for recovering the predisturbance community.

Forest management practices are planned disturbances that are intended to speed up succession, reverse it, or slow it down depending on the manager's objectives. This is a fundamental concept of forestry and is the foundation of silvicultural practice.

The preceding brief discussion about forest succession is a gross oversimplification of a complex process. Although our understanding of the process is incomplete, there are three generalizations about forest succession that are important to keep in mind. First, climax communities are stable, but only in the absence of disturbance. Yet disturbance is the rule in many forest areas, not the exception. For example, pine forests of the intermountain regions of the western United States (and the chaparral forests in the hills of California) are periodically disturbed by dry conditions and fire; the same is true of the pine forests in the Southeast. In New England, forests are periodically disturbed by rain-wind events, usually the remnants of hurricanes. Although there are some forests of the world where severe disturbance regimes are lacking, in areas where forest management for wood production is feasible there are usually one or more natural sources of disturbance that drive forest succession. In these areas, a climax forest is a temporal phenomenon; it is not a question of if a forest will be disturbed, but when it will happen. Positive impact forestry attempts to mimic natural disturbances so as to provide benefits.

Second, drastic disturbances tend to favor intolerant species (remember, a drastic disturbance is mimicking a catastrophic event). The formation of intolerant complements of species is nature's way of dealing with change. Pioneer species tend to stabilize exposed soils and promote the formation of topsoil; the humic layers, rich in carbon, support organisms that use carbon for energy and bank essential mineral nutrients used by species that follow. Forest succession is a process of accumulation, of carbon and nutrients, to support communities that are eventually able to reproduce, establish, grow, and maintain themselves in the absence of disturbance.

Finally, natural catastrophes—tornadoes, hurricanes, fire, insects, and disease—tend to topple climax communities, seriously, which calls into question the concept of a climax forest. In some forest types, especially in the Pacific Northwest, stands composed of pioneer and early-successional species can grow to immense proportions. These stands may look like ancient forests but are actually far from a climax state. Although there are many exceptions to this rule, generally speaking if the species in the understory of an undisturbed forest are different from the species in the canopy, the forest will continue to move toward a climax association. Light, periodic thinning in these stands will tend to move succession forward, mimicking the circumstances in which old, sentinel trees gradually drop out of the canopy due to insect or disease depredations, or for other reasons.

Form and Function in Trees

If an organism's measure of success is the extent to which it is capable of passing on its DNA to subsequent generations, trees are a model for success. They are elegantly simple (although a plant physiologist might not agree), with no moving parts, no delicate internal organs that suffer wear and tear, an ability to regenerate new tissues each year, and they require very few demands of the environment that surrounds them. Simplicity is the key along with their tendency to grow in layers that are constantly renewing themselves (fig. 2.4).

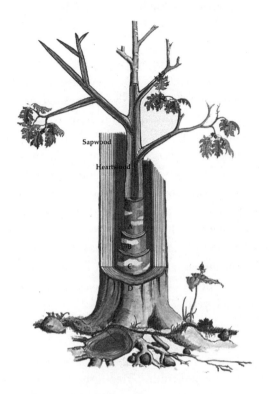

The appearance of the tree with bark when it was
A—8 years old.   B—10 years old.
C—12 years old.   D—22 years old.

FIGURE 2.4 Trees grow in layers. Illustration by David M. Carroll. Reproduced by permission from Shigo 1979.

Trees belong to one of two major classifications of species: *hardwoods* and *softwoods*. Unfortunately, these terms have little to do with the relative hardness or softness of the wood, so a brief explanation is in order. There are major differences in form and function between the two groups.

Hardwoods include all tree species classified by botanists as *angiosperms*. They are generally broadleaf and deciduous (and thus are sometimes referred to as *deciduous*), except in tropical and subtropical climates. Their flowers are complex and they produce a seed that is protected by a skin or a husk. Another interesting fact about hardwoods is that their growth form is strongly controlled by sunlight. One of the challenges of growing good hardwoods for timber is to control the amount of light a stand receives: too much and the trees are squat and branchy, but too little and trees will sacrifice diameter growth for height. Softwoods, or *conifers*, include species classified as *gymnosperms*. They are usually needle bearing and evergreen, although not always, and they have simple flowers that produce "naked" unprotected seeds, usually in cones. Of the two groups, softwoods evolved earlier than hardwoods and their growth form is controlled by gravity, not light. In other words, softwoods grow opposite the pull of gravity. No one knows why this is so, but it may be because they evolved at a time when the earth was far younger and sunlight was diffused through thick clouds and haze. The growth form of softwoods is very different from that of hardwoods and much easier to control. They also tend to utilize site resources more efficiently and grow faster and straighter on a wider range of sites than most hardwoods. For these reasons, softwoods have been a favorite of the wood-using industry, especially in the softwood forests of the Pacific Northwest and in the Southeast where many thousands of acres are planted with pine each year.

Less than 5 percent of a tree's weight (in both hardwoods and softwoods) is living tissue; the balance consists of support structures laid down in such a way as to improve efficiencies, to connect roots with leaves, or to overcome environmental difficulties. Trees grow from meristematic cells—theoretically capable of propagating indefinitely—which surround the entire organism. At the tips of branches, trees form perennating buds during times of dormancy. When conditions are right in the spring, buds expand and meristematic cells begin to divide rapidly. Meristem in roots act the same way, with one important difference: it does not form perennating buds during times of dormancy. Instead, growth will slow almost to the point of cessation until environmental conditions signal that its time to start growing again.

Between root tips and branch tips, the entire surface area of a tree is lined with two very thin layers of meristematic cells known as *cambium*. The first layer, just below the bark, is called the *cork cambium*. It is responsible for forming protective layers, the most external of which is known as *bark*. Inside the cork cambium is a layer of conductive cells called *phloem*, whose role is to bring the products of photosynthesis to living cells throughout the tree (fig. 2.5). Just inside the phloem is another layer of meristematic cells called the *vascular cambium*, which is largely responsible for controlling the way trees grow in girth. Cells that divide outward from the vascular cambium develop into phloem; those that divide inward become conductive and storage tissue known as *xylem*. Even though the vascular cambium is protected by bark, any injury sufficient enough to damage the bark will also injure the vascular cambium, disrupting growth at the point of injury but also exposing living tissue to disease-causing organisms (Shigo 1979).

Xylem is mostly nonliving tissue composed of cellulose and lignin that provides physical support to the vessels that transport water and nutrients from roots to leaves. Surrounding these transport vessels throughout the active xylem are living cells called *parenchyma*, some of which are designed to store photosynthate but some of which form a specialized transport network known as the *symplast*. The symplast connects living cells in the xylem with the phloem (strictly speaking, the phloem is part of the symplast); it is the transport mechanism that supplies these living cells with energy. In xylem, symplast is commonly referred to as *ray cells*, a type of parenchyma capable of moving photosynthate both around a single growing season's xylem and across many years of xylem.

Meristematic cells are also capable of differentiating to form flower buds and other tissues that can react to special circumstances. For example in many deciduous hardwood species, meristem will form dormant buds surrounding the entire tree. Known as *adventitious buds*, their normal condition is dormancy, but when conditions are right—usually the result of a

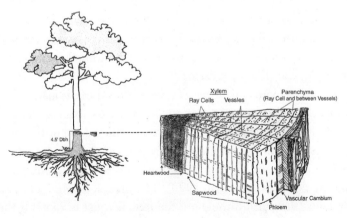

FIGURE 2.5 Important internal components of a tree stem.

disturbance of some kind—the buds are activated, causing them to develop as though they were ordinary buds. The purpose of adventitious buds is to react to disturbances. It is a sort of backup mechanism for trees that have been injured or are suffering stress. Species vary widely in their ability to form and make use of adventitious buds. For example, most softwoods do not form adventitious buds.

There are two important facts to remember about how trees grow:

1. Growth originates from the vascular cambium just under the bark and surrounding the entire tree. When this sheath is breached or injured, it not only interrupts the pattern of growth, but it also creates an opening for pathogenic organisms, which is far more serious than the injury itself. Stem injuries later in the life of a tree can negatively affect timber values far more than similar injuries on saplings.

2. Aboveground parts of trees will form resting buds during periods of dormancy (cold periods in northern climates, or during dry seasons in areas that do not freeze), but roots do not. Instead, roots slow the formation of new cells until growing conditions are favorable again. Even though roots are protected by soil, they are very susceptible to injury, which can hurt the tree by decreasing root area and by exposing tissues to disease-causing organisms. In some ways, root damage is far more injurious to tree health and vigor than stem injuries that lower timber values. Protecting roots and residual stems when silvicultural practices are applied is one of the most important aspects of positive impact forestry.

A tree is composed of four primary systems: roots, stem, branches, and leaves. There are also other specialized structures, such as flowers and seeds that develop periodically for reproduction, and buds that contain meristematic tissues, as described earlier.

Twenty percent or more of the mass of a forest-grown tree is made up of roots. Their role, in addition to anchoring the tree, is to obtain water and nutrients, and—for most hardwoods—to store a portion of the products of photosynthesis, especially during dormancy. Roots also produce hormones that serve as a form of communication between aboveground and belowground parts (Hartmann et al. 1990). The precise function of these hormone systems (that form throughout the tree, not just in roots) is the subject of another book, but suffice it to say that the presence, absence, or relative concentration of these chemical products serve the tree in much the same way a nervous system serves an animal. For example, the root-suckering response of poplar or aspen species (also known as *popple* in some areas) results from the sudden development of adventitious buds on roots. Those buds are triggered to break dormancy by the absence of a hormone produced in the tree crown that normally suppresses bud growth on roots. When a catastrophic event disconnects aboveground from belowground parts, adventitious buds on roots begin to develop. And—if conditions are right—before the end of a growing season, a single stem is replicated by scores of clones. This is an example of just one mechanism used by pioneer species to quickly regenerate a site that has been severely disturbed.

The hormone system used by trees and other plants is a highly effective mechanism to communicate conditions throughout the organism (Kossuth and Ross 1987). Some trees even produce toxins that prevent other trees from competing for space and resources. This phenomenon is known as *allelopathy* and varies widely between species. For example, black walnut is well known for the toxins it produces (leached from roots and aboveground parts) that prevent other plants from growing near it.

In the plant kingdom, and within the realm of forests in particular, communication is achieved through the use of chemicals, mostly within a single tree but also between individuals. For example, some species may have developed ways of communicating the impending threat of an insect defoliation or a serious disease outbreak, both between individuals in a stand and at a distance, through the use of chemical substances that act similarly to pheromones (chemical sex attractants) in animals. This is a gross oversimplification of communication paths in trees, but the main point is this: trees do not have nervous systems or centralized ganglions or brains. (Tompkins and Bird 1973). So far as we know, trees do not use electrochemical pathways known as *nerves* in animals. Thus, trees do not think (at least not in the fashion of humans); they don't ponder their circumstances, develop strategies, or feel pain despite the fact they are perfectly well adapted to the sites on which they live.

Forest tree roots are usually far more extensive than may appear to be the case. In most forest stands, roots extend as much as two to five times beyond the crown spread of any given tree, but the more coarse-textured and nutrient-poor a soil, the greater the extent of roots (Daniels et al. 1979).

The pattern of rooting is dendritic, although far more extensively so than branches in the crown, and some species form a central tap root while others develop a more fibrous root system. Most of the surface area of roots is composed of fine, hairlike structures also known as *feeder roots* that reside within a few inches of the soil surface. These fine roots account for a relatively small proportion of total root mass but most of the total root length and almost all of root surface area. Virtually all nutrient and water uptake is performed by fine roots.

The roots of forest trees also rely on a symbiotic relationship with a group of soil-dwelling fungi called *mycorrhizal fungi* (or simply *mycorrhizae*), that form nonpathogenic infections, both within root tissues and surrounding them, that greatly increase their surface area and ability to take up moisture and nutrients, especially phosphorus (fig. 2.6). A tree shares a portion of photosynthate with the fungus in exchange for enormous benefits the association provides. Mycorrhizal associations are common in the plant world, but they are especially important to forests. Trees that readily form mycorrhizal associations are far more productive than trees that do not, for a variety of reasons. For example, when soil oxygen is limiting due to compaction from logging equipment, the formation of mycorrhizal roots is inhibited. This is the primary reason why harvesting in stands to favor conditions for residual trees (such as when thinning) must avoid soil compaction. Mycorrhizae-forming fungi represent some of the most important species in the "hidden" forest below the soil, discussed in greater detail later in this chapter.

Another significant fact about forest roots is that they readily graft into one another—even between species—so resources, toxins, and pathogens are shared widely. Below ground, roots are everywhere and the fine roots that are most sensitive to damage are also the most susceptible *and* the most crucial to tree health. The importance of protecting roots is discussed in greater detail later in this chapter and again in Chapter 5.

The main stem of a forest tree, from the *root crown* (where the stem emerges from the soil) to the first scaffold branches in the crown, comprises about half of a tree's total mass. It is primarily composed of cellulose, a carbohydrate that is a major constituent of the cell walls of plants and the most abundant naturally occurring organic substance on earth. Another important constituent of wood is *lignin*, a noncarbohydrate polymer that stiffens and binds cells that form the primary vessels in wood. In fact, it was the development of lignin in trees that allowed them to evolve into arborescent forms (Morey 1973), which in turn assured that they would grow

FIGURE 2.6 The fruiting body of mycorrhizal fungi grow on top of and within tree roots, greatly increasing their surface area and ability to take up nutrients and moisture. Photograph by D. Moore, 2002. Reproduced by permission of ForestryImages.org.

cylindrically (tree stems take the form of a tapering cylinder called a *parabola*). A cylinder is far more aerodynamic than any other form and stronger per unit area, since any force perpendicular to the cylinder—from any direction—is resisted by what amounts to the strength of a balanced arch (Shane 2003). A tree's shape allows it to withstand the forces of wind, except in extreme circumstances or when a formerly closed canopy is opened exposing residual trees to high winds for the first time. As strong and well formed as they are, trees still rely on strength in numbers to survive. Nevertheless, high winds, not stem failure, commonly cause blowdown.

The main stem of most trees is composed of two different types of wood: the outer rings consisting of active conductive tissue (xylem), known as *sapwood*, and the central core consisting of xylem that has been abandoned, known as *heartwood*. The presence or absence of heartwood is often a function of tree age, and vigorous trees of a few species are capable of delaying the formation of heartwood until very old age. For example, sugar maple seems to delay the formation of heartwood on good soils, except in circumstances where an earlier injury caused the tree to abandon its sapwood. Even though this species is also capable of "walling off" infections (as are most trees, including both softwoods and hardwoods), which effectively stops the spread of disease into wood layers accumulated after the initial infection, early injuries will spawn the formation of heartwood in sugar maple. A log defect that commonly forms in the heartwood of sugar maple, known as "mineral stain," is often associated with poor sites. But the presence of stain is less evidence of a poor site than a poor logging job. Mineral stain is caused by injuries, commonly from old logging wounds that leave a legacy of ruin for the next owner to discover. The internal effects of stem injuries are discussed in greater detail in Chapter 3.

Sapwood is the equivalent of a first-order plumbing system for leaves, and it also serves to store a portion of the complex sugars produced by photosynthesis. Active xylem in sapwood is infused with living parenchyma cells, including the current year's tissue plus those of the past five to twenty years, depending on the physiological activity of the tree, its total leaf area, and its storage needs. The delineation between sapwood and heartwood is not obvious in all species.

Heartwood is usually darker than sapwood (especially in many hardwood species, but less so in the conifers—spruce and pine species in particular) because of its role as a dump for metabolic byproducts that stain wood. The presence of heartwood also offers some structural support, probably more so later in the life of a tree than when it is growing vigorously. The proportion of sapwood to heartwood is a function of tree vigor and leaf area. The more vigorous a tree the more sapwood, but as trees get older and become less vigorous the proportion of heartwood increases. In some timber species the amount of heartwood in proportion to sapwood increases the value of logs for lumber (black walnut, for example); in other species the opposite is true (e.g., sugar maple). Also, as a general rule, species that lay down xylem vessels that are coarse and large (such as in the oaks) tend to form heartwood more readily than species that rely on a finer, smaller xylem vessels (such as the maples).

In temperate regions of the world where trees experience a period of dormancy, the rate of xylem formation is easily read in the annual rings of a tree. In spring, when physiological activity is at its highest, the conductive vessels in xylem are straw-like, thin-walled and relatively large. But as the growing season progresses, vessels are noticeably smaller, more densely packed, and progressively darker (with a higher proportion of parenchyma cells for storage) until growth ceases during dormancy. These changes, triggered by decreasing day length, are a mechanism to help the tree prepare for dormancy. The pattern of *springwood* followed by *summerwood* (or *latewood*) represents a single growing season, or one year in the life of a tree.

Physically, a tree's branches are just like the main stem but the proportion of sapwood to heartwood increases from the main stem to branch tips. A branch is a second-order plumbing system between roots and leaves, but branch xylem tissue forms differently from that in the main stem to support a less-than-vertical weight. Softwood species tend to bolster cells on the same side as gravity, while hardwoods reform the cells under tension. This same differential in cell walls occurs in the main stem when a tree is leaning and forms what is called *reaction wood*: in softwoods, it is called *compression wood* and forms on the side toward the lean; in hardwoods, it is called *tension wood* and forms on the side opposite the lean. In both cases, even a slight lean can produce reaction wood, which causes lumber to warp during drying and has a significantly negative effect on lumber values.

Branches and leaves usually represent less than one-quarter of a grown tree's total mass, but the differences in branching strategies between softwoods and hardwoods is so great that it is impossible to generalize about the formation of branches without considering them independently of one another. In softwoods, buds are formed in a distinct and regular pattern consisting of a terminal bud at the tip of a branch, or at the top of the tree, surrounded by lateral buds. Terminal buds produce a hormone that controls the development of lateral buds. If a terminal bud is injured or killed, the surrounding lateral buds will compete to become the new terminal bud. In the very top of the tree, the same drama plays out: the terminal bud forces buds below it to grow laterally. If the terminal bud dies, stopping hormone production, the formally subordinate lateral buds will vie to become the new terminal. This mechanism is known as *apical dominance*. The apical bud at the top of a conifer (or at the end of a branch) dominates buds below it by producing a hormone that suppresses the tendency of subordinate buds to compete for the terminal position. In this way, branching is very regular and predictable in softwoods.

If the terminal bud of a softwood and its complement of lateral buds are removed, the branch terminal buds at the first whorl or node below the top will vie for the dominant position until one bud becomes apically dominant. When such an injury happens early in the life of a tree, the main stem will develop a permanent crook near the point where the injury occurred. Repeated injury to a terminal bud, or to buds vying for the terminal position, can permanently damage a tree, completely destroying its potential timber value. For example, eastern white pine in the Northeast is highly susceptible to the white pine weevil, an insect that lays its eggs under the scales of a terminal bud so that larva can tunnel down through the developing bud, killing it, and emerging just above the first set of lateral branches. Laterally terminal buds just below this injury will begin to grow vertically and will compete with one another until one achieves apical dominance, suppressing the buds below it and forcing them to continue as laterals. Infestations in succeeding years can quickly turn an arborescent tree into nothing more than a shrub.

Hardwood trees use the same hormone-signaling system as softwoods, but the mechanism is different. Softwoods rely on apical dominance primarily because they are more sensitive to the pull of gravity (i.e., they are *geotropic*). Hardwoods are more sensitive to the location of light (i.e., they are *phototropic*), so buds tend to develop and grow into areas where light is available. The communication between buds effected by varying hormone concentrations is the same in hardwoods as in softwoods, but it tends to play out more *between* branches in most hardwoods and this allows crowns to develop so as to take best advantage of light conditions and other environmental factors. For this reason, hardwood trees require relatively crowded stand conditions as *saplings* and *poles* (2–10 inches dbh) to favor terminal buds that must develop in a vertical direction to obtain light. Once trees have reached 30–40 percent of mature height, hardwood stands are thinned for the first time, allowing crowns to expand. With hardwoods, crown shape is always a function of light availability, and height growth is far more plastic than in conifers, where all branches are subordinate to the leader, which is growing opposite gravity regardless of light conditions.

Branch form in hardwoods is very plastic, since they tend to develop to position leaves where there is light. When the canopy closes in, shading lower branches to the point where leaves can no longer produce enough photosynthate to "pay" the energy costs of the branch, lower branches stop producing buds and die (Schulze et al. 1986). Cambium in the main stem continues to form layers around the now dead branch until it falls away. In time, the cambium covers the branch stub and begins growing again as a uniform layer, just as though the branch had never existed. Eventually, the former branch location is invisible to all but the most seasoned log buyer. The presence of branch stubs as defects in logs is discussed in greater detail in chapter 3. Logging injuries to branches are generally inconsequential (when branching begins at a height above merchantable limits, as discussed later) or are certainly far less damaging than injuries to the main stem or roots. Although the goal of the logger should be to leave as little residual stand damage as possible, a manager concerned with future value in a residual stand spends more time looking for value-threatening injuries on the main stem than for broken branches in the crown.

Leaves are the factories of trees, using water from the soil, carbon dioxide from the atmosphere, and light from the sun to produce sugars, one of which is a complex carbohydrate known as *cellulose* that represents about half the weight of a tree. The process common to all green plants is called *photosynthesis*. It is the conversion and storage of light energy to chemical energy. In addition to photosynthesis, leaves also serve trees as sites for the exchange of gases, producing oxygen as a by-product of photosynthesis and carbon dioxide as a by-product of respiration at night. Leaves also transpire moisture vapor, serving both as a kind of wick to help pull water and nutrients to leaves and as a cooling mechanism to protect leaves from exposure during hot summer days.

Most of the *intermediate treatments* in forestry, practices to improve the growth and value of trees from saplings to maturity, are intended to allocate space to the crowns of trees that are good candidates for the future. The trick is to increase the rate of photosynthesis in selected trees with periodic thinning while avoiding potentially damaging impacts from extracting products.

One of the most serious threats to leaves is defoliation from a wide variety of insects. When softwoods are defoliated, it usually leads to mortality. Fortunately, there are not many defoliators of coniferous trees, since trees defend themselves by exuding a sticky pitch at the point of injury. In hardwoods, a single-season defoliation is rarely fatal. In fact, healthy hardwoods can usually withstand a couple of years of complete defoliation, but not without stress. As a general rule, early-season defoliators are far more harmful than those that tend to attack in mid- to late summer. Why? Because when leaves are destroyed early in the season many hardwood species will produce a second set of leaves, seriously depleting the tree's reserves, whereas a late-season defoliation will usually hasten dormancy, or, rarely—the worst-case scenario—a late-season flush of leaves killed by an early frost. Fortunately, this third scenario almost never happens thanks to the triggering effect of an increasing dark period that signals trees to prepare for dormancy.

Defoliations of any kind are a serious stress to trees, so much so that thinning and other silvicultural practices should be postponed for at least two to three seasons after the most recent defoliation. And, if an infestation is predicted for an area, the manager should attempt to suspend thinning at least two years before the first defoliation. This conservative guideline is predicated on the fact that thinning and other types of stand entries are usually stressful to trees during the first season following treatment, sometimes longer. And, although trees can withstand a single stress (or disturbance), when stresses are compounded it can lead to crown dieback and mortality (fig. 2.7).

To survive, a tree must be capable of producing at least as much as it consumes, and it must have adequate control over water. So long as a tree can maintain a healthy cambium and parenchyma cells, allowing it to continually replace essential tissues, it will persist. In fact, a number of species are capable of persisting as individuals for many hundreds of years. The bristlecone pine, for example, in the White Mountains of east central California is capable of living in excess of four thousand years (the oldest specimen, which makes it the oldest known tree, is almost 4,800 years old). And among species that clone, such as aspen, it is quite possible there are

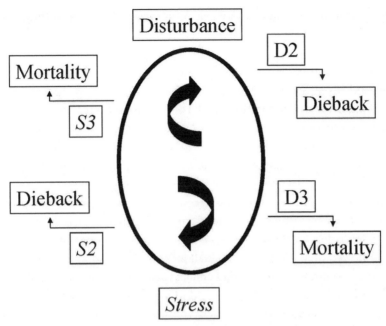

FIGURE 2.7 Stress and disturbance in forests are related phenomena that trees
are well adapted to survive. But when stresses and disturbances are compounded,
trees are apt to show symptoms such as crown dieback and—with increasing
severity—even mortality.

individuals that are far older than this (only because cloning replicates an
individual that exists for a period of time as a single stem).

Stress is a big factor in the lives of trees, especially when they reach a
point where size itself is stressful. Pioneer species reach this critical point
much sooner than midsuccessional or climax species (Kozlowski et al.
1991). No one knows why, but it may have to do with the pioneer's strategy of devoting resources to the stem, flowering, and fruiting portions of the
tree at the expense of roots. Heavy flowering and fruiting is a potentially fatal stress to the pioneers, and in this way they are "programmed" to give
way to mid- and late-successional species. Giving way in this sense means
either a gradual or abrupt dying back of the crown (depending on other coincidental stresses), increasing light availability for more tolerant species in
the understory.

Longevity is a characteristic of climax species primarily because its strategy is opposite that of a pioneer. As suggested by the term they were named after, climax species are the last to arrive in the successional cycle of an undisturbed forest. They are capable of photosynthesis in low light conditions and tend to "spend" resources on critical support structures, like roots and strong stems (Huges 2003). Climax species are programmed to idle along in the understory, for dozens of years if necessary, until a fatal inefficiency causes a senescent, early- or midsuccessional species to cease forming meristematic cells in the crown, causing dieback and thereby increasing light availability to a climax understory (Grime 1979). Again, crown loss is gradual or abrupt, depending on other stresses.

Once climax species reach the overstory, they continue to "spend" resources wisely by furthering the development of roots, stem, branches, and leaves while delaying flower and seed formation. When tolerant species begin to flower, they do so in a gradual, measured way so as to not tax the support systems. Since the seed of climax species is capable of germinating and establishing in the understory and idling along in the same fashion as the parent, trees do not need to rely on producing high seed volumes. Seeds that do germinate grow very slowly, developing further only as gaps in the canopy allow more light. Survival is a question of fate since parents in the overstory can remain in those positions for scores, even hundreds, of years longer. Eventually, further longevity is a function of stress; any combination of stresses that tip the energy balance, such as insect or disease depredations, drought, excessive temperatures, or even sheer size, can become a stress. The older and larger a tree, the less capable it is of weathering stress; even grand old sentinels eventually reach a point where the expense of coping with stress exceeds a critical balance point and the cost of persisting is more than the tree can afford. It succumbs to a combination of small stresses—or one larger event—that tips the scales, and the meristem stops dividing. A tree's demise is mostly a function of energetics. It becomes less and less efficient with size, sacrificing crown area as inefficiencies build, increasing susceptibility to stresses, until one or more additional stresses combine to create circumstances the tree is no longer capable of resisting.

Stress and Disturbance in Forests

A forest is far more than trees. It is a complex ecosystem—ever changing and defined by the interactions of living organisms and the surrounding environment. For this reason, active management decisions for any particular stand should also consider potential impacts not only on timber values, but also on surrounding forests. Decisions that prescribe disturbances must address the possibility of unforeseen impacts, both good and bad; and those who make decisions need to acknowledge that the true value of any forest ecosystem is something that far exceeds the sum its parts. The first concern of positive impact forestry is to protect, maintain, and even enhance the health and integrity of forest ecosystems over and above opportunities to generate income or enhance investment.

Ecosystems can exist at any scale, from microscopic to global. Wherever plants and animals interact with their environment and each other, and the original source of energy is sunlight, the association is described as an ecosystem. Oceanographers have recently discovered an exception to this primary rule, having located bottom-dwelling ecosystems living near volcanic vents. Thousands of feet below the surface, under incredibly high pressure and temperatures, live organisms that have adapted to sunless conditions. In areas once thought inhospitable and completely devoid of life, bacteria take the place of green plants as *primary producers*, capable of converting geothermal energy into chemical energy and supporting a food chain of higher-level organisms that until recently no one thought possible. This is a discovery that has redefined the concept of *ecosystem* as we know it. Yet, notwithstanding a wholly different source of energy and complements of organisms capable of harnessing it in possibly the most harsh conditions the earth has to offer, these ocean vent-dwelling communities seem to follow the same patterns and processes as ecosystems that rely on the sun as a source energy, and on photosynthesis as a means of harnessing it.

The study of terrestrial ecosystems is mostly concerned with the way different species interact, changes in communities over time, and the flow of inputs and outputs, such as energy, nutrients, and water. Even microscopic ecosystems are complex, yet minor changes of single factors can lead to changes throughout. The same is true in forests: almost regardless of the disturbance, whether caused by fire, drought, disease and insects, hurricanes, or human activity, it will spawn change in soil organisms, in wildlife populations, in productivity, and often in tree species composition. The direction and degree of change is a result of the way organisms react to one another and to new site conditions. Positive impact forestry endeavors to create desirable changes capable of providing human benefits while maintaining ecosystem integrity. It is predicated on the idea that humans are a part of forests and therefore have an interest in maintaining them as more than merely places for gathering fiber. Managing forests for the sake of forests is reason enough.

Stress can fuel changes. Yet, in many forests stress is the rule rather than the exception, and not all stresses are bad. Forest-dwelling organisms, and trees in particular, are well suited to cope with stress, but when stresses are compounded—either simultaneously or sequentially—it can translate into unfavorable changes that affect human use, such as reduction in tree growth, partial defoliations, and crown dieback. A severe compounding of stresses can lead to mortality (see fig. 2.7).

Climate-induced stresses and disturbances, such as drought, hurricanes, and ice storms, are expected but unpredictable events. The same is true for disturbances caused by insects and disease. Sometimes, environmental stress will predispose trees to depredations from other organisms. Vigorous trees are known to fend off attacking organisms, but trees already suffering a compounding of stresses cannot. In fact, some predatory organisms may be capable of detecting stress in trees and using it to advantage.

Human error is behind some of the most serious stressors caused by forest pests in North America:

Chestnut blight, a wind-borne fungus that decimated possibly the most important tree species the world has ever known—American chestnut—which once comprised nearly half of the forests east of the Mississippi River, arrived on infected seedlings imported from Europe.

Dutch elm disease, a vascular fungus spread by the relatively minor feeding habits of native bark beetles and by root grafts, causes infected trees to plug their vascular system, cutting off the delivery of water and nutrients to leaves and killing a tree in a few seasons or less (ironically, vigorous trees succumb more quickly). It arrived on infected elm logs from the Netherlands, destroying one of the most popular shade trees planted in the United States.

Gypsy moth, brought to the Boston area just after the Civil War by a self-described "naturalist" who was also interested in silk production, was allowed to escape and within ten years developed populations that defoliated almost all trees in the town, spreading throughout New England by the 1930s and throughout the Northeast by the 1960s. It is especially destructive to oaks, one of the region's most valuable species, and is still spreading across North America in a fan-shaped infestation to the south and west.

Each of these destructive organisms has had a tremendous impact on the species composition of eastern forests. For example, forests now principally composed of oak were formerly chestnut stands and—since oak is a favored food of gypsy moth—the higher proportion of oak in the canopy has probably fueled the spread of gypsy moth. It was hubris and ignorance that brought these destructive species to North America (species not known to be pathogenic or pernicious in their native ranges), launching a veritable plague of invasive exotic species that are now one of the greatest threats to forests in the United States. The nature of the problem for woodland owners and some practical guidelines to avoid the risks of exotic species is discussed in greater detail in chapter 6.

Even correctly timed logging practices, although one of the most important tools for managing forests, can stress stands in a number ways, including (1) opening the canopy, increasing light, temperatures, and wind speeds, but lowering humidity; (2) disturbing and compacting forest soils when heavy equipment is used for extraction; and, the most serious, (3) causing wounds in residual trees, both roots and stems, disrupting important physiological processes, and leaving them susceptible to decay and disease-causing organisms. Other potentially negative effects from practices such as *high grading* (i.e., "take the best and leave the rest") reflect poor silviculture but often do not cause any more stress than logging to improve a stand.

Stands with closed canopies (highly shaded conditions) that are abruptly opened by logging may experience a phenomenon known as *thinning shock*. Although it is not exactly clear why this happens, it may be that trees divert energy into crown growth to take advantage of openings at the expense of providing adequate nutrition to other parts of the tree. A changed environment can also be a factor. Thinning shock by itself is not bad. Usually a stand recovers after a growing season or two. But when thinning shock is coupled with other stresses, crown dieback and even mortality are possible. Forest managers who learned the hard way now know that thinning in tightly spaced stands is risky, especially if trees have suffered from stress in recent years. Thinning shock is avoided by treating only healthy, relatively stress-free stands with light but frequent thinning.

Frequent stand entries, however, can stress stands in other ways, such as by wounding residual stems, which leaves them candidates for damaging infections, or through soil compaction from logging equipment. When heavy equipment eliminates air spaces in soils, it also decreases the rate of water percolation and moisture-holding capacity of soils. These effects are discussed in greater detail in chapter 5. Positive impact forestry always considers the risks associated with management treatments, proceeding only when potential human benefits are possible without putting ecosystems at risk.

In the eastern forest, a general guideline on gaining access to stands for silvicultural treatments is this: No more than 10 percent of a stand's area is devoted to roads, landings, and skid trails. Experts insist that with proper planning and good felling techniques, even this conservative figure can be cut in half. Good planning not only lessens the potentially negative ecological impacts of logging, it also makes timber extraction considerably easier and cheaper. This means that in areas where forest soils freeze, harvesting activities should be scheduled during winter to prevent soil compaction and root disturbances, and to minimize the risk of soil erosion. Exceptions to this role are discussed later in this chapter.

Even though logging is usually perceived as bad for forests, there are many positive results when loggers use good practices and good timing (Landsberg and Gower 1997). Almost regardless of the objective—be it for wildlife habitat, recreation, timber production, or a combination of uses— logging is the principal means of effecting and controlling change in forests. But it also has the potential to do great damage, some of which might take years to recover from; or impacts may be irreversible, such as when soils erode from access routes. Fortunately, most practices that lessen the negative impacts of logging are common sense. Couple a well-informed woodland owner with a knowledgeable forester and skilled logger—all committed to protecting forest ecosystems even if it means delaying income production—and it is easy to convert potentially debilitating practices into positive impacts.

The Hidden Forest of Soils

Those who learn even a few things about soil usually develop a healthy respect for the important role it plays in forests. It is composed of varying proportions of minerals, organic matter, and air, and it is home to an almost immeasurably diverse population of bacteria, fungi, and other organisms, many of which are essential to healthy forests (Leak and Riddle 1979). In addition to anchoring trees to the earth, soils provide virtually all of the essential nutrients and water used by trees (Armson 1977).

The one characteristic of forest soils that distinguish them from agricultural soils is the vast complement of organisms—flora, fauna, vertebrates, and invertebrates—residing in upper soil layers, rich with organic matter. Fungi and single-celled bacteria predominate in topsoil and are organized into microscopic communities representing hundreds, if not thousands, of species only a small fraction of which science has isolated and identified. Phenomenal diversity coupled with a complexity of interactions that has, so far, defied sophisticated scientific inquiry makes forest soils a tantalizing puzzle, one that will take thousands of scientist-years and computing power far beyond the capacity of even the most advanced systems today to understand. It is distinctly possible that exploitive practices may have caused the extinction of microscopic species on a level equal to, or far exceeding existing diversity, fatally compromising processes about which we can only speculate. Nevertheless, forest soils are a biological and ecological treasure, and still a mystery. Bacteria and fungi are to this hidden forest, what trees are to forests in the landscape.

Some bacteria are capable of fixing atmospheric nitrogen and converting it into forms trees can use. Others are capable of unlocking essential nutrients bound in minerals. But some of the most important functions of bacteria and fungi involve recycling nutrients from leaves and other debris. They obtain energy from cellulose shed from trees but passed down from larger organisms like earthworms, newts, and others. In the process of consuming complex carbohydrates, fungi and bacteria release nutrients in forms roots can use. For example, if we could flag a single atom of magnesium in a forest soil and trace its path from roots to leaves, where it serves as the only mineral constituent of chlorophyll, when leaves are shed, the magnesium atom would return to the forest floor surrounded by carbonaceous compounds. After a few growing seasons (more or less depending on climate, temperatures, species, and biological activity), the atom will have passed through an unknown number of soil-dwelling organisms—probably culminating in bacteria—that release the atom (either by itself or as an *oxide*, combined with oxygen) in a form available to roots. Once it is within the vascular system of the tree, it is quickly incorporated into a chlorophyll molecule where it will reside until the leaf is shed.

Although greatly simplified, this example is intended to illustrate an essential process of forests known as *nutrient cycling*. If not for the ability of trees to convert light energy into chemical energy to fuel a system largely dedicated to recycling the essential ingredients of photosynthesis, forests could not exist. Trees are both the source of energy for the hidden forest in soils and the primary beneficiary of their combined actions. The relationships between aboveground and belowground forest organisms are far more complicated than this, but, in essense, the processes are intended to conserve essential nutrients (Pritchett and Fischer 1987). Nutrient cycling is a primary function of soil flora and fauna, and without the actions of these unseen organisms ecosystems would fail.

Aside from the considerably important but largely unknown biological associations in soils, there are four other important characteristics that affect tree growth and productivity: soil depth, texture and structure, soil reaction, and natural fertility (McEvoy 2002b).

Forest trees do not require a tremendous volume of soil to grow, so long as there is enough to meet basic needs mentioned earlier—especially anchoring. But shallow soils generally do not support productive forests. Trees growing on bedrock, also known as *ledge*, or above an impervious layer caused by clay, or by a hardened soil layer found in glacially derived soil known as *hardpan*, or even on top of a high-water table, are incapable of reaching full potential. Forests will grow in these shallow soils, but it is highly doubtful they can provide sustainable wood supplies. In some circumstances where shallow soils cause roots to grow in the form of a flattened mat, trees are susceptible to *windthrow*. Where these conditions occur, periodic thinning of trees to promote diameter growth can open the canopy sufficiently to cause blowdown. Even judicious thinning on shallow soils is risky in areas exposed to high winds.

The texture of a soil refers to the relative proportions of sand, silt, and clay, while soil structure is defined by the aggregation of particles. Generally, fine-textured soils have a higher level of natural fertility than coarse soils, which tend to be nutrient poor. The most productive forest soils are those characterized as loams. A loam is an almost perfect combination of sand, silt, and clay. It is a soil that drains well but is not droughty, allowing roots to develop without restrictions, yet it is strong enough to provide solid anchoring and is capable of holding high levels of essential nutrients in forms that trees can readily use.

Particles of sand, silt, and clay form *aggregations* with organic compounds in soils, which arise from byproducts, or wastes, of soil organisms.

The aggregation of particles is essential to a healthy forest because the more aggregated a soil, the more air space it has and the more water it can hold. Well-aerated soils also supply oxygen to soil organisms and to tree roots. And, when it rains, aggregates (and organic layers) act like sponges, holding water in the rooting zone of trees for extended periods. This is one of the reasons forests can withstand dry conditions better than many agricultural crops. Aggregations, however, are easily broken when soils are compressed (Tisdale et al. 1993).

When aggregations are broken by soil compaction, water absorption rates are diminished, as is total water-holding capacity, and there is significantly less oxygen for soil organisms and roots. Heavy equipment used to extract timber is one of the primary culprits of soil compaction. But even the weight of a horse or that of an adult displaced over the sole of boot can cause compaction on some fine-textured soils, especially when saturated. The effects of compaction are primarily a function of weight, and it appears that impacts are usually temporary. Soil aggregations are reformed in healthy forest soils by the actions of soil organisms. Long-term negative effects from soil compaction (on healthy forest soils) appear minimal, but a lack of baseline data from areas that have not experienced the effects of timber extraction makes comparisons difficult. We do, however, know enough about the effects of heavy equipment on forest soils to always warrant caution, especially on fine-textured soils and when soils are saturated. Positive impact forestry practices advocate harvesting when soils are least susceptible to physical changes; on frozen snow-covered soils or—in areas where soils do not freeze—when soils are dry. Regardless of soil conditions, timber extraction trails should always be kept to a minimum.

Soil reaction is an indicator of soil chemistry and the availability of essential nutrients. Sixteen elements are considered essential for plant growth, which means they have a functional role in plant nutrition. Of these, thirteen are considered mineral nutrients obtained mostly from the organic or mineral components of soil. The other three—carbon, hydrogen, and oxygen—are building blocks of carbohydrates, the primary product of photosynthesis. Trees obtain carbon from carbon dioxide in the atmosphere, and oxygen and hydrogen are obtained from soil water. These elements are never lacking, and since they are not gathered from organic or mineral portions of the soil, technically, they are not considered mineral nutrients.

Seven of the remaining thirteen essential nutrients are called *micronutrients* because adequate levels of these elements are on the order of ounces per acre, not pounds or tons. Micronutrients are almost never lacking in healthy forest soils.

The final six nutrients, used in relatively large quantities, are called *macronutrients*. They are further categorized as *primary* and *secondary* according to relative needs. The three primary macronutrients are nitrogen, phosphorus, and potassium; the secondary nutrients are calcium, magnesium, and sulfur. Although trees are capable of taking up some of these nutrients from atmospheric inputs, most are obtained by roots from the organic and mineral components of soil, and this is where the importance of soil reaction comes into play.

Soil reaction, also known as *pH* (potential hydrogen), is an indicator of a soil's ability to hold ions of essential nutrients so that roots can take them up. Most forest soils have a slightly low pH, primarily because of the biological actions of micro-organisms and secretions from tree roots. When pH is too low, essential mineral nutrient ions with positive charges are incapable of being held by soil particles, while those nutrient ions with negative charges are held so tenaciously that they are effectively locked up and unavailable to roots. When pH is too high, the tables are turned but the effect is the same: nutrients are either locked up or washed through the soil.

By itself, soil pH is nothing more than an indicator of the acid or base intensity of a soil. It does not say anything about the amount of acid or base. which is also known as *buffer capacity*, or the degree to which a soil will resist a change in pH. For example (and by way of analogy), consider two containers of water, one large, the other small, both at exactly the same temperature. The larger container will require more energy (British thermal units [Btu]) to achieve an equal change in temperature. In this example, pH is to temperature what buffer capacity is to Btu. Fine-textured soils have more nutrient exchange sites and thus are more highly buffered than coarse soils. This fact is one of the reasons why acid deposition in forests of the Northeast is so injurious. Sites that show the most serious injuries are usually shallow, coarse-textured soils incapable of buffering acidic atmospheric inputs. The result: trees show signs of stress, tree crowns begin to die back in situations where stands are already stressed from other factors, and when other stresses appear, trees die.

The last important characteristic of soils in this brief discussion of the impacts of soil characteristics on potential forest productivity, is natural fertility. As discussed earlier, in northern climates a site's nutrient pool tends to reside in soils more so than in vegetation. In tropical rainforests, the opposite is true. But even forests in northern areas accumulate nutrients in aboveground tissues as forests get older. Generally, nutrient accumulation in aboveground tissues is in inverse proportion to the size and extent of that tissue. Smaller parts like leaves, buds, and twigs have a higher nutrient concentration.

The relative concentration of essential nutrients in the main stem is so low, that stem harvesting—on most sites—has only a minor impact on the total nutrient pool, assuming that branches, twigs, buds, and leaves are left on the site. Whole-tree harvesting systems that process the entire aboveground parts into biomass, will accelerate the nutrient-mining effect that any form of vegetation extraction has on sites. For this reason, any harvesting system that removes tissues smaller than primary-order branches (in hardwood stands, primary-order branches are commonly processed into fuelwood) is not considered a positive impact practice, with the following two exceptions: instances in which diseased stands are being reproduced (during dormancy) by clearcutting methods and it is necessary to remove tops for sanitation purposes, and instances in which clearcutting methods are used to regenerate premature, defective stands on good-to-excellent sites and the manager is sure that the overall impact on the site's nutrient pool is minor.

Soils vary widely in fertility, from almost inert sands in glacial outwash plains to deep, loamy soils derived from limestone and other mineral-rich bedrock. Natural fertility is a function of all the factors described above—soil depth, texture, structure, and pH—in addition to origin of minerals and how well developed the organic layers are. Over time, the nutrient pool of any forest soil will build, primarily in organic layers. And trees adapt to the nutrient-suppling capacity of a site. This idea of *nutrient balancing* is a relatively new concept that explains why even trees growing at high elevations on harsh, nutrient-poor sites can produce healthy but extremely slow-growing trees. In these circumstances, trees have balanced nutrient uptake with the site's ability to supply nutrients (Ingestad 1974).

Virtually all of the biological activity in soils, most essential nutrients, and tree roots reside in the organically rich top layers of soil. The actions of forest floor and soil-dwelling organisms—from newts and earthworms to fungi and bacteria—incorporate leaves and other organic debris into the mineral component of soils. They use carbon from the debris as a source of energy, and they recycle mineral nutrients tied up in these tissues. They also produce chemical compounds (mostly as by-products) that help break down mineral particles, releasing essential nutrients while at the same time promoting the formation of aggregations of organic and mineral particles. The more aggregated a soil, the better its ability to supply oxygen and water.

The proportion of organic to mineral compounds decreases with depth from the surface. Depending on forest type, climate, and other factors, a single inch of well-aggregated topsoil consisting of equal parts organic particles, minerals, and air requires from a few years to many hundreds of years to form. Similarly, the thickness of topsoil layers varies from a few to many inches, depending mostly on the length of time that has passed since the last disturbance severe enough to affect the processes that convert leaves and other organic debris into humus. A well-developed organic horizon is an indicator of an old forest, one that has not experienced the effects of logging in quite some time. Old-growth forests that have not had any major soil-related disturbances for two hundred years or more develop organic layers that are so deep and spongy that the physical experience of walking on them is almost more memorable than the visual grandeur of the canopy.

Although forestry professionals have always understood the importance of soils to healthy forests, only recently have they begun to suspect that soils are far more important than once thought. Foresters know soil fertility develops in forests over time, and they have come to accept that periodic harvesting of stem wood (not branches, twigs, and leaves) has only a fairly minor impact on all but the most nutrient-poor sites. But only recently have managers learned that some nutrients, calcium and phosphorus in particular, are "mined" from sites at rates that will one day exceed the capacity of soils to replenish. With even conservative harvesting intensity, essential nutrient levels will reach a point where inputs are necessary. Unfortunately, our knowledge about the effects of mineral supplements on beneficial soil organisms is not sufficient enough to advocate widespread fertilization in natural forests. Until we know more about the impacts of periodic harvesting on nutrient pools and develop cost-effective and ecosystem-safe methods to replace essential nutrients, woodland owners should manage timber on poor soils extensively—or not at all—and should manage stands dedicated to timber on productive soils using longer rotations but with fewer stand entries, and then only when soils are frozen or dry.

The Importance of Avoiding Injury to Roots

On the subject of roots, "out of sight, out of mind," is a figure of speech that comes to mind, but roots are as important to tree health as the crankshaft is to the function of an engine. Most car owners never actually see an engine's crankshaft, nor do they think much about it. But if the crankshaft fails, there is no way to translate energy from pistons to the driveshaft, and the engine dies (usually violently so if an oil seal blows and the engine seizes up or if the shaft breaks). In trees, when roots fail the tree suffers, and if the failure is severe enough the tree will die.

The "don't see it, don't think about it" analogy between roots and crankshaft also fits in another way: failures are subtle, such as when a bearing between the shaft and the engine block begins to wear. If an operator misses a very slight change in engine pitch or a subtle but annoying clunky noise, disaster is only minutes, hours, or days away. When a bearing starts to go, it is not a question of if the engine will fail, but when. The same is true with tree roots. Seemingly subtle disturbances of roots from the effects of harvesting equipment, from livestock hooves—even human foot traffic at the wrong time of year—can result in a negative effect on tree vigor. Although the effect of root injuries or soil compaction may not be directly fatal, when a tree loses vigor it is more susceptible to other stresses, such as insect defoliation, disease, drought, or even stresses associated with opening the crown during a partial harvest.

The surface area of roots is many times that of aboveground parts, which makes sense because roots rely on surface contact with soil to perform three of their five main functions: water uptake, nutrient uptake, and anchoring. A fourth function of roots is storage, a place for the tree to hold resources during dormancy so that they are immediately available when aboveground parts start growing again in the spring. The importance of anchoring is obvious, but the fact that trees have developed adaptations to improve anchoring in harsh situations is nothing short of miraculous. The fifth function of roots is hormone production, as described earlier.

Water and nutrient uptake are such important functions of roots that the distribution of these resources in the soil will determine the extent and pattern of rooting. On good sites, roots tend to be branchy and compact, but the opposite is true on poor sites where roots are more extensive and lanky. Where soils are good, a tree's strategy is to create as much surface area in roots as possible, which makes sense. On poor soils roots need to forage for resources, but at the expense of surface area.

Regardless of site, most roots reside in the top few inches of soil, below the leaf litter. The top layer of soil is mostly humus, an organic salad of leaves, twigs, and other woody debris in various stages of decay. High carbon content in these layers provides energy for many different species of bacteria, fungi, and other organisms. Just below the humus layer is a very high concentration of fine roots, also known as *feeder roots*, tapping into mineral nutrients that are by-products of decomposition.

When the leaf litter and humus layer in a relatively undisturbed forest soil are carefully pulled back, a veritable mat of roots appear. Most of the important biological activity in roots takes place in these fine roots. If it were possible to look below the soil surface in a forest with the same clarity and detail of the woodland scene above, it would look like a randomly woven tapestry in three dimensions with a lot of loose ends. About the only noteworthy pattern to this scene would be an increasing order of size for roots to the point where they join individual stems at ground level. Pick any fine root, or even any root several orders larger in size, and it is a guess to determine which tree it belongs to. The beauty of this otherwise chaotic scene is that it doesn't matter. Roots graft onto one another at will and virtually everything is shared For example, if an essential nutrient is chemically flagged and placed in one isolated pocket of soil, eventually it would show up—in varying concentrations—much further from the source than expected. This sharing, coupled with the multiple functions roots perform, is why scientists coined the term *root systems*. In forests, roots are everywhere below the surface and the parts that are most biologically active are also the parts that are most sensitive to disturbances.

So what is the best way to protect roots from human activities? Avoid disturbing roots as much as possible, but especially in the spring when roots systems are becoming biologically active. On many forest sites, roots never become completely inactive. But there is a time just before the growing season when roots are setting the stage for the coming season. Forest soils should not be disturbed at this time (even to the extent of avoiding foot traffic, if possible; especially on saturated, fine-textured soils).

One of the best ways to limit site disturbances is with good planning that keeps heavy equipment on established trails, with a configuration that drags logs to the trail, also known as *pre-bunching*. Highlead cable systems in mountainous areas can be an effective way to avoid excessive site disturbances. But the problem with this type of harvesting system is that the expense of setting it up usually requires extraction of all merchantable timber.

Depending on the site, soils, species, and silvicultural objective, heavy cutting to justify the expense of a harvest system is nothing more than market-driven silviculture and should be avoided. Helicopters and balloon logging are possible alternatives in these circumstances so long as the expense of extraction does not prostitute good, positive impact forestry practices. Some timber is simply inaccessible without systems that can extract trees one at a time. Harvesting alternatives are discussed in greater detail in chapter 5.

In areas where soils freeze and there is a reliable snow cover, the best way to protect roots is to schedule timber harvesting during these conditions. Where soils don't freeze, schedule harvests during dormant conditions and when soils are as dry as possible, especially on fine-textured soils. Coarse-textured soils are less susceptible to damage from logging equipment even when soils are wet. But as a general rule, if soils are soaked, keep heavy equipment out of stands where there are concerns about residual trees. This guideline also applies to livestock, which should be kept out of stands from the time wildflowers first appear until leaves have completely expanded. Despite the fact that many woodland owners believe it is impractical to exclude grazing animals from forests, livestock and healthy forests do not mix. At a minimum, animals should be excluded from the most productive stands.

Unless it is the manager's intention to regenerate forests to favor early-successional species using clearcutting methods, intermediate treatments that leave a protective canopy should be used. Light cutting can be balanced with a cycle that disturbs stands as infrequently as possible. In other words, stands should be entered no more frequently than once every ten years or longer, and only when soils are frozen (preferably) or dry. And heavy equipment should stay on established trails, unless there is good reason to do otherwise.

Practical Applications of Forest Site Concepts

Under guidelines of traditional forestry in the United States, forests require from 30 to 150 years—seedling to sawlog—to grow useable products, depending on a number of factors. This is the equivalent of from one to four human generations, which is a long time considering that most forests are held in a single family for a generation or less. Variability in the age of maturity is due to local markets and to differences in species and site quality. A forest site is the sum of all the conditions that influence tree growth potential, but the most important factors are climate and soils. Climatic conditions include temperature extremes and rainfall. The local expression of broad climatic patterns as influenced by factors like topography, elevation, and aspect (i.e., the direction a slope faces) determines which locally indigenous trees grow where, but the rate at which trees grow within a particular microclimate is mostly influenced by soil. All other factors being equal, the effect of soil quality on forest productivity is exactly the same as for croplands. The difference is that a farmer harvesting one crop every season knows exactly what to expect from a particular soil. And the farmer can affect yields by applying soil amendments. A forest crop, however, takes many years to mature, so a manager needs to use a predictive tool to estimate how much wood will grow on a particular site, and how long it will take. Soil amendments are used on some forest soils, especially on played-out agricultural lands in the Southeast and in plantations of the Pacific Northwest. But forests in most other parts of the country rely on natural fertility, and even on sites where nutrients are lacking, soil amendments are not usually practical.

Almost anyone who knows even a little about local forests can correctly choose the more productive of two sites composed of the same complement of species. Paying attention to visual clues such as tree heights and bark characteristics, or to the presence or absence of understory plants, is the trick. But sometimes the stature of a forest is confused with production—large-dimensioned, older forests look more productive than dense sapling stands. Knowing how to assess forest site quality is one of the most important skills a forester possesses because it helps in deciding where time and effort is most apt to pay off. Thinning an unproductive stand is not only a waste of time, it is expensive—assuming the owner considers the cost of thinning an investment and takes into account the time-value of money. As a general rule, a manager will only thin stands where future value of the treatment exceeds the future value of a next best alternative investment (assuming ecosystem risks are minimal). A good decision to thin is the financial equivalent of buying a certificate of deposit that pays 6.5 percent when the next best alternative is a passbook savings account that pays 3 percent.

Trees grow in temperate regions by putting down a new layer of wood each year. On the main stem, this new wood increases the girth of the tree, but in the top of the tree the same layer elongates the stem, increasing total tree height. Diameter growth rate is controlled by stem density: the more crowded it is, the slower trees will grow in diameter. This is because in crowded stands a higher proportion of wood is devoted to elongating the top of the tree, probably to improve its chances of positioning leaves in sunlight. When stands are not crowded, trees will lay down proportionally more wood lower on the stem, possibly as a way of improving transport of water and nutrients to leaves. This relationship between top elongation and girth means that if tree density is held constant in closed forest conditions, the height of a tree expressed as a function of its age is a good indicator of site quality.

Within a species, the relationship of height to age is relatively constant throughout the life of a stand. On a good site, for example, one can expect to find trees 30 percent taller than trees of the same age on a poor site, and the relationship holds true from sapling to sawtimber. Since it is, however, unlikely that a manager will encounter trees of the same age on different sites to allow a direct comparison, foresters use an index based on height, or predicted height, of trees when they have reached an "index age." That age varies around the country; twenty-five years is common in the Southeast with fast-growing pine species; fifty years is the index age in the hardwood forests of the East; and 80–100 years is usually the index age in the West.

This relationship of height to age is known among foresters as *site index*. It is based on the direct measure of total tree height and age (obtained from a count of annual rings at breast height), but is expressed as the predicted height at an index age of 25, 50, or 100 years (fig. 2.8). For example, a tree that is 60 feet tall at the index age of fifty years is said to have a site index of 60. That same tree at 30 years old has the same site index, and one would expect it to be 60 feet tall when the tree is fifty years old. Site index curves allow a manager to use total height and age to predict site index for almost any combination of tree heights and stand ages. One limitation of site index is that it is species specific, so it is correctly stated as, for example, "sugar maple site index," or "red oak site index." Site can sometimes be compared across species, but not always. An excellent site for red oak may prove only average to good for sugar maple, and a great pine site is usually not as good for most hardwood species. A good soil *is* a good soil, but site index integrates a number of other factors that influence growth. Site index is more comparable among species that are common associates—sugar maple and yellow birch, for instance—than between species that do not usually grow together.

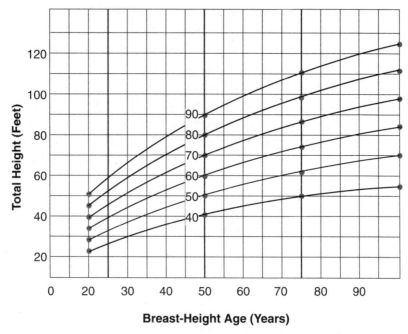

FIGURE 2.8 Site index is a species-specific method of estimating relative productivity of a forest site based on total height growth of a tree grown in forest conditions. By comparing actual height and age measurements to a tree's predicted height at a given "index" age, a forester can estimate relative productivity (for that species) across a range of different sites. This figure applies to sugar maple in the Northeast. A tree that is 100 feet tall and 75 years old (at dbh) has a site index value of 80 ("80 feet")—a good-to-excellent site for this species.

Another limitation of site index is that the user must assume trees have not been suppressed but have always had competition from surrounding trees (which is the same as saying the stand has always been fully stocked). The concept of site index does not apply in uneven-aged stands or in stands that have had drastic changes in stocking due to earlier trimming, or insect- and disease-related mortality. The most common error is overestimating productivity, predicting a site index that is higher than a site deserves. But because site index is mostly used on a relative scale to evaluate how one site compares to another for a particular species, precise measurements are rarely necessary.

Site index evolved as a way for managers to quickly identify productive forest sites back when most woodlands in the East were young sapling stands recovering from heavy cutting to fuel foundries and for building. In the 1930s, Luther Schnur, a silviculturalist working for the U.S. Forest Service, developed a way to use site index to predict yield in upland oak stands (Schnur 1937). Yield is the production of useable wood fiber per unit time; the higher a site index, the greater the yield. Tying site index to yield was no easy matter, especially since Schnur had a great deal of data on young stands but almost no information on older stands. The result: although Schnur proposed a very useful tool to assess relative forest productivity, his lack of data points in older stands made it almost impossible to predict yield later in the life of a stand. Today, site index is mostly used to determine the range of potential productivity in a particular forest and to help prioritize silvicultural decisions.

Site index is typically measured as follows: Total tree height is estimated using a clinometer and principles of basic geometry (similar triangles). A tool called an *increment borer* is used to remove a straw-sized piece of wood at *diameter at breast height* (dbh) that includes growth rings from the current year back to when the tree was 4.5 feet tall. Almost all measures in forestry are based on dbh, because it eliminates the effect of flaring where the stem meets the ground (also known as *butt swell*). Extracting an increment core damages the wood but if done correctly does not injure the tree. Unfortunately, it is the only way of aging hardwoods, short of cutting the tree down. Pines in northern climates are easy to age without boring since they produce one whorl of branches each year. It is a simple matter of counting branch whorls to the top of the tree (a *whorl* is a group of branches that come out from the stem all at the same height, separated by clear stem for a foot or two until the next year's whorl). The values for total height and age are plotted on an appropriate set of curves to obtain a value for site index.

Finding the age of a site index tree is hard work, especially in the dead of winter when wood is frozen. For this reason, and because the hole created by the tool represents a lumber defect, foresters are reluctant to take too many samples. In addition to aging the tree, an increment core is also used to estimate current growth rate. By averaging the thickness of rings over the last ten years, a forester can predict growth rate and estimate future yields. Of the two, current growth rate is preferred because it requires less boring and the extracted core does not need to extend into the stem any deeper than the thickness of the first slab, when the log is squared off on the headsaw during conversion to lumber.

Sometimes knowing what to look for in a site is as good as knowing site index. For instance, sites located on toe slopes—where the sidehill makes a transition into a valley—are almost always more productive than side slopes. Deep, relatively fine-textured but well-drained soils usually support productive forests, especially if the mineral component is derived from limestone. Shallow soils, or soils derived from shale, schist, sandstone, or poorly drained, wet soils are usually less productive. In mountainous terrain, look for more productive sites in places where you would expect soils to accumulate: saddles, benches on sidehills, and valleys are usually much more productive than sidehills and ridgelines. South- and southwest-facing slopes also tend to be slightly less productive than north and northeast slopes, because the former experience higher temperatures and are dryer.

Managers must also watch for sites where a species is highly productive but off-site. This can occur when past disturbances allow some species to occupy sites that they are not adapted to persist on. An example of this situation is the occurrence white pine in parts of northern New England where it grows on toe slopes and is extremely productive. Just how white pine came to dominate these sites is not entirely clear but is probably related to agricultural abandonment over the past hundred years. A traditional site index measurement would show an excellent site for white pine, but a thick northern hardwood understory belies the fact that pine is actually growing on a hardwood site. A positive impact approach to this situation is to let the pine grow on a longer-than-usual rotation and remove the overstory gradually, a few trees at a time, to allow hardwood saplings to develop in the understory. Most of these pine-dominated toe slopes are excellent sites for northern hardwoods.

A positive impact approach to forestry advocates the following: the better the site, the longer the rotation, almost regardless of species. So long as the value growth rate exceeds the next best investment alternative, a manager is probably better off to let sawtimber-sized trees grow larger on a good site, using periodic thinnings to keep stem diameters growing. The trick is to keep site and stem damage to a minimum during intermediate treatments.

CHAPTER 3

Creating Disturbances
in Forests through Silviculture

Silviculture, a term already used a number of times in this volume, is described by foresters as the "art and science" of growing and tending forests for the production of human benefits. As noted in the opening chapters, the term and concepts were originally proposed by Saxons in northern Europe nearly two hundred years ago. The word literally means *tree culture*, and it is a science that developed to deal with dwindling supplies of timber from forests that had been misused.

Although it may seem a contradiction to describe an endeavor as both art and science, since art is borne of creative inspiration and science of facts, there is no question but that silviculture is a creative expression of practices that are based in science. The alternative, of course, is that when the art of silviculture fails to achieve the desired results, it is the fault of science (in jest), and vice versa.

When the concepts of silvicultural practice, well established in northern Europe, were imported to the United States a few years before the twentieth century, almost all of the forest in the eastern half of the country had been harvested at least once, and highly accessible portions of the western forest were being cut hard. For a country on the verge of exposing the bottom of an "endless" supply of timber, the practice of silviculture was disturbingly slow to catch on. In the East, cutover hardwood forests proved to be highly resilient, regenerating under natural conditions to complements of valuable species almost regardless of the practices used to remove the presettlement forest. In the West, emphasis was placed on replanting the original softwood forest.

The contemporary goal of silviculture is to tend forests for benefits, but when the concepts were originally imported, the emphasis was on wood fiber. Even today, the focus of silviculture is primarily on trees: on selecting and cultivating valuable species and products, shortening rotations and increasing yields, improving efficiency, and protecting site productivity. All of this is accomplished by devising a reasonable approach to answer these questions: Which species will have the most value in future markets? What are the most reasonable practices to favor and allocate site resources to those trees? Where are the risks, and what are the best methods of weighing them against benefits? And, with the potential negative impacts from logging in mind, how best to limit those impacts or—better yet—convert them to positive impacts?

As discussed in chapter 2, the principal unit of silvicultural practice is the *stand*, which is commonly defined as an area where the forest is uniform enough in one or more characteristics (such as species, age, structure, site quality, health, etc.) so as to make it distinguishable from surrounding areas (Smith 1997). In other words, managers implement silvicultural practices in stands, and the collective management of all stands in an ownership (or other defined unit) is forest management. This distinction may seem minor, but it is actually quite significant when it comes to making decisions, especially for nonindustrial private forest (NIPF) owners who own and control the majority of forests in the United States.

Silvicultural methodology is based primarily on the forest structure a manager wants to promote and the means by which the existing forest cover is to be reproduced or regenerated. Under the German system, there are two primary structures—even-aged and uneven-aged—and five regeneration methods. Even-aged structures work best with pioneer to midsuccessional species, while uneven-aged structures tend to favor midsuccessional to climax species. Of the two, far more work has been done to manage for even-aged structures, because the severe cutting practices that predated the arrival of silviculture in the United States left us with largely even-aged stands. An even-aged structure is generally defined as a stand where the difference in age between the oldest trees and the youngest is 20 percent or less of the rotation age. For example, if the rotation, or the average age at which the stand is to be reproduced is one hundred years, an approximately fifty-year-old stand can have trees that vary in age from forty to sixty years. But the range of ages is far less significant to a manager than the vertical and horizontal structure of a stand.

In an even-aged stand, the featured trees all share the canopy, to a greater or lesser extent. As noted earlier, canopy position has a significant bearing on how well a tree will grow, and so managers have developed a system to describe the relative canopy positions of featured trees. There are four positions: *dominant*—a canopy position in which the tree crown has never been overtopped and is clearly above its neighbors; *codominant*—a canopy position in which the tree appears to share canopy space equally with immediate neighbors; *intermediate*—a canopy position in which only the top of the tree's crown (or a small portion of it) receives direct sunlight and the balance of the crown is affected by surrounding codominants; and *suppressed*—a canopy position in which the tree's crown has developed wholly under a canopy of surrounding trees for most of its life. Being able to quickly assess canopy position is easy for those who want to learn the system, but only if the observer can also identify species and their relative tolerance to competitive conditions, as described earlier.

Under even-aged structures, virtually the entire realm of silvicultural options boils down to two choices: (1) the manager is attempting to improve growing conditions for trees that have yet to reach maturity, or (2) the stand has reached maturity and the manager is applying practices to reproduce or regenerate the stand. The former are called *intermediate treatments*, and the latter are referred to as *reproduction methods*.

An example of a very common intermediate treatment is *timber stand improvement* (TSI). The purpose of TSI is to match species to the site—or to anticipated markets—or allocate space to featured trees, or both. Intermediate treatments early in the life of a stand are said to be *noncommercial*, which means that the practice does not yield salable products. Older stands usually call for treatments that yield products like pulpwood, firewood, or small sawtimber and are therefore said to be *commercial* treatments. A noncommercial treatment represents an expense to the woodland owner, or, rather, an investment since the outcome usually translates into faster-growing, more valuable trees even though treatment costs are an out-of-pocket expense.

All silvicultural decisions are driven by the goals and objectives of the property owner, and the process of applying practices should be hierarchical. In other words, a husband and wife who state that their primary interest is to manage woodlands principally for wildlife are initiating a process whereby all subsequent silvicultural *prescriptions* are first assessed for their potential impacts on wildlife. It does not mean wasting stands capable of high-value timber products. Rather, it requires the manager to craft prescriptions, even in stands that are dedicated to timber, in such a way as to provide the greatest benefit (or the least negative impact) to wildlife species that use the stand in question. This is an extremely important concept because one of the differences between silvicultural practice and cutting trees is the presence of objectives to guide decision making. Without objectives, especially at the stand-level, it is impossible to measure success or failure of a prescription. Wildlife, and other alternative benefits are discussed in greater detail in chapter 6.

The term *forest management* used to be synonymous with *timber management*, but this is no longer the case. The word *management* implies control and allocation of benefits and when preceded by the word *forest*, it encompasses all the potential benefits forests are capable of providing. For example, even woodland owners who decide that their goal is to leave nature to its own devices are—by the act of controlling forests in ways to

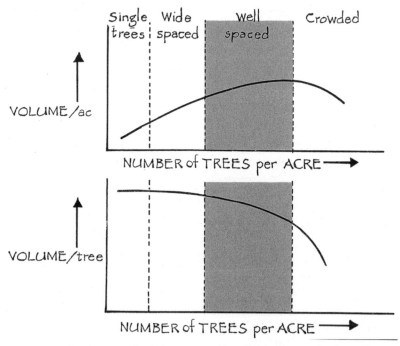

FIGURE 3.1 Volume growth rate per tree and per acre are controlled by tree density. Thinning sacrifices volume growth per acre to maximize volume growth per tree. The goal when growing timber is to maintain stocking so as to maximize volume growth per tree but without wasting space.

achieve this benefit—managing lands, provided they do all that is necessary to ensure that their goal is carried into perpetuity. Simply stating a goal is not management.

If the objective of an even-aged stand is to maximize timber values, intermediate treatments in the form of periodic *thinnings* are essential. Thinning is TSI intended to reduce the number of stems per acre, thereby reallocating space, soil nutrients, and moisture to residual trees. The purpose is to open the canopy, giving crowns of featured trees room to grow, with the goal of maintaining or increasing diameter growth rates on those trees. But there is a hitch: when stands are thinned there are fewer trees available for harvest at a later date.

Thinning is a choice between growing many trees of relatively small diameter or fewer trees of larger diameters. In silvicultural terms, the forester is managing a trade-off between maximizing volume growth per tree and maximizing volume growth per acre, both of which are controlled by stem density (fig. 3.1). The trick is to maintain *stocking*, or stem density, within a range that maximizes value growth on selected trees but without sacrificing—to an unreasonable extent—growth per acre.

The Impact of Stocking on Growth

Stocking is an indication of the average girth and number of trees in a stand as compared to an optimum, usually to achieve a timber objective. Most often, and certainly within the context of managing forests for timber, stocking is lowered periodically to improve diameter growth rates. In traditional silvicultural terminology, *stocking* only applies to even-aged stands, despite the fact that some well-known forestry experts in the United States have used the term to describe structure in uneven-aged stands (Duerr and Bond 1952).

Optimum stocking is difficult to maintain and it changes as stands develop. For example, in hardwoods, young stands are carried at higher densities (sacrificing volume growth per tree) to "train" stems for the purpose of achieving vertical growth. Later, stem densities are lowered (sacrificing volume growth per acre) to promote diameter growth. Adding to the complexity of deciding when to thin and by how much is factoring in the impacts of damage to the residual stand from tree falling and extraction. Injuries to stems and roots from even one incident of careless and poorly timed logging can more than wipe out the benefits of thinning, destroying a stand's future timber potential. Early injuries of this nature are not always obvious since trees are capable of sealing off infected tissue and growing new layers on top (fig. 3.2)

Once a stand is established, there are in most forests only two things a manager can do to improve growth rates and increase timber volume and value: (1) adjust species composition to favor trees well suited to a particular area (and apt to be in demand when they are mature), and (2) lower stocking periodically by thinning—removing trees not well suited to the site, or trees that are poorly formed or diseased—to allocate site resources to the best and most productive trees. Since height growth, as discussed earlier, is mostly controlled by soil and site conditions, only species mix and relative spacing of trees are left for a manager to manipulate. For this reason, foresters are often obsessed with stocking, especially when stands are composed of trees of a similar age with the potential to produce valuable timber.

To say that manipulation of stocking is the only tool available to a forester is not completely correct. In some parts of the country, managers can use applications of soil amendments to correct known nutrient deficiencies. And there are instances, usually in plantations or in areas that have been replanted with seedlings, where fertilizer applications can have an enormous impact on yields. For most natural forests of the United States, fertilizer applications are the exception rather than the rule, but where amendments are used, the effects of treatments generally decrease the interval between thinnings. In other words, stem growth is faster. Nevertheless, too little is known about impacts of fertilizer salts on forest soil organisms to warrant widespread use. Maintaining healthy populations of soil organisms is probably a far more important practice than broadcast applications of mineral salts.

Stocking is a measure of tree density. When stocking is high, wood growth is distributed across many stems; when it is low, almost the same amount of growth is distributed on fewer stems. More trees mean higher stem densities and slower diameter growth rates. Total stand volume (by weight or by cubic volume) may not be affected by high stem densities, but usable wood volume—especially when the final product is sawtimber—is almost completely controlled by stem density. From the time trees are large enough to measure until the final harvest, stocking (and tree volume and value growth) is controlled by periodic thinnings. The idea is to maximize

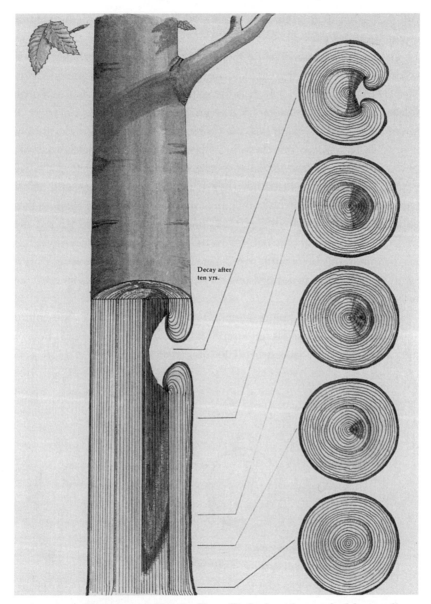

Decay after
ten yrs.

FIGURE 3.2 Trees are capable of walling off infections that resulted from earlier logging injuries, sometimes hiding serious defects. Illustration by David M. Carroll. Reproduced by permission from Shigo 1979.

volume and value growth per tree, but without overly sacrificing volume growth per acre.

The most commonly used reference to stocking is *basal area*, which is actually a measure of stem-area density, or the proportion of an acre occupied by tree trunks (fig. 3.3). It is the sum of the cross-sectional area of all trees measured at 4.5 feet above the ground, also known as *diameter at breast height* (dbh). Taking stem measurements so high up from the ground may seem ridiculous, but there is a reason. As noted earlier, measuring girth at dbh eliminates—for most species on most sites—the effect of stem swelling, or fluting, where the trunk disappears into the ground. Also, equations used to predict wood volume in trees assume stem shape is parabolic, that it tapers like a bullet from a point 4.5 feet above the ground and up to the limits of merchantability in the crown. Diameter measurements taken consistently below dbh will exaggerate timber volumes, usually more so on poor sites where fluting is exaggerated than on good sites where taper is less.

Unless the manager knows something about the age and structure of the stand, basal area by itself is not a very useful measure of stocking. There is, after all, a big difference between 100 square feet of trees averaging 16 inch-

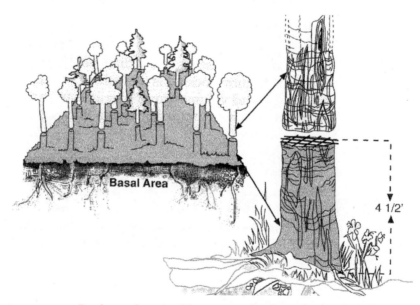

FIGURE 3.3   Basal area, the sum of the cross-sectional area (square feet) of trees on an acre, is a measure of tree density.

es dbh, and the same stem-area density of trees averaging 6 inches dbh. For example, seventy-two 16-inch trees have approximately the same basal area per acre as more than five hundred trees averaging 6 inches dbh. These two stands have the same basal area but very different structures, and thus require drastically different treatments to achieve the same goal. In short, if basal area is the only known measure of density in a stand of timber, it is analogous to agreeing to meet someone at "8 o'clock" without specifying "a.m." or "p.m."

Another common measure of stocking is stem density, or number of trees per acre. Young stands generally have high stem densities. As the stand matures, some of the trees—in fact, most of them—succumb to the forces of nature and gradually drop out. For example, left unmanaged, a young stand of northern hardwoods (sugar maple, American beech, yellow birch, and other associates) will—over the course of 200 years, depending on site quality—"naturally" thin from more than one thousand trees when dbh averages 4 inches, to forty to sixty trees when dbh averages 20 inches. Periodic thinning can cut this time in half, but not without the risks discussed earlier.

An inventory that reports stem densities of two hundred trees per acre could represent an adequately stocked stand of trees averaging 8 inches dbh or a severely understocked stand averaging 4 inches dbh. Number of trees per acre alone is just as inadequate for measuring density as basal area alone. The best measure of stocking in even-aged stands is a combination of both numbers of trees per acre and their total basal area.

Figures that illustrate number of trees per acre as a function of basal area are known as *stocking charts*. A stocking chart allows the manager to take into account stand basal area and numbers of trees per acre to develop guidelines for periodic thinning. Charts are specific to forest type or to species. For example, white pine diameter growth is less affected by high stem densities than most hardwoods. One can grow white pine at higher stem densities without sacrificing volume growth per tree.

Standard stocking charts, used mostly in eastern forest types, identify three different levels of stocking, known as the *A-line*, the *B-line*, and the *C-line* (fig. 3.4). The goal is to maintain stocking during the rotation between the B-line and A-line. In other words, stands with stocking above the B-line are candidates for thinning. When stocking goes above the A-line, the stand is severely overstocked, and the manager is sacrificing volume growth per tree. When densities drop below the B-line, the stand is

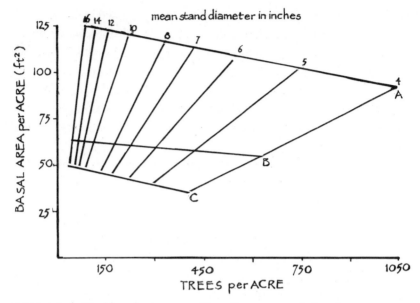

FIGURE 3.4 Stocking charts are specific to forest type and allow foresters to compare tree density in a stand (as a function of basal area and number of trees per acre) to an optimum density so as to maximize volume growth per tree but without overly sacrificing volume growth per acre.

slightly understocked, although individual tree growth is maximized. Thus, the stand is not fully occupied and is sacrificing volume growth per acre. Below the C-line, the stand is grossly understocked and, by definition, will take at least ten years to reach B-line stocking. It is the equivalent of allocating ten spaces in a parking lot to each vehicle and closing the lot when it has reached 10 percent of actual capacity. Managers who thin to the point where residual stocking is below the B-line are wasting space, unless there is another reason to do so, such as to leave room for regeneration.

Stocking charts are a useful tool to plot basal area and number of trees per acre to help assess potential to improve growing conditions in an even-aged stand. The purpose of thinning, as noted earlier, is to concentrate a site's growth potential on selected trees without wasting space. Periodic thinnings, most often scheduled at 10–20-year intervals (depending on species, site quality, and current stocking) can have a dramatic effect on merchantable volume growth. And, when trees exceed 16 inches dbh, increases in value are disproportionately higher than increases in volume. It is tempting to cash in on timber when it reaches this size, but the return on investment in trees from 16 inches to 22 inches dbh will, on many sites, exceed the return on even the most impressive portfolio of stocks and bonds.

Standard stocking charts are available for virtually all of the major timber types in the United States. Not too many years ago, stocking charts were the cookbook of forestry, but such is rarely the case today, at least among seasoned managers. Most foresters use the charts to help develop marking guidelines for implementing intermediate treatments in even-aged stands, and the charts have been used in some states to define logging statutes. A keyword search on the Internet will most likely discover charts for every important timber type in the United States, or you can call one of the sources listed in appendix C.

Forest Reproduction Methods

As noted earlier, silviculture in the Teutonic tradition consists of five reproduction methods that result in one or the other of two stand structures: even-aged and uneven-aged (figs. 3.5a to 3.5e). The methods vary in severity of disturbance used to achieve regeneration, from the most severe—clearcutting—to the least severe—when widely scattered, single, mature trees are harvested. Severe treatments are intended to mimic catastrophic conditions and thus tend to favor pioneer and early-successional species, while the single-tree methods favor mid- to late-successional species that are capable of idling in the understory for years, waiting for their moment in the sun. The reproduction methods are described below in decreasing order of disturbance (from most to least).

Clearcutting

Although this reproduction method is arguably the least understood by the general public and therefore the most maligned, it is an invaluable silvicultural method intended to mimic the conditions of a severe disturbance. Unfortunately, it is also the easiest and cheapest method of extracting timber, which tends to justify its use more for the sake of efficiency and expedience than for silvicultural merit. By definition, a clearcut removes all trees within a designated boundary of sufficient size so that at least two-thirds of the treated area has the light and temperature regimes of an open field. It is the only way to reproduce early-successional species like aspen (or *popple*) whose buds and bark are a preferred food for important wildlife species such as deer, ruffed grouse, and others. Clearcutting methods are used to

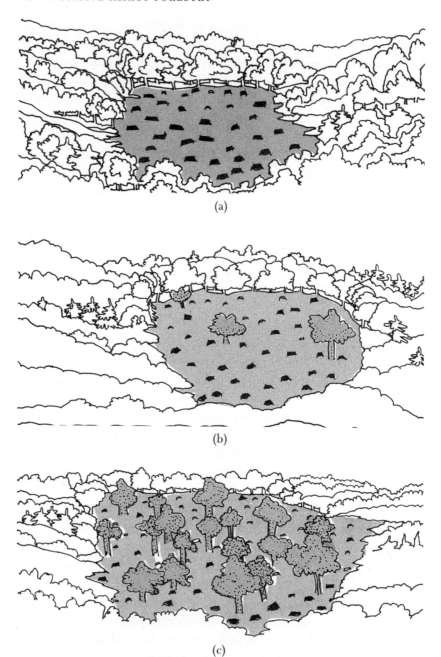

(a)

(b)

(c)

FIGURE 3.5 Traditional silvicultural methods arranged from the most disturbance to the least: (a) clearcut, (b) seed tree, (c) shelterwood, (d) group selection,
and (e) single-tree selection. Methods A, B, and C are even-aged systems, while D
and E create uneven-aged forests.

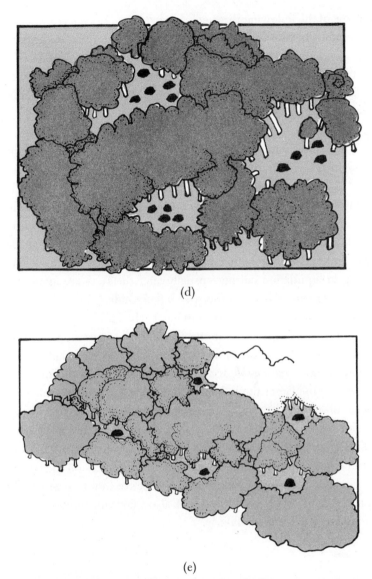

(d)

(e)

FIGURE 3.5 Continued. The two uneven-aged methods.

create one of the following three conditions: (1) an open environment that favors establishment of pioneer species which will develop under exposed conditions (by root-suckering or by natural seeding), (2) an open environment favoring further development of small saplings already on the site (also known as *advanced regeneration*), or (3) a cleared area to be planted (or *artificially regenerated*).

When clearcutting is used principally as a means of converting trees into fiber, it is not a silvicultural reproduction method. Areas so treated are easily recognized by few to many, usually damaged, residual trees that have been left standing. Clearcutting as a reproduction method removes all trees and may even disturb upper soil levels to prepare a seed bed. Commercial clearcutting, also known as *liquidation cutting*, is less concerned with silvicultural outcomes than simply converting trees into cash. The one should not be confused with the other, and those who try to connect silvicultural meaning to liquidation cutting—usually after the fact—are attempting to cover poor practices that are otherwise indefensible.

Clearcutting is a positive impact practice when it is employed—at a reasonable scale—to reproduce pioneer and early-successional species in even-aged stands to achieve more than one objective. On small holdings of 100 acres of less, *reasonable scale* is defined as patches of from 0.5 to 5 acres in size; the larger the holding, the more expansive "reasonable" can become, up to a maximum of 40 acres (or more if the manager has good reasons). Also, as a general rule, a silvicultural prescription of any kind should attempt to fulfill two or more objectives simultaneously. This rule is especially pertinent when imposing severe disturbances on the landscape. For example, clearcutting is not only an effective tool to regenerate trees adapted to catastrophic conditions, it is also a fantastic tool to create habitats for many species of wildlife.

Seed Tree

This reproduction method is a slight variation of the clearcut, leaving widely scattered mature trees as a source of seed from species the manager wants to reproduce. Timing to coincide with a good seed year, and creating the proper conditions for seed germination and establishment, make this system mostly prone to failure. It is, however, used in the southeastern United States to regenerate pine. In most circumstances natural seeding fails and the manager ends up replanting with seedlings.

Shelterwood

The last of the reproduction methods intended to regenerate even-aged forests leaves a sheltering overstory to provide a degree of protection to seedlings and saplings. The method tends to favor mid- to late-successional species depending on the amount of overstory left in place. The traditional shelterwood is implemented in two phases: the first phase is a *seed cut* that opens the canopy and secures regeneration; the seed cut is followed by a second phase called the *removal cut*, which completes the overstory harvest but is implemented only after sufficient regeneration has been achieved.

There are many variations of this popular regeneration method. For example, when implemented in three phases, the first treatment is called a *preparatory cut*, with the objective of removing species that are not wanted in the future stand while stimulating favored species to reproduce. The next two phases are implemented as usual.

Another shelterwood variation delays overstory removal to coincide with the first thinning of the new stand coming in underneath, or later. Known as a *deferred shelterwood*, it is intended to favor more late-successional species in a "two-aged" stand. When a widely spaced overstory is carried on a very long rotation with an understory composed of species capable of asexual reproduction via sprouting—usually from stumps—it is possible to harvest two or more rotations of understory while the rest of the stand is left to grow. This variation, used more frequently in Europe than here and traditionally described as a separate reproduction method, is called *coppice with standards*. The objective is to identify trees of seed origin, called *standards*, and cultivate them over long rotations in very low densities, leaving space for an understory of sprouts, which are managed on much shorter rotation usually for fence posts, poles, and firewood.

The shelterwood variations are favored for two reasons: their flexibility and the fact that the overstory is never completely removed until midway through the next rotation, which makes it more aesthetically pleasing. Scheduling the final harvest, once it has served to reproduce a new stand, can be delayed until there are favorable markets or until it is necessary to do other work in stands nearby. Shelterwood methods can even take the form of a series of thinnings late in the rotation that gradually opens the canopy, favoring a late-successional understory. The one fatal flaw of the shelterwood method, caused by impatience, is the tendency to remove the overstory before regeneration is well established, leaving seedlings to succumb to overexposure from sun, high temperatures, and wind.

Group and Single-tree Selection

An uneven-aged stand is composed of trees that range in age from seedlings to fully mature, a structure believed to closely mimic old-growth forests that have escaped catastrophic disturbances. Depending on scale, however, an old-growth, uneven-aged forest could alternatively be viewed as a cacophony of even-aged patches (fig. 3.6). Nevertheless, the goal of both group and single-tree selection is to duplicate the processes that lead to a gradual replacement of old-growth trees as they fall out of the canopy. These methods are intended to reproduce the same complement of species currently in the overstory by encouraging reproduction in small gaps. The two methods are combined because they are often implemented together in the same stand; small groups of usually -two to five trees are harvested in some areas while in others only single trees are removed.

It is possible to convert even-aged stands to uneven-aged (or, more cor-

FIGURE 3.6   Undisturbed old-growth forests usually exhibit a distribution of tree diameters and age classes that is the goal of uneven-aged reproduction methods. Depending on perspective and scale, an uneven-aged forest is actually a random collection of even-aged stands.

rectly, uneven-structured) stands, but the secret is patience. Conversions work best on good sites in stands composed of a midsuccessional, fairly mature overstory with a well-established understory of late-successional species.

For all the advantages these methods can offer, group and single-tree selection is difficult to implement successfully. It requires frequent stand entries—usually every five to ten years—and extremely careful logging methods. For example, it is almost impossible to fall a mature tree without damaging nearby saplings and poles even for loggers trained in the newest directional tree-falling practices described in chapter 5. The potential for excessive damage from tree falling, coupled with the need to protect residual stems and root systems, means that effective selection reproduction methods require frozen ground conditions, or dry soils.

Artificial Reproduction

The silvicultural reproduction methods discussed so far are also called "natural methods" because harvesting disturbances are intended to create conditions that will allow trees to regenerate on their own. When natural methods fail, or when the complement of species desired in the new stand is not already present, clearcutting is usually followed by planting. The result, of course, is an even-aged stand managed to optimize stocking and growth rates, as discussed earlier.

Artificial reproduction is the most common method of reproducing coniferous stands, especially when the new stand will feature early- and midsuccessional species. This method can involve the application of seed, but most often two- to four-year-old seedlings are planted, usually by hand or—if the terrain is not too steep—by machine. Although hardwood stands almost never require replanting if natural methods are employed correctly (timing of treatments is always crucial), a growing number of woodland owners in the eastern United States have been experimenting with the establishment of small plantations of valuable hardwoods. The most serious risk to these plantings is browse damage from deer, but a fairly recent development has allowed managers to grow seedlings in protective, opaque plastic tubes. The tubes protect buds from browsing and because of a sheltering effect inside the tube they can also prolong the growing season. The relative cost and merit of using "tree shelters" for artificial regeneration is discussed later in this chapter.

Planting, in addition to ensuring a new crop as soon after cutting as feasible, also allows the opportunity to improve growth rates and timber values by using genetically improved seedlings. In the years following World War II, the forest industry and the U.S. Forest Service invested heavily in tree-breeding programs, and both have relied mostly on artificial methods in the coniferous forests of the West. Planting is also the predominant regeneration method on the pine lands of the Southeast. Although the artificial methods work well to quickly replace forest cover, the stands that result from these methods are dangerously uniform—in structure, species composition, and even DNA. The silvicultural advantages of uniformity (improved access, faster growth rates, and tremendous timber extraction efficiencies) are primarily economical and run the risk of sacrificing the ecological benefits of diversity in forests for the sake of expedience. Positive impact practices do not necessarily exclude planting as a reproduction alternative so long as the ecosystem-related risks of planting described above are addressed and when the purpose of planting is to reproduce natural forests and their complement of benefits, both tangible and intangible. Planting solely for timber production (or any single-use purpose) is not positive impact forestry.

Trading Timber Volume for Value

The opportunity to obtain periodic income from wood production is one of the most tangible benefit of forests, but not necessarily the most important. Some owners prefer to manage woodlands to effect changes in habitat for favored species; others simply want to improve access or to create a network of trails for recreation; and some want it all. Almost regardless of an owner's primary interests in forests, timber opportunities will figure into the mix at some point. Forest owners need to know about managing forests for timber even if timber production is the most subordinate objective of all.

There are two choices available to a manager who decides a particular stand or area is suitable for growing timber: manage for volume production, or manage for value. The two are related to a certain extent; strategies that increase volume growth will also increase value, and larger trees are generally more valuable than smaller ones. But the volume manager is concerned with fiber production—how to grow the maximum amount of useable wood fiber in the shortest amount of time. For example, paper companies are mostly concerned with volume production from their lands. Tree size and form is less important than growth rate. Although paper manufacturers are concerned with wood quality—especially as it affects the pulping process—a crooked tree is just as valuable as a straight one. The value manager, on the other hand, is concerned not so much with wood volumes but, rather, tree form and how much the marketplace will pay for wood when it is ready for harvest.

While the volume manager is focused on time and efficiency, the value manager is concerned with timber appreciation for end uses like veneer or high-quality, defect-free lumber. Which perspective is correct: volume or value? The answer is, it depends; on product markets, site quality, and the woodland owner's objectives. Most managers fall somewhere between the two extremes, balancing the need for cash to pay the current expenses of owning forest land with future gains when timber has reached its maximum value.

Does it pay to manage for value? Absolutely, if an owner can wait long enough and is not overly concerned with who reaps the benefit when timber values mature. For example, in parts of Europe where stands have been managed for much longer periods than anywhere in North America, a single two-hundred-year-old tree is worth more than an entire acre's worth of trees in some parts of the United States. Values are likely to have stayed within the family, but it is a sure bet that the person who first decided to favor that tree is not around to see it harvested.

Growing valuable timber takes time, and patience—above all else—is the virtue of a value-oriented manager. A forest owner growing value is willing to bear the cost of management while passing the opportunity for income to future generations. For most people this is a difficult, if not impossible, choice. The value manager is a true altruist.

Focusing silvicultural decisions on value requires predictions about future markets, which are not always easy to make. For example, who could have guessed fifty years ago that in New England red oak would be more valuable in today's market than, say, sugar maple? Certainly not the people who then advocated "weeding" red oak from northern hardwood stands to favor other more valuable species. Heeding this advice at the time might have seemed reasonable, but to have done so would prove to have had a tremendously negative effect on forest timber values today. The assumptions of value managers are not always correct and consumer trends are fickle. Although it is impossible to predict how consumer demand will affect future timber values, it is reasonable to assume that today's commercially important species will be even more valuable in future markets, due primarily to scarcity. Less timber from public lands, and less timber from private lands owned by people who do not want to cut trees, means that timber from well-managed lands will be much more valuable in future markets. The value manager can take advantage of these trends by employing practices that grow straight, defect-free trees on good sites using long rotations: 50–100 percent longer than current guidelines, depending on the species, sites, and prospective markets. Better sites are capable of longer rotations.

Aside from time, patience, and generosity toward future generations, what are the best methods to grow valuable timber? The ideas suggested below apply mostly to eastern U.S. hardwoods, but the concepts are universal. It is possible to grow coniferous species into high-value trees, but with current market trends, favor has shifted to the hardwoods.

A first consideration is site quality. Trees will grow almost anywhere in the United States where there is adequate soil and moisture, but only the best soils are capable of growing valuable timber. These sites are located in coves and valleys, on the toe slopes of hills (the transition between the side-hill and the valley), and especially in areas where soils are derived from limestone or other nutrient-rich bedrock. Although it is impossible to say how much forest land in the United States meets these criteria, it is probably less than 20 percent. On some forest properties the extent of productive soils is higher, especially in the geographic center of the hardwood region. But on many properties the extent of productive soils is much less than one acre in five. Sites that are not suitable for growing high-value timber are ridgetops, side slopes, and sandy, excessively drained soils that are usually also nutrient poor. Wet soils, or soils that are poorly drained, are also not suitable for long-rotation timber production.

The easiest way to locate productive soils is with the use of soil maps that are available from the USDA Natural Resources Conservation Service (formerly the Soil Conservation Service). Not all areas in the country have been mapped, so the next best alternative is to "read" site productivity from the trees in a stand. One of the best predictors of site quality is tree height. A tall stand of young sapling or pole-sized trees is a great indicator of a potentially excellent site. As discussed earlier, foresters use a measure based on tree height and age called "site index" to predict a site's ability to grow timber.

Once potentially productive sites are identified, the next task is to make sure the site is not susceptible to storm winds. Look for the telltale pit-and-mound topography that results from the root ball of an upended tree next to a hole where the roots used to be (fig. 3.7). Careful examination of the site will reveal hints about storm frequency and even the direction of storm winds. When storms are funneled down valleys, sites near the mouth of a valley show more evidence of blowdown than sites farther up the valley. This is caused by *venturi effects*, a sucking turbulence that develops when landforms compress and accelerate wind. Evidence of pit-and-mound topography on a site is a sign that storm winds may damage or blow down a stand before it reaches full value (maybe not in the current owner's lifetime, but at sometime during the life of that stand). Risk of blowdown is not necessarily a reason to always avoid these sites, especially if soils are highly productive. A manager who thinks strategically is able to recognize the risks and plan for the possibility of nature moving up the harvest date.

Depending on when in the life of a stand a manager makes the decision to focus on long rotations and high value, the principal cultural activity is periodic thinning. In young stands, thinnings are delayed to take advantage

FIGURE 3.7   Evidence of pit-and-mound topography is proof that a stand has been affected by storm winds. Photograph by Robert L. Anderson, USDA-Forest Services.

of competition from surrounding trees, also known as "trainers." High stem density in a young stand promotes height growth and helps lower branches prune naturally. When to start thinning is species dependent, but in northern and central hardwoods the first thinning is delayed until the stand is at least thirty to forty years old (on a good site), with subsequent thinnings at ten- to forty-year intervals. The manager must always weigh the potential benefit of a thinning with the risks of damage to soils and to residual trees. Even minor stem injuries can destroy future timber values. In the South, the first thinning is scheduled earlier and the interval is less. In all circumstances, thinning should be scheduled when trees are dormant or when soils are dry, or both. In the North, schedule thinnings that involve timber extraction during frozen-ground conditions. The next best alternative is when soils are dry.

Careful tree felling and extraction practices are essential in high-value stands. Even a minor bark scrap in the butt log of a residual tree can reduce stem value by hundreds—sometimes thousands—of dollars. Make sure logging contractors are skilled in directional felling practices discussed in chapter 5. Most loggers profess complete control over falling trees. But directional felling ability is not a matter genetics, bravado, or luck. It is a skill, learned as a set of practices that enable a logger to safely and accurately fell trees. Positive impacts from logging are impossible if residual stems are damaged in the process.

Evaluating Timber Investments

Woodland owners often want to know the investment value of trees, especially when intermediate treatments are called for. "Which trees should I harvest, which do I leave, how much will I make on the sale, and how does thinning improve investment?" are common questions. Making these kinds of decisions is never easy because trees, unlike other kinds of assets such as stocks and bonds, have intrinsic values that are impossible to evaluate in dollars and cents. For example, a particular tree growing in value at a rate that is less than the rate of inflation may provide wildlife benefits, or it may have value for some other reasons that are impossible to evaluate in monetary terms but valuable nonetheless. A good manager never makes silvicultural treatment decisions solely on the basis of economics, but understanding rudimentary economic analysis is absolutely necessary to the decision-making process of those who endeavor to grow valuable timber.

The first step in any economic analysis is to recognize the *alternative rate of return* of a forest investment. It is considered the next best alternative to owning and managing forest lands, and is an answer to the question, "If money were not tied up in forests, how else could it have been used to obtain a similar rate of return?" Bonds? The stock market? Rare books? It is a rate of return that, by definition, would compel an investor (in a purely economic analysis) to convert timber into an alternative investment. The rate of return on an investment is compared to a benchmark, and that benchmark is the opportunity cost. Most forest economists use very conservative rates for such comparisons; for example, the average rate paid on a ten-year Treasury note, or a thirty-year bond over the life of a timber investment. The good news is most forests in the United States are better investments than these conservative-but-safe alternatives. The bad news is, but not by much.

There are many variables that factor into economic analysis of forest land in addition to an alternative rate of return. But one fact about forests is inescapable: it is a very long-term investment, and one can not ignore the power of compounding if economics plays a role in decision making. Compounding works like this: $100 put into a savings account that pays 5 percent interest will have grown to $105 at the end of year. By the end of the second year, the original amount has grown to $110.25. This does not seem like a fantastic rate of growth (which is one of the reasons explaining the importance of saving to children is so difficult), but only because the investment period is so short. What is the future value of $100 deposited today and compounded at 5 percent for, say, one hundred years? A whooping $13,150! When Benjamin Franklin said, "Time is money," he was probably referring to the power of compound interest, not wasting time.

The power of compounding interest is truly awesome. A good business calculator is necessary to compound a sum over a period of years, but here is a useful rule of thumb: When the interest rate is 7.2 percent compounded annually, the value of an investment doubles every ten years. At half this rate (3.6%), an investment doubles every twenty years. The inverse of these figures is also true. In other words, an investment at 10 percent compounded annually doubles in about 7.2 years. Using these numbers, it is easy to do mental approximations on different figures.

Time is the bane of forestry investments, where even insignificant costs at the beginning of a rotation grow by Herculean proportions to when trees are ready for harvest. For example, a $3 plastic tree shelter (described earlier in the "Reproduction Methods" section), installed over a seedling with an alternative rate of return of 5 percent and an investment period of 120 years, costs $1,046 and change. But, if using a tree shelter can produce logs that are worth even slightly more than this amount, it is a good investment.

So what is the lesson of compounding as it relates to timber investments? Managers should try to delay timber management expenses until later in the rotation, but not if the delay will have a substantially negative effect on value. For example, on some sites it is impossible to grow hardwood seedlings without tree shelters to protect seedlings from deer browse, as described earlier. In these circumstances, tree shelters are a necessary cost, and chances are that timber prices 120 years from now—even in current dollars—will make that cost inconsequential. Economic analysis is weighing the benefits of an expense against an alternative, assuming the investor could have used the same money somewhere else.

There is one other significant aspect about forest growth and investment that deserves mention: although the power of compounding applies to tree value, the way trees change in value is not a smooth transition from year to year. Trees experience a market phenomenon known as *ingrowth*, which is an abrupt change in value as trees grow from one product category into another (fig. 3.8). Ingrowth is due to an increase in diameter and a concomitant increase in value. In most timber markets, there are three ingrowth phases. First, when trees reach pole size at about 6 inches dbh (this varies widely by region and markets), value goes from essentially zero to whatever someone will pay for fuelwood or pulpwood (or post, poles, or some other local specialty market). Second, there is a jump in value at about 10–16 inches dbh, or whenever local markets first recognize trees as sawtimber. Timber value jumps from a few dollars per thousand board feet (converting cords to board feet) to ten or twenty times more. Third, when diameters exceed 18–26 inches, trees have surpassed the threshold of the highest value the market recognizes—veneer timber. When stems—especially hardwoods—reach this threshold, and they are perfectly straight with no obvious defects (obvious to a veneer buyer), values can jump to thousands of dollars per thousand board feet. Prices are even higher for favored local woods.

Variation in stumpage is positively correlated with tree value; there is a very wide range in veneer prices but comparatively little variation in fuel and pulp prices. For this reason, the more valuable a timber stand is, the more bids an owner will want when it is time to sell. But sellers should also

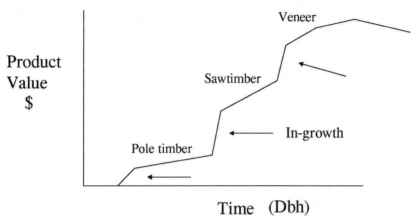

Product
Value
$

Time   (Dbh)

FIGURE 3.8   Ingrowth is a stepwise progression in value as trees grow from one product class into another.

keep in mind that there are enormous variations in bids for high-quality timber and—to effect positive impact practices—should seriously consider the possibility that the highest bidder is often not the best candidate.

Ingrowth is essentially a rapid change in value over a short period, and one of the most common mistakes of woodland owners is to sell timber before or during a period of ingrowth. It is the financial equivalent of selling a common investment instrument of banks, called a *certificate of deposit*, before the certificate has matured. People who buy these instruments from banks are cautioned that "there is a substantial penalty for early withdrawal." This penalty for early conversion is exactly analogous to selling timber at the wrong time. For example, a tree that is now 16 inches in diameter with a radial growth rate of five rings per inch will be 20 inches dbh in ten years—a fantastic growth rate. Assuming the tree has only minor surface defects (that are easily covered with ten years of growth), a buyer might pay $60 to take the tree today. In ten years the same tree could be worth $600 or more (in constant dollars; which means inflation is not factored in). During the ten-year period of this example, the tree is growing in value at an average annual rate of nearly 30 percent, a rate of return that far exceeds the performance of the stock market's S&P 500 Index during any of its best decades.

Answering the question, "Which of two trees is a better investment?" is a comparison that depends on species, health and vigor, site suitability, and growth rate—both in terms of volume and value. It is impossible to predict with any degree of accuracy how wood preferences will change in the future, and it may not matter. The better of two trees is the one with the best prospects for changing in value over time, both in terms of volume and grade, holding all other factors equal.

"Are the trees in question healthy and vigorous, and are they suitable for the site?" In other words, what are the chances that current management decisions will have a positive impact on future forest condition? Again—all other factors equal—investment quality is a function of tree volume and value, and the prospects for these variables to improve with periodic thinning. For example, consider two trees sharing crown space: one is 12 inches dbh, the other 16 inches. The larger tree has about 20 percent more volume, but it also has a seam up one side and a fork at the top of the first log (at 16 feet). The smaller tree is perfectly smooth and straight to a height of 24 feet with no obvious defects. Both are adding volume at the same rate, but which is the better investment? The 12-inch tree. Why? Because it has better prospects than the other and it is increasing in value *at an increasing rate* due to ingrowth.

Notice the assumption about growth in the example above, that both trees are growing at the same rate. This is, in fact, an enormous assumption, one that if not true might change the decision. Unfortunately, the only way to estimate the real growth rate is to "read" the way trees lay down annual growth rings, in one of two ways: (1) counting rings on a stump (in which case the decision to cut has already been made), or (2) using an increment borer to extract a straw-sized core from the stem. Both methods are destructive (one obviously more so than the other), so managers are reluctant to measure growth rate directly. Sometimes destructive sampling is unavoidable, such as when a manager must extract cores to age trees for site index estimates as well as to estimate growth rates. But it is not necessary to bore every tree, nor is it absolutely necessary to know growth rates when deciding which of two competing trees to cut. What is far more important is judging value growth. A smaller tree about to experience a period of ingrowth is a better investment than one that has already grown into a product class, provided the manager is sure about the ability of the smaller tree to respond. As discussed earlier, there are many circumstances in even-aged stands where the larger of two trees is the better investment.

Another important aspect of forest investment is that trees are connected to land, and it is almost impossible to analyze a timber investment without considering land. In a legal sense, trees are an "interest" in land, which means they are part of the "bundle of rights" by which land is defined. But the asset value of land is different from the asset value of timber, and to avoid comparing apples to oranges, changes in timber values are always considered separate from changes in land values. For example, a forestry investment might be an excellent opportunity because of the appreciation of land, if an investor is simply speculating. But if the goal of the investor is to grow timber, it is necessary for taxation purposes to separate the value of timber investments from that of bare land.

Income from timber is considered a long-term capital gain if it has been held for the requisite period and the method of sale demonstrates the conversion of standing trees into logs and other products. Generally, income from capital gains is taxed at a lower rate than other sources of income, and social-security-related assessments do not apply to sales of capital. For these reasons, it is absolutely essential that owners use proper timber sale practices (discussed in chapter 4), avoiding methods that might disqualify timber income from long-term capital gains status.

Another, often overlooked, advantage of arranging timber sales so as to allow capital gains treatment of income is this: Internal Revenue Service rules allow taxpayers to use capital gains to fully offset capital losses, and up to an additional $3,000 of other income (for married taxpayers). Excess losses in any particular year can be carried over into subsequent tax years and the same rules apply. This means that a woodland owner can unload shares of equities that have plummeted in value and use the loss to fully offset capital gains from timber. The result: no tax paid on income from timber sales. Timber sale methods and tax implications are discussed in the next chapter.

In areas undergoing urbanization, it is not uncommon for land values to increase at rates that exceed the return on investment in timber. Another way to look at it is this: the factory is more valuable than the products it is capable of producing. A decision based strictly on money in this case would compel a timber investor to liquidate a timber investment, not because the timber has matured, but because someone wants the land for another purpose. Decisions of this nature are all too common in urbanizing areas, and investments that involve short-terms gains on conversions of forest land to nonforest uses do not involve silviculture.

It is difficult, if not impossible, to factor intangible values of forests into a meaningful economic analysis. Yet, for many forest owners, wildlife habitats, recreation, aesthetics—even the spiritual value of forests—are far more important than money. An intangible is something that has value, but it is difficult to evaluate in terms of dollars. The pride of ownership and sense of fulfillment to those who manage their lands is almost impossible to measure as investment. Nevertheless, these intangible values are—for many families—worth more than money. Often the dilemma these families face is how best to pass forest lands and management legacies on to future generations, a subject discussed in chapter 8.

So just how good are timber investments? The answer is, it depends; on a number of factors such as the cost of forest land, timber values on the date of acquisition, the cost of maintaining a timber investment (property taxes are one of the big expenses in most states), length of the investment period (or, in silvicultural terms, rotation), the time value of money or opportunity cost, and, last, the status of markets at harvest time. When comparing timber investments to alternatives, investors need to account for the effect of inflation. Timber has a "real" growth rate independent of inflation, and it is this number that an investor would use to compare with an alternative. For example, a timber stand growing in value at an average annual rate of 4.5 percent looks like a poorer investment than a certificate of deposit (CD) that pays 5.0 percent. But if you subtract a 2.5 percent rate of inflation from the CD, timber wins. "A dollar in your pocket today is worth more than a dollar tomorrow" during inflationary times.

For young, fully stocked stands of valuable species on good soils and accessible sites, timber is an excellent investment, especially if a woodland owner's time horizon extends into the next generation. The secret is to not overmanage woodlands and to invest only in the best sites. Delay investment-related expenses as long as possible and take a long view. Some of the best timber investors know far more about how to enjoy the intrinsic values of forests while also leaving a solid legacy for heirs.

Focusing on Value in Crop Trees

In silviculture there are two broad classes of treatments: *regeneration treatments*, which remove mature trees to favor the reproduction of seed and seedlings, and *intermediate treatments*, which include a variety of treatments that improve growth rates and values between the last time a stand was regenerated and the next final harvest. The goal of intermediate treatments is to match species to the site or to improve growth rates or value of trees for whatever the purpose, or both. Intermediate treatments include such practices as thinning (to give trees space to grow) and timber stand improvement (TSI), which is almost the same as thinning but favors trees that are both suitable to the site and capable of increasing in value during the rotation.

When implementing regeneration treatments, foresters are concerned with ensuring successful flowering and seed crop production of favored species, adequate sunlight availability, and favorable soil conditions. But after an intermediate treatment, foresters are more concerned with the growth and vigor of residual trees, which are those left standing after TSI. Another way to view the difference between intermediate and regeneration treatments is this: Following regeneration treatments, a forester's attention is focused on the ground to assess the composition and health of the future stand. After an intermediate treatment, attention is focused on the crowns of residual trees to assess their future prospects and to gauge competition from neighbors.

A good rule of thumb for thinning is to release—or open—a tree's crown on at least two sides, providing enough space so that it will take ten to fifteen years for crowns to grow together again. During the next thinning cycle, the process is repeated, always leaving the best trees and giving them room to grow.

Intermediate treatments are popular on private lands partly because most second-growth forests are not fully mature and because people are reluctant to convert nearly mature forests into seedling and sapling stands. Intermediate treatments are gradual and regular, yielding periodic income from cordwood and sawlogs. If the manager follows the standard rule of always favoring the best trees and removing those that compete with them, and employing the best tree-falling and extraction methods, then each successive thinning results in felled timber that is increasingly valuable. Eventually, after three or more thinning cycles, the manager's concern shifts from residual trees to getting a new stand started, and a series of intermediate treatments culminates in regeneration. The result is an even-aged forest, and the process starts all over again.

Any practice that removes 40 percent or more of the overstory is probably best characterized as a regeneration treatment; when less of the overstory is removed, it is probably an intermediate treatment, but there are plenty of exceptions, *crop tree management* being one of them.

In the mid-1980s, a group of U.S. Forest Service scientists in the Allegheny region discovered that hardwood trees thinned by conventional means (opening the crown of a residual tree on at least two sides) resulted in half the growth rate improvement of trees thinned more heavily (opening the crown all around). Because this approach is such a radical departure from traditional and conservative thinning regimes, they called the system "crop tree management," and it has since attracted the interest of foresters throughout the United States (Perkey and Smith 1993).

One of the advantages of crop tree management is that it forces managers to look for potential early in the life of a tree. When a tree is designated a crop tree, it is given special treatment for the rest of its life and never again will it have to compete for space. Thinnings are scheduled when competing crowns touch, and only those trees that interfere with crop trees are removed. The underlying philosophy is to "select the best and ignore the rest."

Aggressive thinning is the key to success with crop tree management. Proponents argue that it is better to select fewer crop trees, say ten per acre, and thin heavily around those than to select more crop trees (as many as fifty per acre) but thin less aggressively. Why? Because the advantage of selecting crop trees comes from the extra diameter growth one can expect when crowns are released on all sides. The purpose of selecting crop trees is to identify and cultivate favor in specific trees for specific reasons, which may include timber, nut production for wildlife, and other values. Lucrative premiums for high-grade logs, however, make timber the premiere product of crop tree management. When the crop is finally harvested, the payoff is handsome.

Managers who use crop tree methods are banking on the final value of crop trees exceeding the sum of the value of timber harvested in periodic traditional thinnings plus the value of timber at the time of final harvest. If heavy thinning early in the life of a stand (when trees have reached at least 40 percent of their height at maturity) more than doubles the diameter growth rate of residual trees, one can easily afford to carry half the inventory. And crop tree management—even on the best sites—usually requires fewer stand entries because the crown-release thinning given crop trees lasts much longer than the effects of partial thinning. Fewer entries means less expense, less chance to damage residual trees, less disruption to wildlife populations, less soil compaction, and fewer disruptions to beneficial belowground microflora and microfauna.

But there is a downside: the more crop trees per acre, the heavier the cutting and the more a stand is opened up. For instance, when there are more than fifty crop trees per acre, the removal of four to six surrounding trees per crop tree leaves the forest looking like a carefully tended golf course. Another risk: the crowns of crop trees, without the protection of neighboring crowns, are more susceptible to breakage from storm winds and ice. Finally, the requisite heavy thinning around favored trees is tantamount to "putting all your eggs in one basket." Years of careful tending can be lost to an insect or a disease, or a single storm. For these reasons, crop tree management is best employed on highly productive deep soils, in young, healthy stands of valuable timber species that are both wind-firm and not especially susceptible to ice damage.

In crop tree management, it is the residual trees—not cut trees—that are marked either with flagging tape or with a nontoxic, permanent paint. Choosing crop trees is not as easy as it sounds, but after they are marked, thinning guidelines are simple: remove all trees competing with a crop tree for crown space and ignore all other trees. There are exceptions, for instance, when two beautiful trees are growing side by side and it is impossible to favor one tree over another. In this situation, the manager is likely to keep both trees and completely thin around them as though they were a single tree.

Some of the nicest features of crop tree methods are the open guidelines. A crop tree is selected on the basis of any number of user-defined factors ranging from the obvious—the tree is vigorous and healthy—to personal—the owner happens to like a tree and wants to favor it. Crop trees are the "best of the best," so managers look for those that possess the following characteristics: valuable species that are apt to increase in value at an acceptable rate until the time of final harvest; long, straight, clear stems with few or no defects at any point along the stem; and balanced, healthy crowns that are at least one-third of total tree height. A *balanced crown* is one in which the weight of branches and leaves are evenly distributed on all sides of the tree.

If stand age is within twenty years of final harvest, it is too late to utilize crop tree methods, although not too soon to think about regenerating the stand. The uneven-aged regeneration methods, described earlier (single-tree and group selection), that favor shade-loving species create a forest structure that is very similar to the crop tree stand. But remember, when regenerating a stand, attention shifts from the canopy overhead to what is happening on the ground. Crop tree methods are intended to increase tree value but not necessarily to regenerate stands, although crop tree stands will begin to regenerate when the canopy is opened and so the manager will want to watch for promising young trees.

Young to middle-aged stands, on highly accessible sites of good to excellent soils are candidates for crop tree management. In this type of situation, there are usually plenty of trees that meet crop tree standards, and the manager can ease into crop tree methods without converting the stand all at once. A gradual approach would work like this: Identify and mark up to fifty crop trees per acre, but in the first thinning release only ten of them and thin the rest of the stand by conventional means (opening residual trees on at least two sides). By selecting crop trees gradually, the manager can maintain a higher stem density (and a more closed canopy) while hedging against potential losses from unforeseen circumstances. When the next thinning is scheduled (ten to twenty years hence), another twenty crop trees are selected and released. The last batch of crop trees is released during the next thinning cycle after which the manager is left with fifty trees per acre (or more, but none of the extra trees are in competition with the crop). In the last cycle, the manager should start looking for crop tree candidates for the next rotation and mark them with tape or paint.

Don't give up if an initial search for crop trees results in fewer than fifty trees, which is likely to happen, especially in older, second-growth hardwood stands. When working with fewer trees, simply adjust the proportions in the example above accordingly. In some stands of high-value species, crop-tree methods can be used on as few as ten trees per acre while treating the rest of the stand by conventional thinning.

An excellent book on the subject is *Crop Tree Management in Eastern Hardwoods* (Perkey and Smith 1993), a Forest Service publication, which is available online at no charge. Although written as a technical guide for foresters, the concepts should be comprehensible to most experienced woodland owners.

Common Silvicultural Misconceptions

Popular interpretations of forest management have led to some very unfortunate myths and misconceptions about silviculture. The term *clearcutting*, for example, describes a valid and important silvicultural practice the purpose of which is to create forest openings that are often beneficial to wildlife. Yet most people believe clearcutting is exploitive and bad. Although clearcutting solely for the purposes of converting forest ecosystems to fiber can yield undesirable results, as described earlier, it is misapplication of the practice—not the practice itself—that is bad.

Some of the most common misconceptions about silviculture arise because of difficulties inherent in planning for events that extend beyond a lifetime. Most people have difficulty planning their lives into next week, yet basic tenets of forestry expect woodland owners to plan for a resource that takes nearly two lifetimes to mature. Couple this with the fact that humans are inherently impatient, and it is easy to see how myths are spawned.

One of the most egregious myths is that *selective cutting* is a valid silvicultural treatment. This is not true, yet the term *selective cutting*, or *selective harvest* has become popular in North America, even among forestry professionals. It means nothing more or less than "trees have been designated for harvest," but it is now a common term used by timber buyers, consulting foresters, and even academics.

Such a term evolves because of a misapplication of terminology. As discussed earlier, under the uneven-aged silvicultural systems there are two regeneration methods known as *group selection* and *single-tree selection*, the purpose of which are to reproduce stands with late-successional species or trees capable of growing in the shade of parents. The criteria used to choose trees for harvest under the selection methods are usually associated with size or maturity, or to take advantage of circumstances in which seedlings on the forest floor will respond to more light.

The term *selective harvest* is not an adequate substitute to describe uneven-aged silvicultural methods. It is instead an official-sounding term used to justify a logger's (or forester's) choice of cutting methods or to pass off 'high-grading' (take the best and leave the rest) as silviculture. Any time the word *selective* is used as an adjective in the context of timber harvesting, chances are it has nothing to do with positive impact forestry. Those who use the term should be challenged to explain it.

Arguably, the most common mistake of people who are new to forestry and logging, especially in eastern forests but also in even-aged stands elsewhere, is assuming that bigger trees are older and more mature than nearby smaller trees. An incorrect observation such as this is often used to justify harvesting the "ripe" trees to make room for smaller ones, despite the fact that bigger trees are about the same age as smaller associates. Moreover, size in these circumstances is a proxy for vigor and faster growth, and a more sensible thinning prescription would be to leave larger trees and remove smaller associates. But there are exceptions to the general rule. In an even-aged stand composed of trees that are dramatically different in size, smaller trees should either be (1) removed from the stand if they are an early- or midsuccessional species that have been overtopped and suppressed, or (2) retained in the stand. But retain trees only if (1) they are late-successional species with excellent form, no hints of earlier wounds, and there is a good chance they will reach the overstory before the end of the rotation; (2) they will be carried to maturity if the stand is to be converted to an uneven-aged structure; or (3) they contribute to other management goals, such as improving wildlife habitat.

If a prescription calls for an intermediate treatment like timber stand improvement, described earlier, smaller trees should be removed to improve growing conditions for larger trees—the ones that have already proven to be good competitors. From the perspective of a timber buyer, this is exactly the opposite of what he or she would prefer to do.

Sometimes a timber buyer will propose harvesting according to diameter-limits, that is to say, harvesting only trees that exceed a certain size. If the limit is low; for example, when all trees that are 12 inches dbh and larger are to be harvested, 80 percent or more of the stand's merchantable volume can end up on the landing. This is an extreme case of "making space for smaller trees" and is usually a gut-wrenching surprise to the woodland owner who agrees to it. Generally, diameter-limit cutting is a ridiculous guideline intended to assuage a reluctant woodland owner. But it, too, is a form of high-grading that a buyer is misrepresenting as silviculture. Nevertheless, there are situations, especially in old-growth forests, where a diameter-limit guideline might make good sense. For example, in Costa Rica, forestry authorities use diameter limits to enforce harvesting statutes. Only trees *less than* a diameter limit in designated areas are harvested, contrary to the use (or misuse) of diameter limits in the United States.

Another egregious myth in forestry is that a timber sale composed of trees that have been marked for harvest (usually at face height and again on top of the root collar) is a silvicultural prescription waiting to happen. The fact is that anyone with a paint gun can designate trees for harvest, and just because a stand is "painted" does not mean the person who did the painting had a silvicultural objective in mind. Unfortunately, woodland owners have become conditioned to accept paint marks as a sign of careful deliberation. But if marking guidelines were developed without silvicultural objectives, the paint simply designates trees to cut. Tree marking for the purposes of implementing silviculture and for controlling timber sales is discussed in greater detail in chapter 4.

Most uninitiated woodland owners assume their woodlands will look better following a timber harvest. Some may even have been led to believe that one of the objectives of harvesting is to enhance the visual appeal of forests. Although there are circumstances where valid silvicultural prescriptions can improve aesthetics, most good silviculture does not always look good. This is especially true immediately following a harvest and for the next few years. Regeneration treatments—especially using even-aged methods—look worse than intermediate treatments, especially where deer populations are high and tops have been left to protect regeneration. Yet many woodland owners equate good silviculture with a parklike appearance. A careful manager is always concerned with aesthetics, but not to the point of compromising a silvicultural objective simply to make it look good. Woodland owners should be prepared for the visual impacts of disturbances caused by harvesting and should remember the important role of disturbance in forests. Nevertheless, in areas that are visually critical, buffer strips (untreated areas) are called for, especially along roads and high-profile areas such as ridgelines. It is easy to protect the visual quality of woodlands without compromising silviculture.

Another myth of forestry, which is slow to die, is the belief that thinning will help a stand suffering from stress. In other words, a great way to help a stand overcome the effects of drought, disease, or insect depredations is to thin it out, the theory being that competition for resources is stressful. We now know, however, that thinning is itself a stress that, when compounded with other stresses, can lead to crown dieback and even mortality. The negative effects of harvesting (probably due to increased exposure) in an already stressed stand are far more deleterious in the near term than are the positive effects of more space, light, nutrients, and other resources in the long term. As discussed earlier, trees suffer not so much from single stresses as from a compounding of stresses. Opening the canopy of a stand is stressful to residual trees and is best avoided if the stand is already stressed by other factors. If a stand has been recently defoliated, for example, or has suffered from dry or excessively wet conditions, or any other combination of extreme stresses, the best thing to do is nothing until the stand shows signs of recovery. And, if it appears as though a stand may suffer some biological or environmental depredation in the near future, delay thinning until after the stand has experienced the stress and has had a chance to recover. Also keep in mind that perfectly natural biological events can be stressful. For example, a heavy set of seed in a bumper-crop year is a stressful event. Although it is difficult to consistently predict with any degree of accuracy when a really good seed year will take place, flowering is a good indicator. Heavy fruiting may be cause to delay harvesting, unless the goal is to reproduce a stand.

Finally, the ultimate myth of modern forestry is that nature is wasteful and silvicultural treatments make forests more productive. If the measure of productivity is useable wood products, then carefully timed and executed silvicultural practices will increase lumber yields. But if the measure is biomass or some other measure of carbon accumulation, the long-term effects of repeated harvests is a gradual lowering of a site's ability to grow fiber; by how much, no one knows. Soil disturbances, nutrient removals, creation of disease infection courts from logging wounds, and other harvesting impacts conspire to lower productivity over time, more so on shallow soils, excessively dry sites, or on soils that are nutrient poor. But even highly productive, fine-textured soils are at risk from the effects of heavy equipment at the wrong time of year, which is usually spring or anytime soils are saturated.

Silvicultural intermediate treatments are intended to lessen the negative impacts of harvesting while concentrating site resources on fewer, well-suited trees. Good, well-timed silviculture can increase productivity of stands for lumber production, but productivity overall is gradually lowered as a result of repeated harvests. The effect on most sites is small, but who knows what the cumulative effects will be five hundred or a thousand years from now. Perhaps by then we will have developed a substitute for wood, or a safe mineral supplement for natural forests. But until then, positive impact practices weigh risks against benefits, placing long-term ecosystem integrity and health above short-term financial gains, always treading lightly.

CHAPTER 4

Harvesting and Selling Timber

The single most important element of any timber harvest is the forest management plan. It is a written document that minimally includes the owner's objectives, descriptions of different stands in the forest, and a chronology of major management activities. The amount of detail in a plan varies according to the owner's objectives: those who engage in timber harvesting need far more information than those who are primarily interested in values other than timber. In addition to the elements mentioned above, management plans that involve periodic timber sales should also include stand maps with existing and proposed access routes; timber inventory data, including growth estimates; wildlife habitat assessments; and an objective for each stand that is to be treated.

It is impossible to practice positive impact forestry without good planning, which is the difference between silviculture, as discussed earlier, and cutting trees. Forest management planning is one of the principal services of consulting foresters and often takes place in advance of a sale from which a portion of the proceeds are used to pay for the plan. Although it is preferable to do planning well in advance of scheduling activities that disturb forest stands, most woodland owners are reluctant to pay cash for these services and thus planning usually immediately precedes a timber sale. Nevertheless, any plan that gives careful consideration to the impacts of timber harvesting and extraction is better than no plan. More detailed discussion of forest management planning can be found in *Legal Aspects of Owning and Managing Woodlands* (McEvoy 1998); information on planning can be obtained through cooperative extension and state forester's offices. A state-by-state listing of public service forestry resources is included in appendix C.

Effecting change in forests is accomplished by manipulating vegetation. Managers are primarily concerned with species composition and physical structure of forests, in both vertical and horizontal planes. *Vertical structure* refers to the arrangement of vegetation from ground level to the top of the canopy. *Horizontal structure* refers to the relative positions of vegetation on the ground, in the same sense that chess pieces relate to one another on a board. Changing forest structure alters the ambient conditions of light, temperature, relative humidity, and wind speeds in predictable ways. When vegetation structure changes, so do the environmental conditions.

Manipulating horizontal structure affects the rate at which trees grow in diameter. A manager can choose between growing a large number of thin stems or a fewer number of thicker stems. The manager who is trying to have a positive effect on growth rates wants to grow as many thick stems as possible without overly sacrificing volume growth per acre. At the same time, the manager is also trying to choose species that are best suited to a particular site and that have a potential to yield valuable timber in the future. This may or may not be the species that is already growing there, since much of the forest in the United States today is second growth and there are higher proportions of some species than would be the case if not for cutting practices used in the past. For example, in the East, white pine is found commonly on toe slopes, where it does extremely well. It became established on these sites as they were abandoned for agricultural purposes early in the twentieth century. In presettlement times, many of these sites supported highly productive stands of hardwoods. The act of clearing land for pasture and then abandoning it years later provided the perfect conditions for white pine to invade these sites, where it too does extremely well. Today, a highly productive white pine stand with a towering coniferous canopy provides nearly perfect conditions for presettlement hardwoods to invade the understory. The manager who recognizes these circumstances knows that the site *wants* to grow hardwoods, even though the pine does very well. A positive impact approach in this situation is to grow the white pine on a long rotation but very gradually and carefully remove the overstory through a series of single-tree and group-selection treatments to cultivate the hardwood understory. The only way to effect this kind of silviculture is through periodic timber sales, which is the subject of this chapter.

The Realm of Forestry Professionals

There are four types of forestry professionals who offer services to woodland owners: procurement foresters, public service foresters, consulting foresters, and loggers. The question is, of the four, which is the best service provider? Choosing is not always easy and the credentials, skills, and motivations of each type of professional vary widely. Since few woodland owners have the knowledge, expertise, and equipment to manage lands on their own, at some point owners who manage their lands are faced with a choice: How to find the right advisor or service provider?

The key words to remember are credentials, skills, and motivations. Many states do not define forestry credentials, so anyone who works in the woods can use the title of forester; and more than a few, usually unscrupulous individuals, do just that. So what exactly is a forester? According to the Society of American Foresters (SAF), a professional organization that represents about seventeen thousand individuals in the United States, a forester is someone who qualifies for regular membership by having completed a four-year undergraduate (or graduate) degree in forestry from an SAF-accredited university. In other words, an individual who qualifies for regular membership in SAF can use the title of forester, whether or not the person is also a member. SAF estimates there are about fifty thousand foresters in the United States, so it represents about one-third of the total population.

The first thing to look for in a person using the title of forester is a diploma in forestry or a closely related field. There is no amount of experience in the woods that will substitute for the blend of science and math, thought and language, and management that comes with a solid university background in forestry. Nevertheless, educational credentials alone do not guarantee skills, and a degree in forestry does not come with experience. Look for forestry credentials and experience. Also consider that choosing the right person is often a matter of understanding the *motivations* of those offering services, assuming credentials and skills are not an issue. Deciding if a person is capable of using positive impact forestry methods is another matter altogether. Just because a person has forestry credentials, it does not mean he or she automatically subscribes to the concepts of positive impact forestry.

Procurement Foresters

A forester whose job is to purchase timber for a local sawmill is known as a *procurement forester*. Although a forester with procurement responsibilities is perfectly capable of developing silviculturally sound forest management prescriptions, it is impossible for this person to hold the interests of a woodland owner above those of his or her employer. A forester who buys logs for a local mill has an obligation to the employer that may or may not conflict with the interests of a particular woodland owner. In other words, a procurement forester may have the credentials and skills to offer sound management services, but because his or her employer wants access to an owner's timber, the person's motivations are obviously tilted toward satisfying monthly log quotas. An owner who decides to work with a forester representing a local mill needs to make sure this potential conflict of interest is fully disclosed. A woodland owner should not be obligated to sell timber to a forester's employer. By the same token, this same owner should not accept free services unless also willing to consider selling timber to the forester's company. This is known in the business as "a right of first refusal."

In some parts of the country, wood-using industries are trying to develop fidelity with local woodland owners. In exchange for management services, and sometimes other management-related expenses like tree planting, or timber stand improvement, a woodland owner agrees to allow the company to lease the land for growing timber. These types of long-term arrangements generally allow the company to call the shots when it comes to harvesting decisions. The terms of timber leases vary depending on the needs of the woodland owner and the company. Such arrangements are far more common in the Southeast pine forests than elsewhere.

Public Service Foresters

A service forester is a public employee whose job (although it varies from state to state) is to offer forest-use education programs, information, and some limited services to private woodland owners. As public servants, their mission is to help woodland owners make well-informed decisions about forests, but not to make decisions for the owner or to offer services that are available for hire in the private sector. In other words, do not expect the local service forester to inventory woodlands, write a management plan, mark a timber sale, or help locate a logger. These services are far beyond the scope of a public servant, and those few public foresters who do act as personal advisors run the risk of accusations of favoritism from people who sell the same services for a living. A service forester is, however, an impartial advocate of good forest management and an excellent source for second opinions. The service forester is probably also an excellent source of information on local positive impact forestry practices. It is the public forester's job to keep up to date in forestry trends and to help bring innovations to local woodland owners. The first task of anyone who acquires forest land is to call on the local service forester (see appendix C).

Consulting Foresters

Consulting foresters sell forestry services to private woodland owners, or they represent the woodland owner in forestry-related transactions. The basis for fees can vary widely from a daily rate to a contract rate, an hourly rate, a fixed fee for services or—one of the most common and troublesome basis for fees—commissions from timber sales. Services typically offered range from locating boundaries to timber inventories, and management planning to timber sale administration. For most consultants, the primary source of income results from timber sale administration and forest management planning; credentials and skills are almost never an issue. The source of a forester's motivation, however, can be another matter, and it is very important to recognize the circumstances under which a potential conflict of interest might arise.

When a consulting forester also serves as a woodland owner's agent, the forester has a fiduciary responsibility to the owner. In other words, the forester has a legal obligation to act for the sole benefit of the owner, and under no circumstances can the forester benefit directly from the relationship. The forester gets paid, of course, for services rendered, but none of the forester's actions should have any bearing on the rate of pay. This means no commissions, which obviates the most common method of payment for forestry services in the United States: an agreed upon portion of the proceeds from a timber sale.

A forester who is paid commissions is legally incapable of acting as the owner's agent because the rate of pay is based on income from the sale and herein lies a conflict of interest. Even though the woodland owner still receives his or her fair share when a forester works on commission, there is an opportunity for the forester to increase the rate of pay by designating more timber for harvest than is prudent. It is the *opportunity* for a service provider to improve his or her circumstances at the expense of another—not the act itself—that creates a conflict of interest. And when a conflict of interest arises, it is impossible for the service provider to act as an agent of a client. Conflict of interest and other ethical pitfalls common to forestry are discussed in greater detail later in this chapter.

Special contract forms are not necessary to establish an agency relationship between owner and forester so long as the circumstances show favor to the owner. For example, the person selling tires at a Sears automotive shop is acting as an agent of Sears. If a client buys a defective tire, Sears is expected to honor the warranty, not the person who sold the tire. And even though the salesperson may receive a commission for the sale, in this case the commission does not create a conflict of interest. Why? Because selling more tires benefits Sears, and the management is fully aware of the commission and the power of its incentive to motivate the sales force. Commissions on timber sales, however, are predicated on selling timber. The more timber marked for sale, the more a consultant stands to make. Consultants who use commissions have an obligation to explain the conflict of interest inherent in stumpage commissions even when there is no intention of taking advantage of the situation.

There is a big difference between working with a forester as an independent contractor and working with the same person as an agent. If a forester is operating as a contractor, the woodland owner is buying the results of that person's actions and thus has little or no say in how the forester goes about obtaining those results (except as outlined in the contract for services). If the forester is operating as an agent, the owner—as principal—has a right to control the agent's actions. An agent's duties to the principal generally include the following: loyalty, performance, obedience, information, care, and accounting. The principal's duty to the agent include compensation, compliance with the terms of the agency, reimbursement for expenses sustained by the agent, and indemnification—to "save and hold harmless" the agent in his or her dealings with third parties (remember the tire salesman from Sears?).

A contract with a forester to establish an agency relationship should describe the compensation the forester is paid as consideration, which is an essential element of a legal contract. Consideration in this type of contract takes the form of a *retainer*, a fee paid to the agent upfront but credited against compensation when the agent acts in the principal's behalf. It is an advance and represents only a portion of the compensation the agent might expect doing work for the principal.

Since an agency authorization is commonly viewed as an employer-employee relationship, the contract should also clearly describe the special nature of the relationship between parties. Unless it is the woodland owner's intention to hire the forester as an employee, the contract should state that the agent is not an employee but a person entrusted to act on the owner's behalf and according to the terms of the limited power of attorney.

The owner wants to avoid the employer-employee relationship for three reasons: to avoid Social Security liability, to avoid the necessity of worker's compensation insurance, and to avoid employment actions for wrongful termination, sexual harassment, wrongful death, or any other worker's rights that could be invoked when the relationship is terminated.

Creating an agency relationship without hiring an employee is tricky, so legal advice from a local attorney who has experience with employment law is essential. For a more detailed discussion on agency relationships with consulting foresters and other legal aspects related to forests, see *Legal Aspects of Owning and Managing Woodlands* (McEvoy 1998).

Loggers

A logger may or may not have forestry credentials. Most do not, but the situation is changing, and it is mostly changes in education and skills of loggers that have enabled positive impact forestry in the United States. Increasingly well-informed woodland owners, sensitive to the impacts of logging on forest ecosystems, are also demanding better services from loggers.

A successful logger has a good reputation and is highly skilled, but unless this person also has forestry credentials, he or she is in no position to offer silvicultural guidance. A logger also has the same type of conflict of interest as a procurement forester, the difference being that for most loggers it is personal interests that come before those of anyone else. When a logger is also the timber buyer, it is—in principle—impossible to act in the best interests of the woodland owner.

In most circumstances, it is inadvisable for a woodland owner to work directly with a logger, unless the logger or the owner, or both, have forestry credentials. A forester-logger with a good reputation and who is skilled operating in local timber types is an invaluable asset to local woodland owners. It is, however, essential that any potential conflict of interest has been disclosed and accepted by the woodland owner. Only then can an acceptable business relationship evolve between logger and woodland owner.

Keep in mind that the better the logger, the more demand for his or her services and the longer it will take to obtain a commitment. Good loggers are always in short supply, so be prepared to wait up to year or more and be very cautious of one that is available "next week."

WORKING WITH LOGGERS

Unless a woodland owner knows *exactly* how to proceed in all aspects of the timber sale and also has explicit reasons to trust a logger—both in terms of technical ability and to deal fairly—the owner should seek a second opinion. Family, neighbors, friends, or friends-of-friends are not valid "explicit reasons to trust" an individual's abilities as a logger. "He seemed like a fair guy, and I assumed he knew what he was doing," is a poor excuse when the trees are gone, soils from poorly planned skid trails are muddying the brook, and the forest is a mess.

"*Assume* is the only word that will make an *ass* out of *u* and *me*," an attorney friend of mine is fond of saying. But it is easy to remember and very good advice: Never *assume* anything in business dealings, especially when the outcome involves changes in forest structure and composition, and will ultimately affect long-term ecosystem health.

Sometimes just a call to the local service forester or the county cooperative extension office will provide enough information to determine if it is reasonable to work with someone. If this is an owner's first timber sale, however, he or she may want to seek guidance from a local consulting forester. Consultants charge fees, but it has been well established that the increase in income a consultant-advised owner can expect more than offsets the added expense for services. Forestry consultants know the markets, the players, and—most important of all—the forest and how it will respond to harvesting disturbances.

A very common pitch of independent loggers to potential timber sellers is, "Why share income from your timber with a middleman—the consultant? Work with me and you'll get the same job and more money." Although there are circumstances in which this might be true, if a primary concern of the owner is to ensure that positive impact practices are followed, there is little chance of this happening without services from a forestry consultant.

CREDENTIALS AVAILABLE TO LOGGERS

An emergence of logger education programs in the United States has had more of an effect on the availability of positive impact forestry services than any other single factor. In the early 1990s, increases in timber prices, a growing controversy about harvesting on public lands, parcelization of ownerships, and an increase in public sensitivity to environmental issues were conspiring to make the logging profession more challenging than ever. For most loggers, knowing how to wield a chainsaw, fell trees, and haggle with log buyers was not enough.

In addition to a strong background in business management, a successful logger needs to know how to communicate effectively with all sorts of people, including crew workers, foresters, equipment suppliers, woodland owners, and the general public. Equipment technologies are changing so rapidly that a successful logger must keep current on innovations, and he or she must also understand the complexity of forests and how to protect ecosystem values during timber extraction. Above all, a logger must know how to operate safely and how to provide aid when someone is hurt. The days when logger was the vocation of choice for the pariahs of rural America have come to a close. Only those committed to the *profession* of logging will survive in the new millennium.

In 1992, a national steering committee consisting of people representing a broad range of interests—from the wood-using industry to mainstream environmental groups—that have a stake in good logging practices proposed a "model" curriculum for loggers. It is composed of workshops in five areas: forest ecology and silviculture, business management, safety and first aid, forest operations, and professionalism. The model curriculum was called LEAP, an acronym that stands for "Logger Education to Advance Professionalism."

State extension service specialists were invited by the steering committee to submit competitive proposals describing how they would import LEAP and develop the necessary local alliances to make logger education a success in their states. The USDA Extension Service eventually funded fourteen projects (in Idaho, Michigan, Minnesota, Mississippi, Missouri, North Carolina, Oregon, Pennsylvania, South Dakota, Tennessee, Virginia, Vermont, Washington, and West Virginia) selected from more than thirty submissions, representing every major forest ecosystem in the United States. Each state project was a variation on the LEAP theme, but all developed and offered a comprehensive curriculum covering the five subject areas.

These early efforts laid the ground work for LEAP-like logger education programs that exist in these states today. Only a few of the pilot states still use the LEAP acronym to describe their logger education programs, preferring instead names like Master Logger, or Professional Logger Program, or some other more locally meaningful name. But the original concepts of LEAP are still visible in these and other logger education programs that have spread to surrounding states.

Before the 1990s, loggers were the underclass in forestry communities. Viewed mostly as a necessary evil—since someone has to get the wood out—loggers were portrayed as uneducated, greedy, and uncaring, and almost no one came to their defense. If something went wrong in forestry, we always blamed the logger, and so those who chose to work in the woods—conscientious or otherwise—became forestry's lightening rods. Most in forestry at the time saw loggers as nothing more than tools, ironically somewhat analogous to the chainsaw: fast and efficient if used correctly, yet deadly if careless. But in less than ten years, logger education programs have changed this image so that loggers are now viewed as an essential link with foresters and woodland owners, and many private woodland owners now ask for a logger's credentials before signing a contract.

It is no surprise that one of the most prominent requirements of the Sustainable Forestry Initiative (SFI), sponsored by the American Forest and Paper Association (AF&PA), is logger education. Companies that are members of the Association are required to purchase wood only from loggers who have completed state-certified logger education programs. This requirement was a difficult, but necessary, step for AF&PA, and the LEAP national pilot project was a point of departure for it. Now, each state SFI Implementation Committee has different specific requirements that are variations on the original LEAP theme. Some states require only a couple of day-long workshops to obtain SFI certification, others offer a comprehensive curriculum that looks more like a college degree program than a series of workshops for loggers.

There are no education programs that can take larceny out of a person's soul, and more than a few loggers use education certifications to cover bad practices. This failing is one of the major controversies of such certification programs, especially among conscientious loggers. But there is a significant difference between certifying that someone has completed an educational program and certifying "good" behavior. It is the responsibility of state-wide logger education committees to help the public understand the difference until state statutes change the little "c" in certification to a big "C." Despite almost revolutionary changes in logging and forestry over the past ten years, more regulation is inevitable, a trend discussed in greater detail in chapter 7.

The Nature of Stumpage

Before wood markets were well developed, the price paid for standing timber was figured as a residual calculation from the value of green lumber. In other words, starting with the market value of lumber off the sawmill's green chain, the costs of sawing, handling, hauling, and harvesting logs were subtracted all the way back to the stump. Whatever was left, after subtracting all the costs of production, was the imputed value of standing trees. But since the trees were gone and only the stumps remained, the price of standing timber acquired the inglorious name "stumpage."

Prices paid today for standing timber from private lands are not usually based on residual calculations, but the term *stumpage* still applies. It is the price paid to a woodland owner for the right to fell and harvest designated trees, usually just the logs in the main stem unless the contract also specifies that tops are included. Most buyers do not base their bids strictly on residual calculations, but they do take into account some or all of the ten factors that affect standing timber prices: market demand, timber quality, accessibility, total volume offered for sale, species mix, average tree size, per-acre harvest volume, distance to public roads, distance to market, and the seller's knowledge of timber markets and prices.

The weight given these factors varies from sale to sale, but each factor affects every timber sale transaction to some degree, so much so that a more detailed description of each is in order.

Market Demand

Standing timber is a raw material that requires a considerable amount of effort to convert into a useable product, and it is the demand for wood products that ultimately affects the demand for standing timber. A key indicator of wood demand in the United States is housing starts. They are also known as *derived demand*, because when housing starts are down, the demand for framing lumber and plywood eventually drop, followed closely by a drop in the demand for flooring, trim, and cabinet stock. Fewer new houses means less demand for appliances that are shipped on wooden pallets and in cardboard boxes padded with paper. Consumers cut back on furniture purchases. The net effect of a decreased demand for wood products eventually trickles down to the timber owner in the form of reduced stumpage prices, or few or no timber buyers at all. When the economy improves, housing starts go up and in time this creates a greater demand for timber. Competition among stumpage buyers coupled with increased demand for timber fuels higher stumpage prices. But the effect is much more complex than this, and there is usually at least a six-month time lag between cause and effect.

Timber Quality

The main determinant of a tree's timber quality is the size and condition of the first 16 feet of the stem, also known as the *butt log*. As much as 70 percent of total tree value is in the butt log, and the higher the average quality of butt logs on trees offered for sale, the more a buyer is willing and able to pay. Of course, the highest-value butt log is used for sliced veneer, followed by peeled veneer. Logs that make it into veneer classes are thick and straight with no outward defects such as seams or branch stubs. But veneer logs are rare, usually no more than five or ten percent of a total sale volume, and many sales yield no veneer-quality logs. The apparent quality of trees to potential buyers has a significant effect on stumpage prices, but it takes a trained eye to predict quality based on the outward appearance of trees. Trees often look better in the woods than they do at the yard or on the headsaw at the mill after the first pass.

Accessibility

The more it costs to extract timber from steep slopes or nearly inaccessible coves, the less a logger is willing and able to pay for timber regardless of its quality. Gaining access to timber is a cost of production so that inaccessible high-value timber is worth less than more-accessible timber of similar quality, and inaccessible low-value timber may be worth next to nothing (at least to a timber buyer). Not factoring in the cost of access is one of the most common mistakes of woodland owners (and young timber buyers) as they try to assess the value of timber. Notwithstanding this fact, some buyers suggest there is no such thing as inaccessible "good" timber. But there is much timber better left where it is because poor quality does not cover extraction costs. It is a sad irony that almost all of the ancient forests in the United States have been preserved, not as a conscious decision to protect the intrinsic values of untrammeled forests, but for lack of good access.

Total Volume Offered for Sale

Closely tied to the total cost of production is the amount of wood offered for sale. The larger a sale, the more a buyer is willing to pay per unit because the cost per unit of production goes down. Another way to look at it is this: A logger loses money in fixed costs when equipment is not extracting timber. Each time equipment is moved to a new site, it costs the contractor in terms of lost production time. Smaller sales mean shorter set times, more frequent moving, and more "no-pay" days. All other things being equal, a prospective buyer will offer less for a small sale volume to help cover the fixed costs of production. Low-volume, high-quality sales are not as severely affected by this factor as low-volume, marginal- or low-quality sales. In fact, a low-volume, marginal-quality sale may not attract any bidders because timber quality can not even come close to compensating for production costs.

Species Mix

A well-informed stumpage buyer knows exactly what species log buyers need to fill orders for lumber, and sometimes even just a few trees of a high-value species will raise the price for timber in the entire sale. In other words, the greater the proportion of high-value species in a lot of timber offered for sale, the more a prospective buyer is willing and able to pay for all the timber. In fact, some seller-agents (consulting foresters) will salt a sale of primarily low-value wood with a few high-value species to make the total sale look better than it actually is, but most seasoned stumpage buyers know this and will adjust their bids accordingly. When this ruse is taken to excess, it can turn into high-grading—the worst form of timber sale.

Average Tree Size

Tree value increases in proportion to tree size (especially girth). Depending on local markets, trees first become merchantable for sawtimber when diameter at breast height exceeds 12 inches. But a doubling of diameter from 12 to 24 inches can result in a disproportionately large increase in sawtimber volume. Since trees require about the same amount of processing to make logs almost regardless of girth, the larger a tree's diameter the greater the volume processed per step of production. Larger trees mean lower costs per thousand board feet processed, and larger logs at the mill mean more efficient lumber production, so everybody is willing to pay more for big trees if they look as though they will yield clear lumber.

Per-Acre Harvest Volume

Per-acre harvest volume is similar to total harvest volume and tree size in that it affects the efficiency of production and, hence, logging costs. The more volume that is scheduled for harvest per acre, the lower a logger's cost per unit of wood processed. One of the major costs of timber production is that of moving timber from stump to landing. Higher per-acre harvest volumes mean less movement and lower costs. Also, when harvest tree density is high, the chances for damaging the residual stand is often less, and this makes working in the stand easier for a contractor.

Distance to Public Roads and to Market

Another major cost of timber production is that of transporting logs from woodlands to mill. Log trucks are heavy and to move at an efficient pace they require hard-surface roads. But the cost of building woods roads is expensive, so the further a landing is from public roads, the higher the extraction cost. Poor woods roads are not only dangerous, but also slow turnaround times, decreasing harvesting efficiency. A loaded log truck can travel five times faster on a paved road than on a woods road, so the shorter the distance between landing and pavement, the better. But once the load hits the pavement, distance to markets is still a factor. For example, reducing haul distance by half can double the rate of delivery, increasing production by 100 percent while substantially decreasing transport costs per thousand board feet. From the seller's perspective, the closer the mill, the more a buyer should be willing and able to pay for a timber sale. Some mills will offer a hauling premium as an incentive to encourage loggers to bring high-value logs greater distances.

Landowner Knowledge of Timber Markets and Prices

A fair market price for any lot of timber is a combination of what a buyer is willing to offer and what a seller is willing to accept, assuming both have equal knowledge about the product and the price. But this is often not the case, since most woodland owners are woefully ill-informed about timber values and local markets. Yet sellers who know more about local timber markets, usually through the assistance of a forestry consultant, c͏ly obtain higher bids for their timber. Although market knowledge does noͅ affect the intrinsic value of timber, it does increase competition among buyers. When good timber is in short supply, paying more for stumpage is inconsequential to serious buyers. Knowledge is money.

Knowing When to Harvest

Every forester has a horror story that goes something like this: A timber buyer visits a widow and presents her with a check for $25,000 that is hers to keep provided she immediately agree to the terms of a timber sale. Since she and her deceased husband had acquired the land years ago for a fraction of the buyer's check, she thinks the deal is too good to be true. And it is too good to be true—a fact confirmed by a brief investigation of her woodland, which reveals timber worth in excess of $65,000.

What would have prompted this woman to seek a second opinion? Aside from instincts telling her that something about the deal seemed wrong, she probably wondered if it was the right time to cut: "Are the trees ready now, or should I wait a little longer?"

It is usually only a matter of time before woodland owners with timber receive a solicitation to sell, usually more than once. For most, it is also the first time they will consider if the timing for a harvest is correct. After all, how does one know if it is the right time to cut? Outside of the context of a long-term forest management plan, it is very difficult to decide if the timing of a harvest is right. Timber harvesting should always be done for silvicultural reasons and within the context of a long-term management plan. Assuming the silvicultural reasons are sound, here are some guidelines.

First, does harvesting timber make financial sense? Timber resources experience an interesting phenomenon known as *ingrowth*, which was discussed in chapter 3. It is a series of points in the life of a stand when timber values take a dramatic jump. When stands jump in size from poles to small sawtimber, local timber buyers appear with tempting offers. Money is a strong seductress to a woodland owner who has waited years for an investment to mature, but just because someone wants to buy the timber does not mean it is the best time to sell. Aside from intermediate treatments for the purpose of allocating site resources to individuals who have demonstrated a capacity to grow in volume and value, it is a silvicultural and financial disaster to liquidate young, sawtimber-sized stands.

A woodland owner in need of cash is usually better off to borrow from a bank than to destroy the investment potential of an asset that could well be outperforming even the most impressive investment portfolio. There is a period during the life of every forest when the value is changing so rapidly that it is sheer madness to cut. And in stands where risk of damage to the site and to residual trees is great, an owner may even decide to postpone thinning, sacrificing diameter growth rates to protect soils, and a long-term timber investment. Intermediate treatments such as timber stand improvement, described in chapter 3, are rarely essential. But the owner must calculate the value of lost income and slower diameter growth versus the benefits of periodic thinnings. Consider, too, that many forestry professionals are reluctant to reveal the long-term effects of prior thinning-related damage that can destroy future timber values from an accumulation of defects. Realistically, residual stem damage should affect no more than 5 percent of the stand, but the goal should be no damage. Is it not uncommon to see injury rates of 20 to 50 percent following sales that are poorly planned and unsupervised.

Prospective sellers must also consider the fact that stumpage prices are expected to increase steadily due to supply shortages in the years ahead. If a buyer says, "Now is the time to sell, because markets will never be better," don't believe it. There are seasonal fluctuations in stumpage prices, but over the long haul, timber in the United States will only become more valuable, because reductions in timber supply will increase the price of standing timber. The basic economic rule of supply and demand (price is a function of supply and demand) is reason enough to shift short-term income production strategies into long-term investment. The one hitch is that owners who decide to postpone harvesting must forego income opportunities, passing value on to future generations. Woodland owners should also consider ancillary benefits of selling timber, such as improved access, hiking trails, or opportunities to create or improve habitat for wildlife. Managing woodlands for timber production on good sites is a worthy investment strategy. But an owner who does not combine a timber investment practice with an opportunity to improve other values is probably making a mistake. In other words, harvesting timber solely for income production is the equivalent of buying a car without brakes.

With a little extra planning (and almost no sacrifice in stumpage income), a timber harvest can yield significant benefits for wildlife and other less tangible, but no less important, values. Some of the best managers consider income from timber a by-product of practices aimed at improving a host of resource values. This is one of the main reasons why harvesting is always executed within the context of a long-range management plan. Without a plan, it is almost impossible to take advantage of other resource opportunities.

So, when is the right time to harvest? If the goal is to improve conditions for residual trees, a practice known among foresters as a *timber stand improvement* (TSI), an *improvement cut,* or an *intermediate treatment,* the best time to harvest is when trees will benefit from thinning and site damage can be kept to a minimum. Unless soils are very coarse and well drained, the best time for TSI is when trees are dormant and the ground is frozen or dry.

If the goal is to begin regenerating a stand, on the other hand, timing is contingent on the species to be regenerated and the silvicultural methods to be used. For example, if the goal is to regenerate a stand of aspen, the prescription would call for patch clearcutting while trees are dormant, but not necessarily while the ground is frozen. Aspen prefers severe disturbances; the more severe, the more dense the regeneration. Late-successional species, however, are best regenerated using uneven-aged silvicultural methods, or using even-aged methods that gradually remove the canopy using a series of harvests that allow seedlings to develop under sheltered conditions.

Stumpage prices commonly go up in the spring, and the prospect for more income makes a sale tempting. Just before frost leaves the ground, loggers and other stumpage buyers (at least those who don't plan ahead) bid up timber prices in anticipation of short supply at local mills when conditions are muddy. In the throes of "mud season" good logs are hard to come by and mills will pay a premium for them. But harvesting during the spring should be avoided on all but the most coarse-textured and well-drained soils because the potential for long-term site damage and injury to residual trees is too great. There are many instances in which harvesting during the growing season is acceptable, but generally speaking, the best time to enter the woods with heavy equipment is when trees are dormant and soils are frozen or dry.

Negotiating a Timber Sale

Woodland owners who report positive experiences with timber sales have one thing in common: they are all good negotiators. They understand that a timber sale is a business transaction and, with few exceptions, they realize and accept the responsibility to protect their own interests. Timber sellers can hire someone to represent their interests, and most of the time that person is a consulting forester. But there are circumstances where even a consulting forester is incapable of having a fiduciary relationship with a woodland owner, and there are many others involved in the timber business who can only represent their own interests or the interests of their company. Knowing who's who is one of the first secrets of a successful negotiator, as is understanding the motivations of people with whom an owner is apt to make agreements.

From the woodland owner's perspective, there are as many as three different players in a timber sale. These include a forester, a timber buyer, and a logger. Confusion sets in when an owner considers the fact that the players can be manifested in a single individual; in other words, the logger is also the buyer who has a degree in forestry. Even though a person such as this may be the most preferable timber buyer in a locality for any number of reasons, sellers must understand that in the final analysis, they stand alone in protecting their interests. The buyer may be the nicest person in the county and the most competent forester in the state, but there is no way he or she can represent the seller's interests in a timber sale. Nevertheless, a seller may still decide to work with this person, but for the seller to negotiate effectively, it is essential that he or she understand and accept the buyer's perspective on the transaction. Commonly in the United States, the timber buyer and logger are one person, but sometimes the buyer is not the logger. The situation among players is not usually so complicated as to require a flow diagram on a piece of paper, but knowing the parties and their different perspectives is essential.

If the seller decides to hire a consulting forester, that person should have demonstrable experience in the seller's forest types and local markets. The forester should agree to work for an hourly rate, a daily fee, or some other arrangement that does not depend on harvest volumes. A very common practice of consultants in some areas is to obtain a percentage of gross income, but this method as discussed earlier is fraught with the potential for a conflict of interest.

For example, suppose the consultant is the victim of a court judgment that requires immediate payment of more cash than he or she has resources to pay, and this happens while marking a timber sale on a client's behalf. The pressure to raise cash to pay the judgment may cause the consultant to make decisions about which trees to cut that are contrary to decisions he or she would have made without financial pressure. The situation would have little effect on an honest person, but the problem lies in the *potential* conflict of interest. A less-than-reputable consultant would mark more heavily, generating more income from the sale and a higher yield on commissions. The best way to avoid a conflict of interest (and the only way a consultant can act as an agent in a timber sale) is if fees are not dependent on volume or value of timber harvested. This point has kindled more arguments with foresters than any other issue. Many consulting foresters disagree with me on this score, but it does not require advanced calculus to show where the conflict lies.

An owner may discover a personable consultant who insists on a commission. It is the owner's choice to work with this person, and as long as the owner understands the nature of the relationship (preferably because the consultant has explained the situation), a commission may be an acceptable and reasonable way to pay for services. The key here is full disclosure: the woodland owner understands exactly how payments are based and has agreed to accept the risks associated with doing business this way. The owner can also negotiate for assurances that the commission is not being abused.

Always spell out a consulting relationship in writing. I once visited with a woodland owner who was working with a well-respected consultant to clean up some ice-damaged timber. Although the consultant promised to send the owner a contract, the sale got started before the contract arrived. When the first check and an accounting came a few weeks later, the owner was surprised at the commission rate, almost 50 percent higher than the last time they worked together. Upon inquiry, the consultant apologized and said he just simply forgot to send the contract. Meanwhile, more timber was extracted than anticipated by the client, fees were much higher than expected, and the sale was history. The circumstances described above seem innocent enough, but the owner was ill-informed and the consultant made some assumptions about the owner that proved incorrect. More important, a long-term relationship based on trust was destroyed for lack of communication and a written contract.

Essential Elements of a Timber Sale Contract

There are many kinds of agreements between individuals that do not require a written contract, but selling timber is not one of them. Not only does the contract spell out the terms of agreement and conditions of a sale—which is nothing less than good business practice—it also proves the existence of an agreement in court if a discrepancy arises. Another reason to get it in writing is this: in most circumstances, selling timber is treated as a sale of an interest in land, and state laws require written agreements when transferring land or any subset of rights to land.

There is no such thing as a standard timber sale contract (except in the mind of the person who says there is), but there are elements that every agreement should include in addition to the "who, what, where, when, how, and how much" of any good contract. A woodland owner who sells timber is entering the local timber marketplace, if only briefly. A written contract is the only means of ensuring that the sale unfolds according to expectations. Described here are some of the elements an owner may want to include in contracts with timber buyers, whether or not a private consulting forester is also involved. First-time sellers should always employ the services of a local consulting forester, preferably one who also subscribes to the tenets of positive impact forestry, if for no other reason than to make sure good silvicultural practices are used.

Owners should always specify the exact location of timber and the marks that identify it in the field, or both. There are three common ways to mark a timber sale: (1) boundaries of a sale area are marked and the buyer is conveyed rights to harvest some or all of the trees within the boundary; (2) residual trees are marked with the understanding that any unpainted tree is fair game—a common method used to thin around crop trees; and (3) designated harvest trees are marked twice, once with a paint spot at about face-height and again—in the same color—below stump height. The stump mark is to ensure after the sale that only seller-designated trees have been removed.

Of the three methods, the last is most common. Using control marks on the stump is a good way to keep buyers honest, but it is not infallible. For this reason, experienced sellers include a clause in the contract that punishes a buyer discovered on the sale area with tree-marking paint of the same color in his or her possession. Violations of these conditions can trigger termination of the contract and forfeiture of any deposits the seller is holding.

The stump control mark is so important in sales where harvest trees are marked that in some sales on public lands it is a matter of policy to use a chemical tracer in paint to resolve questions about the origin of a mark quickly and easily. Such safeguards for private timber sales are usually not necessary, and the manufacturer of the tracer—Nelson Paint Company—is reluctant to sell the technology to private individuals because the number of tracers it uses is limited, and some of its clients (mostly the U.S. Forest Service) would prefer that the formulations were not widely available.

Some sellers will also reference the location of a timber sale with a property map showing the sale area. Doing so not only helps the buyer understand the terrain and the sale area boundaries, but it also protects the seller from liability for a neighbor's claims of timber trespass. In other words, if the buyer ends up harvesting from an abutter's land, the sale area map referenced in the contract proves the seller adequately notified the buyer of the sale area before logging and thus is not, in any way, responsible for the buyer's actions.

Another important element of a timber sale contract is an indemnification clause, to "save and hold harmless" the seller. Logging is dangerous business and the last thing a seller wants to have happen is to be held liable for injury or death of the buyer or an employee of the buyer. In addition to protection from injury claims, the indemnification clause should also protect the seller from damages the buyer might cause to third parties with the seller's timber. For instance, if a log falls off the truck when the driver stops for a cup of coffee en route to the mill, the contract protects the woodland owner from any liability that might result from damages or injuries that are completely beyond the woodland owner's control. There is no legal vaccination for liability, but the seller should always get buyers to acknowledge risks and accept liability when and where the buyer is supposed to be in control.

The contract should also require of the buyer a performance deposit to ensure terms of a contract are met and that all stumpage payments have been accounted for. This can take the form of a bond or a sum of money held in escrow until the contract has been successfully executed. For good reason, buyers are reluctant to purchase a bond or pay a deposit if they can talk the seller out of requiring it. Yet, forest owners should insist on a performance guarantee and an honest buyer will relent. Those owners who are too easily swayed should consider this: If a buyer who is enthusiastic upon signing the contract gradually discovers the timber is not as valuable as originally thought, there is a chance he or she might renege on payments toward the end of the contract, or stop paying altogether. With a performance deposit on the line, this same buyer is less likely to violate the terms of an agreement, but may ask to renegotiate. It is the seller's prerogative to do so.

A good contract clearly describes the method of payment, which usually depends on the type of sale, of which there are three: the lump-sum sale, the mill-tally sale, and the sale on the basis of shares. In a lump-sum sale, the buyer agrees to pay a single sum of money for the right to harvest designated timber. When the sum is more than a few thousand dollars, it is usually divided into three or more payments; one on signing the contract, another midway through the sale, and a final payment when the sale is complete. The lump-sum sale is the most risk-free method for a forest owner to sell timber, provided the owner has an accurate estimate of timber volumes and values.

In a mill-tally sale, the buyer agrees to pay a fixed rate of so many dollars per thousand board feet (abbreviated *MBF*), or per cord, but based on a final tally that occurs in the mill-yard, hence the name. Payments usually take the form of a deposit on contract signing, then periodic certified checks that coincide with log payments from the mill. Regardless of sale type, the seller should arrange for a frequency of payments that at least matches the rate of timber removal. In fact, the seller should preferably have stumpage payments in hand before logs leave the property. Never, under any circumstances should stumpage payments get into arrears, and if they become more than a few payments late, it is cause for termination and forfeiture of the deposit—and the contract should say so. The mill-tally sale is probably the most common method of selling timber in the United States despite the fact that there are many risks for the owner, such as accounting for all loads that leave the landing, poor utilization practices of the buyers, and sharing title to logs even after they have left the owner's forest.

A sale on the basis of shares, also known as a '*consignment sale*,' is the riskiest type of sale for woodland owners and should be avoided. The buyer agrees to harvest trees, process them into logs, and deliver them to a mill. After the mill scales, grades, and pays for logs, the buyer shares mill payments with the woodland owner. One-third of gross mill receipts to the woodland owner is common, but the owner's share can vary usually increasing with timber quality. The same risks as with a mill-tally sale apply and, in addition, the owner runs the risk of losing capital gains status on income. Why? Because the Internal Revenue Service (IRS) allows capital gains treatment only on income from the sale of standing trees, not the products of standing trees. It is a fine distinction but one that can be easily avoided by not using this method of selling timber.

Generally, income from the sale of timber qualifies as a long-term capital gain and is taxed at a lower rate than ordinary income. There are, however, a few caveats. First, the owners must have held timber (or the right to it) for the requisite holding period (not less than 12 months under current law). Second, capital gains treatment only applies to the conversion of standing timber to products; once timber is on the ground, any income from its sale is "ordinary" income. For example, an owner who sells the tops to a firewood buyer subsequent to a timber sale that involved the conversion of trees into logs must treat income from tops as ordinary income. A third caveat that relates to the treatment of income from timber sales has to do with the method of sale. Woodland owners who have frequent sales are required by the IRS to "retain an economic interest" in timber until it is measured and paid for. The mill-tally method described above qualifies, but that does not eliminate the risks of this sale method.

For more information on timber sale methods, see *Legal Aspects of Owning and Managing Woodlands* (McEvoy 1998). For more information on the tax treatment of income and expenses from timber sales, see *The Forest Landowner's Guide to the Federal Income Tax* (Agriculture Handbook 718), available online at: http://www.fs.fed.us/spf/coop/, or at the National Timber Tax Website: http://www.timbertax.org/ (Haney et al. 2001).

Be sure the buyer agrees to abide by any forestry statutes (including those involving acceptable log rules) which apply and that he or she also agrees to accept liability for any violations that might occur. Most of these statutes are written so that the woodland owner is ultimately liable for violations, but unless the owner is actually directing day-to-day operations (and also know the statutes), he or she should include a clause in the contract that requires the buyer to accept responsibility. This type of clause does not vouchsafe the seller from liability, but it does put more responsibility on the buyer to know the laws and to do a good job.

Owners should never allow assignment of a contract enabling a buyer to sell or transfer the contract to someone else without written approval. It is also a good idea to require the buyer to fully disclose names of others who might be involved in helping execute the contract. The buyer may, for example, pay a heavy-equipment operator to install roads, and the owner has a right to know who that person is.

The seller should always reserve the right to suspend or terminate a contract for good cause and with adequate notice to the buyer. If it rains for a week before the buyer shows up with equipment, the seller should be able to call the logger and delay for a few days so the site can dry. And, if soils get soaked while harvesting is in progress, the seller should have the right to close down a sale until ground conditions are more favorable. As discussed earlier, wet soils are much more easily damaged than dry, and moving water over extraction routes can lead to soil erosion and water-quality violations in nearby streams. Buyers are reluctant to agree to these terms since too many wet days in a row can lead to bankruptcy, but the alternative can lead to damages sustained by the seller that can easily exceed the value of timber offered for sale. The guidance of a private consulting forester can come in handy for making decisions about when to suspend or recommence harvesting.

The contract should include a clause that spells out terms under which the agreement is considered fully executed and complete—a kind of summary of the seller's expectations. It should also describe the timing and method for refunding deposits or releasing a bond and procedures to determine if some or all of the deposit is to be retained.

Another increasingly common provision of contracts, and not just for timber sales, is an arbitration clause. It is an excellent method to handle disputes quickly and equitably, but the extent to which arbitration is allowed to resolve conflicts varies by state. Under an arbitration agreement, the parties agree to avoid court and instead appoint a panel (usually three people: one selected by each party and a third person agreed to by the first two) whose decision is final. Arbitration statutes generally require parties to forfeit their day in court unless someone can prove an especially egregious error by the panel, such as a human rights violation. People who can not easily accept the judgment of others should avoid arbitration, even though it can save a great deal of money that might otherwise be spent on litigation.

A woodland owner should never sign a buyer's contract without a thorough and careful review of it with an eye toward the elements discussed here. Those who seek an opinion from a local attorney usually conclude it is money well spent, if only for peace of mind. Novices to the process should also locate a consulting forester who knows local loggers and markets. Most woodland owners sell timber no more frequently than once or twice in a lifetime, so it pays to get professional assistance to do it right. Another reason to work with a forester: higher bids offered for consultant-administered sales, more often than not, offset the cost of services by a wide margin.

Trading Timber for Services

Whenever a forest owner works with a logging contractor, it should be for the purposes of fulfilling more than one objective. This is, in fact, a primary way of achieving positive impacts from forest management activities. An *in-kind service* is a task performed by a contractor who agrees to deliver services in exchange for a break on stumpage payments. Despite the fact that IRS rules require both parties to evaluate services at fair market value and pay tax accordingly, stumpage buyers who use this creative form of payment know that it is easy to discount stumpage dramatically and still fulfill the IRS conditions of "reasonable and fair." The trick is in how services are evaluated, what has been exchanged for them, and how the transaction is documented. From the woodland owner's perspective, it is not receiving services for free so much as at a discount, which is not unreasonable when considering the cost of similar services if the owner were to have hired someone to do just one thing.

Nevertheless, accepting in-kind services in lieu of payment is the same as receiving income, so forest owners should report the value of those services accordingly. The wiggle room is in how services were evaluated and what was exchanged for them. For example, consider the forest owner who wants to gain year-round access to a portion of his or her woodlands the route to which is usually too wet to cross except when the ground is frozen. A contractor hired to build a proper road (geotextile underlayment, a couple of feet of gravel, and drainage) would cost a lot more than if the owner were to hire the same services from a logging contractor. Why? Because the logging contractor (assuming he or she can do the work) already has equipment on the site and is willing to accept less for the prospect of access to timber that would not otherwise have been available, and at lower prices. In the final analysis, it is as though both the woodland owner and logger have an interest in the road. The logger is happy to pay for that interest with services, and the owner pays for services with concessions on timber.

Not surprisingly, most in-kind exchanges in forestry involve cutting trees or moving soil. For example, a very common form of exchange is when an owner wants a site cleared for a camp. An independent crew hired to fell trees, extract products, bury or burn tops, and level the site would cost $150–$500 per hour. The actual exchange for similar services performed by a logger is much less because the logger is interested in timber and the prospect of harvesting wood elsewhere on the land. The future camp site first serves as a log landing, which is an ordinary and necessary expense of a timber sale. After the sale—if the site was laid out properly to begin with—it is an easy matter to convert a log landing into an opening in the forest for a camp. If the owner requires materials in addition to the cost of labor and equipment, such as gravel, road-building fabrics, and culverts, chances are the logger will agree to purchase them on his or her account using contractor discounts that can amount to 10–40 percent less than what someone who walked in off the street would pay.

Even if the forest owner and contractor mutually decide to account for "extras" as a lump-sum credit against stumpage payments, thereby burying the entire expense and income, each must still account for the values they have exchanged at tax time. In most timber markets, however, there are wide variations in stumpage prices—sometimes as much as 200 percent— so a reasonable exchange rate is almost whatever the parties agree to. So long as they avoid excessive differences in stumpage rates (claiming stumpage payments of, say, $50 per thousand board feet in a market where timber more commonly sells for $150), it is doubtful the exchange will be questioned. An egregious abuse of stumpage-for-services evaluations may be questioned during an audit.

Some other ways to exchange in-kind services with a logging contractor: If the owner has a tree near the house that looks like it will take out the master bedroom when it finally comes down, a logger may be willing to fall the tree. Likely, he or she will not want the logs, since trees near homes are notorious for having metallic objects in them that wreak havoc at the sawmill. But if it is a valuable tree, the logger may take a chance, perhaps using a metal detector to identify possible hazards within the tree. The risk for the owner is if the tree falls the wrong way. Most loggers, however, pride themselves on being able to lay a tree anywhere they want. But don't rely on the logger's insurance if the tree falls the wrong way.

Those woodland owners who need firewood but are not comfortable falling trees can make a deal with a logger to skid tree tops (just the primary branches and larger parts) from a harvest area to a central location where the owner can further process the wood. This type of arrangement is very common and almost impossible to easily evaluate for tax purposes, usually going unnoticed. The logger may be unwilling to do the necessary processing to remove second-order and smaller branches, because this type of work with a chainsaw is extremely dangerous. Another drawback to a deal like this is the risk of damaging residual stems when pulling tops even a short distance. Wounding crop trees can lead to value growth losses that far exceed the value of fuelwood. Often, it is best to leave tops where they fall and buy firewood.

Owners looking to create access to woodlands often find willing partners in logging contractors. As long as the road is not too sophisticated, nor too long, most loggers will agree to build it—even into areas that do not have a lot of timber—in exchange for a break on current stumpage prices. But it is essential that both the owner and contractor have a mutual understanding of the specifications for the trail or road. A proper road is not just a path carved through the trees; it is an adequate bed of gravel, with fabric underlayment in wet areas, good drainage, and properly installed water-control features, such as waterbars. Such a road is not cheap. Gaining access to woodlands and protecting exposed soils from erosion is discussed in chapter 5.

Since any in-kind exchange is potentially subject to scrutiny, the terms of such arrangements are rarely put in writing. But this violates the first law of timber sale contracts, which is to always get it in writing. Exchanges work best when people know and trust one another, and they understand the risks and rewards of scratching each other's back. Both parties must also agree on the relative value of a trade. For instance, the owner should have some idea of the actual cost of a service if that service were purchased independent of a timber sale. The owner must also have a realistic knowledge of standing timber values. Most owners have unrealistic expectations, but where are the savings in giving more timber than services are worth?

One final note: owners who decide to negotiate services for timber will likely yield greater savings by trading timber for a reasonable number of small "extras" rather than for one large project. In exchange, it is probably safe to discount stumpage-service rates by up to 30 percent.

Ecosystems and Ethics

Beginning with Aldo Leopold and accelerating since then is a growing awareness and recognition of the interrelatedness of forest organisms and the potentially negative impacts of timber management practices on non-timber values. These concerns have spawned new ideas about how we manage and use forests and are commonly referred to as *ecosystem management* (discussed in chapter 1). Such ideas are not fully accepted by all forestry professionals, some of whom believe that traditional forest management methods when correctly employed also protect and improve forest ecosystems.

The difference of opinion centers on our reasons for managing woodlands and who benefits from it. Proponents of ecosystem approaches say the emphasis should be placed on forest health. In other words, we should concern ourselves with future forests and future generations. Managers, they claim, have a responsibility to control disturbances so as to lessen the negative impacts of logging and to use practices that mimic nature, even if it means sacrificing short-term gains. Human use, above all else, should not be detrimental to other forest organisms—from songbirds to microscopic soil bacteria. Ecosystem management, or ecosystem approaches to management, suggests that responsibility for understanding the complexities of forests rests with those who use them, and our management practices, while attempting to mimic nature, must change as we learn. When we do not know, or can not reasonably predict, the outcome of a practice, we should choose a course of inaction rather than risk subtle but irreversible impacts when we proceed without knowing.

The days of market-driven silviculture are nearly over, as are universal prescriptions aimed solely at increasing timber volume and value to the exclusion of less-tangible, but no less important, ecosystem values. Forests will still provide timber under the guidelines of managing whole ecosystems, but it will be subordinate to the long-term health and sustainability of forests. Fortunately, disturbance—sometimes catastrophic changes brought on by storms, insects, disease, and fire—is the rule in many forests rather than the exception. Practicing ecosystem management means designing disturbances in a way that allows us to use the resource while protecting the integrity of landscapes.

Practicing ecosystem management will eventually challenge our interpretations of private property rights because ecosystems are nested, one within the other, and do not follow geographical, cultural, or political boundaries. Some migratory songbirds, for example, winter in tropical regions of the Caribbean and the Americas but use forests in the United States during the spring and early summer for nesting. Although the reason for migration is still a mystery, it may have something do with a readily available supply of protein in northern forests during the emergence of biting insects in late spring. Relatively undisturbed, old-growth, "deep" forests are important habitats for many of these species. Practicing ecosystem management in such a way as to protect nesting opportunities for

Neotropical songbirds requires guidelines that will limit harvesting in certain forest types for a few weeks each year. This is a small price to pay to ensure the survival of these species. But to some owners who see forests principally as assets—and their ability to use assets as they see fit a fundamental right guaranteed by the Constitution—having to abide by rules that govern behavior is an erosion of sovereignty. The inevitability of more regulation in forestry is discussed in greater detail in chapter 7.

Managing whole ecosystems will require an unprecedented level of cooperation among neighboring woodland owners, municipalities, states, and countries. Uncertainty over how to achieve cooperation between parties, especially at local levels, is a primary concern of owners, managers, and users of forests. Successful implementation of ecosystem management at the international level will require drastic changes in forestry practices worldwide.

A basic tenet of positive impact forestry is that it is possible for humans to use and manage forest ecosystems without destroying other species that rely on forests or the essential functions that keep ecosystems intact. Forest management encompasses practices that mimic natural disturbances to achieve human benefits but without exploiting the natural capacity of ecosystems to support themselves. For example, the practice of thinning woodlands speeds up forest succession; uneven-aged silvicultural systems mimic the formation of gaps in the canopy wrought by disease and insects; clearcutting mimics the widespread effects of fire or hurricanes, and "do nothing" is a valid management strategy so long as the owner grants a permanent easement to ensure his or her decision is legally protected. Forests for the sake of forests supersede human benefit, and those of us who disturb forests do so with great caution, humility, and respect. As good as we know our practices to be, we also know the future will promise improvements, and with knowledge comes responsibility. It is better to err on the side of inaction than to proceed with practices that may have long-term impacts on the integrity, health, and function of forest ecosystems solely for the sake of short-term gain.

CHAPTER 5

Positive Impact
Harvesting Practices

Positive impact forestry is predicated on the idea that human use of forests need not be inherently destructive and that it is possible to achieve an indefinitely sustainable complement of benefits without altering or destroying essential ecosystem functions that support them. In this context, humans are part of forest ecosystems not exterior to them, and we possess an intellectual capacity to realize the importance of protecting ecosystems, both for the sake of forests and for the benefits they can provide. There are several caveats to this assumption.

The first caveat is that long-term health and function of forest ecosystems, including the resources and processes that support all forest-reliant organisms—from mycoplasma-like particles to bacteria and mycorrhizae fungi, amphibians and reptiles to predatory avian species, and mammals from mice to moose—are of primary importance. Human benefit is subordinate to first ensuring that above all else forests provide for the complements of species that make forests what they are.

The second caveat is that short-term gain is subordinate to long-term investment, and forest ecosystems—not timber supplies—are the assets. Our traditional concept of forest management is extended from horizons of ten to twenty years that focus on periodic income opportunities which rarely even cover the cost of owning land to intergenerational planning horizons of two hundred to three hundred years that allow forest owners and professionals to finally think like forests. Effecting such a monumental shift will not be easy because it requires an entirely new way of thinking about forests on the part of industry, universities, taxing authorities, investment institutions, and even families.

John Shane, a friend and forestry colleague of mine at the University of Vermont, recipient of highly coveted university-wide teaching awards for his efforts helping students explore forest ecosystems, recently described a relevant epiphany of his. "It occurred to me one morning on my commute to campus that the word 'forest' is a verb, not a noun," says Professor Shane with the look of someone who has uncovered an essential truth about forests; the equivalent of finally seeing forests without being blinded by the trees. "Forest," he says, "encompasses processes that bring species together and supports their interactions, not the individual parts or even the products we've come to expect." In other words, our expectations of these ecosystems are the *results* of a set of processes, and it is these processes that are important, not the products.

The last caveat is that the act of management is intended to yield benefits from natural systems, not to remake forests in the image of humans. The goal of studying forest ecosystems is to understand patterns and processes more thoroughly and to discover ways people can tap into benefits by mimicking natural disturbances. Positive impact forestry is not intended to follow the path of modern agriculture, to convert forests into farms, especially since there is a very high probability that ingenuity and bioengineering will soon allow us to grow wood fiber in structures other than trees and in places other than forests.

There are five primary risks associated with managing and utilizing timber-related benefits from forests. These risks encompass activities, almost all of which have already been described in lesser or greater detail in chapter 3, that have the greatest potential to effect long-term harm in forests. They are:

- The physical effects of heavy equipment on fragile forest soils, both in terms of altering essential patterns and processes in the "hidden" forest of soil and in terms of the effects of soil loss where the mineral component is exposed to runoff. Secondary—but no less important—are the impacts of silt and sedimentation on benthic communities in forest streams and on the reproductive habits of fish that spawn in forest waters.
- The physical effects of timber extraction on injuries to residual trees, including (1) decreased soil oxygen and damage to fine-root systems from compression and soil shearing, creating infection courts that permit entry of disease-causing organisms; and (2) main-stem injuries

that serve as infection courts for disease-causing organisms. Combined, these effects cause a reduction in productive capacity and in stem strength, and potentially lead to severe degradation of future timber values.

- The environmental impacts of pollution from petroleum products such as hydraulic fluids, engine and sawchain lubricants, and fuels used by timber extraction equipment. Positive impact forestry eliminates the risks of pollution by handling petroleum only in areas protected from spills and by replacing petroleum lubricants, fluids, and fuel additives with nontoxic, biodegradable alternatives.
- The unpredictable ecological impacts of invasive species, especially those that prove to be highly aggressive, pernicious, and capable of spreading widely in forests disturbed for positive impact purposes. The overall effect is one of displacing habitat for native species and interfering with opportunities to regenerate forests by natural means.
- The potential ecological effects of habitat fragmentation when silvicultural disturbances create patterns that are unfavorable to wildlife species that are highly sensitive to changes in forest structure and composition.

The practices to achieve positive impacts are defined by caveats and controlled by risks. But it is important to note that not all forestry professionals and forest owners accept the premise of positive impact forestry that ecosystems are more important than the demands of people. For example, many forest owners are forced by financial pressures to extract timber regardless of risks, simply to pay property taxes. This is a fatal flaw of public policy as it relates to forests. Everyone accepts—even demands—the societal benefits of forests, yet they are taxed as though held in inventory for development. Bad tax policy becomes a self-fulfilling prophecy. Property taxes on forest ecosystems fuel the conversion of forests to higher and better economic uses, which is antithetical to the goals of positive impact forestry.

A forest owner, forced by local tax policies to effect practices on lands that damage ecosystems, has the right (possibly the obligation) to question assessments and to argue with local officials that taxes are too high. Generally, owners who demonstrate that forests are not being held in inventory for development, but for long-term forest benefits, are offered property tax rates based on valuations other than fair market value. There are also a number of strategies (discussed in chapter 8) owners can use to lower fair market value of forest lands that are truly dedicated to long-term positive impact forestry.

Owners who blame "the system" for exploitive practices are usually more concerned with the effect of onerous tax policies on profitability rather than with the long-term health and disposition of forest ecosystems. One of the failures of modern forestry is its obsession on profitability, even in forests that require multiple generations to yield benefits that do not exceed the capacity of forest ecosystems. Positive impact forestry defines profitability in terms of healthy and sustainable ecosystems, not on immediate income production, often requiring owners to forego opportunities in their lifetimes to create a significant and valuable legacy for future generations.

Low-Impact Logging

Among forestry professionals, *low-impact logging* is a somewhat imprecise term that many find hard to define, but they know it when they see it in the field. It is also a relatively new term that migrated upstream through a current of information that flows from developed to third-world countries, with baggage that feeds controversy. Ask any ten foresters to define *low-impact* and expect twelve explanations, all with qualifications. The term is somewhat of a misnomer in the United States, but there is no question that its arrival in the lexicon of forestry has caused virtually all sentient forestry professionals to reconsider the practices they use. Many who do not subscribe to the ideas of low-impact logging, or positive impact forestry, are simply refusing to acknowledge that forestry needs to change.

What is low-impact logging, and how does it relate to positive impact forestry? Most commonly, *low-impact* means lessening negative effects of harvesting equipment on soils, effects that were described in chapter 2. It also means planned avoidance of risks and creating positive impacts where possible. In some areas it has become a standard of practice. Forestry professionals who do not embrace low-impact methods should consider another line of work; especially those younger than middle-aged, who continue to ignore low-impact methods at their peril. It is now highly improbable that "late-adopters" will enjoy careers long enough to allow them to retire from forestry practice.

Low-impact logging methods are intended to protect soils and the communities of flora and fauna they support. Practices are also intended to prevent soil export when bare mineral soil is exposed to runoff. Preventing erosion is discussed in greater detail later in this chapter.

Careless felling and skidding practices can skin the bark off of trees, injure roots, or both, exposing trees to disease-causing organisms. Although trees are capable of containing infections, logging damage to the residual stand can ruin future timber value. Avoiding injury in tree tops is not nearly as important as protecting the first 16 feet of stem, also known as the *butt log*. Injuries to the butt log will translate into future grade reductions, but only for midsuccessional and climax species (trees that tend to reproduce successfully in their own shade). Stem injuries on pioneer and early-successional species, especially in the last quarter of their lives, are usually fatal because infections can spread more rapidly than the trees can contain them. In all species, the effect of injury on grade reduction increases with tree size. Excessive damage late in the life of a stand can destroy 50 percent or more of the stand's final value. As stands get older, therefore, the standard of care during intermediate treatments must increase.

The best way to avoid stem injuries is to use directional felling techniques, such as those taught in the Game of Logging curriculum described later in this chapter, and with well-planned extraction routes that keep heavy equipment on primary skid trails as much as possible. Some low-impact loggers will "prebunch" logs at trailheads using a small crawler, tractor, horses, or some other configuration that limits the amount of off-road travel with the heaviest equipment. Forwarders are another great low-impact tool, but they don't work well where slopes are steep. Equipment configurations to effect positive impact forestry are discussed later in this chapter.

Generally, whole-tree harvesting methods are not considered low impact because of the damage inflicted when dragging tree crowns through the residual stand. Whole-tree harvesting also violates the tenets of positive impact forestry, as described earlier, by removing portions of the tree that hold the highest concentrations of nutrients. Nevertheless, there are circumstances where whole-tree harvesting may be warranted.

Another new concept in harvest area planning refers to "cooling down a job." The three most important concepts to harvest-area cooling are planning, planning, and more planning. The idea is to develop a system in which the components work in harmony and never such that one component must struggle to keep up with the others. For example, a good skidder operator can put a lot of pressure on tree fellers, and this can lead to mistakes and accidents. Cooling down the job means developing a harvest plan where component systems operate independently but in synchrony. Logging contractors who employ these ideas soon discover that there is no such thing as downtime. Even when conditions are too wet to work, the crew can begin laying out the next job or performing scheduled maintenance. This approach to harvest-area planning is very low impact. And, best of all, it keeps crews working, even on rainy days, helping to eliminate the bane of forestry professionals: no-pay days.

Also commonly accepted is the notion that low-impact logging is needed to protect against the visual impacts of harvest areas by using buffer strips to hide areas that most people would find offensive and by making exposed areas look tended rather than hammered. Cutting tops low near roads, judicious tree felling near popular trails, and maintaining clean, orderly landings are all low-impact activities that reduce visual impacts of logging. Although such impacts must be minimized whenever possible, it should not not be done at the expense of sound silvicultural practices. Forestry professionals have an obligation to explain the functional beauty of good practices so owners understand the visual impacts of logging. Generally, people are accepting of disturbances used to effect change in forests, provided they understand their purpose. Surprises lead to discrepancies.

Forestry professionals who advocate, advertise, and use low-impact methods also protect sites from toxic petroleum products such as crankcase and sawchain lubricants, hydraulic fluids, and fuels. The presence of benzene in these products, particularly in hydraulic fluids, makes them dangerous. Toxicity, coupled with the fact that 70 to 80 percent of hydraulic fluids escape from so-called closed systems via leaks, spills, line splitting, and fitting failures means that logging equipment is a high-risk source of pollution (Miller 2002). Fortunately, there are viable vegetable-based replacements on the market for hydraulic fluids, known as *biodegradable hydraulic fluids*, manufactured from rapeseed, sunflower, corn, canola, and soybean oils. They have shorter service lives, about half that of petroleum-based products (due primarily to oxidation), which makes them two to three times more expensive (Rhee 1994), but the environmental and health-related benefits of switching to bioproducts is compelling nevertheless.

Soy-based products and rapeseed oil have also been used with success in engine crankcases. Once again, stability and price are factors that need to be resolved. Equipment manufacturers have generally been slow to endorse nontraditional lubricants and fluids in new machines, primarily because of the lack of market pressure, but some major manufacturers offer guidelines for using biofluids in their forestry equipment and others even market their own brands of biofluids. Thus, the decision to use nontoxic alternatives is left to the owner-operator and the logger.

Petroleum-based bar and sawchain lubricants are known as a *total-loss oil*. When trees are felled and bucked into logs, a fine spray of oil (considered toxic by the Occupational Safety and Health Administration [OSHA] on contact with skin and when inhaled) is spread over an area of a few square feet per cut. Nontoxic, biodegradable alternatives are readily available. Manufactured principally from canola and soy, bar and sawchain oils are probably the most common biodegradable lubricant used by low-impact contractors. These products are generally considered more expensive, but cost comparisons are difficult to make since some manufacturers claim their products last longer than petroleum. Another potentially significant bio-alternative for chainsaws is a nontoxic, biodegradable, two-cycle engine oil that mixes with gasoline and works as well as petroleum lubricants. A short list of sources for nonpetroleum-based lubricants, fluids, and fuel additives is listed in appendix A.

Other low-impact logging practices include the following:

• Establishing protected equipment fueling and servicing areas on landings in the form of plastic-lined revetments (a low soil berm) where fuels, lubricants, and fluids are stored and where all fueling, greasing, and lubricant changes take place. Heavy plastic is covered with sawdust or some other absorbent material, and when the job is completed the plastic is rolled up and disposed of at a facility that can handle these types of waste.

   There are products on the market that use bacteria capable of consuming petroleum hydrocarbons and toxins, but to avoid the risk of introducing exotic bacteria that could prove to be invasive and pernicious in local forest soils, forestry professionals should refrain from using these products on oil spills.

• Outfitting equipment using traditional hydraulic fluids with emergency absorbent pads to staunch leaks and recover spills. Also known as *spill kits*, they are essential anywhere there are risks of petroleum products getting into forest soils. A short list of spill kit suppliers is provided in appendix A. Managers should also develop a written protocol that describes safe and effective procedures for handling fluid leaks. Hydraulic systems that develop leaks under pressure are extremely dangerous and can cause serious injury.

- Avoiding harvesting during the time of the year that forests serve as critical habitat for certain wildlife species, for example during the few weeks each year that Neotropical migrant songbirds breed in temperate forests.
- Avoiding road-building practices that block or attempt to reroute natural drainage patterns.
- Encouraging practices that reduce travel over forest soils, especially in stands undergoing thinning. For example, rather than backing a cable skidder up to each stump, a logger can pull cable from an established trail that will allow bunching of logs without too much extra effort or damage to residual trees. *Prebunching* logs from the stump to the trailhead is another method to limit soil disturbances.
- Logging with draft horses. Properly done, this method is considered low impact, although the weight displacement of a horse over four hooves is many times that of a skidder tire, and hooves are sharp. Multiple passes of a draft horse over some wet forest soils can cause more damage to roots than machines because of the sharp edges on hooves and weight displacement. The same low-impact rules for machine use applies to horses: stick to established trails, prebunch loads, and—if possible—harvest during frozen ground conditions.

Designing Access That Protects Soils and Streams

Virtually all forestry-related soil erosion comes from trails and access roads used to extract timber. So long as the forest floor is left relatively undisturbed, tree removal—even clearcutting (following the positive impact guidelines discussed in chapter 3) on all but the steepest, most risky soils— does not promote soil erosion. This is a surprise to most people who have been lead to believe that canopy removal causes soils to wash away. Nevertheless, an important function of forests is their ability to buffer the movement of water, from raindrop to stream. Forest canopies absorb the considerable energy in falling rain, and undisturbed forest soils—the organic-rich upper layers in particular—have a great deal of pore space capable of holding many times its weight in water. Extensive forest canopy removal, especially in mountainous areas, coupled with soil compaction, can eliminate the buffering effects of forests on rainfall, contributing to flooding when conditions are right.

In 2001, I had an opportunity to observe the effects of heavy cutting in mountainous areas on flooding downstream in a province of northern China bordering with Russia. A torrential rain in 1998 that would have been buffered by undisturbed forests quickly exceeded the capacity of rivers, causing widespread flooding of croplands. Flooding not only destroyed the current crop, but evaporation over the course of months on improperly drained marl soils (limestone-derived) resulted in alkaline surface conditions that have prevented any subsequent planting. Thousands of acres of lowland floodplain that should have never been planted in the first place are now mostly salt flats with a few rough grasses poking through. Millions died that year of famine in a tragedy that was unreported to the western world, triggered by poor forestry and bad agricultural practices. After the devastating floods of 1998, forestry officials in China were demoted from the ministry level to that of an agency, and the People's Republic of China—after investing millions to develop a wood-processing infrastructure—placed a moratorium on harvesting in natural forests.

Sometimes, torrential rains can cause flooding regardless of forest cover because soils become saturated. When soils are saturated, further inputs simply increase the rate of output and can lead to flooding. There is evidence to suggest that this may have been the case during the 1998 rains in northern China. In the United States, the effect of forest cutting on water yields is almost always a consideration of forestry professionals, especially in mountainous areas. Of greater concern to managers than the effects of cutting on total water yields is the potential for runoff to cause soil erosion. When water runs over bare mineral soil surfaces, it picks up soil particles and carries them away.

Traditional methods of gaining access to forests that involve extraction systems that drag logs to landings can expose 10 to 15 percent of a treatment area to the erosive forces of water. Good planning and positive impact practices can cut this figure in half. The trick is to expose less mineral soil during harvesting and sap water of its energy in places where it can erode and carry soils.

Where does silt-laden water go? Usually to a location where it is a problem. Of the 4 billion tons of sediment that are produced annually through all causes of erosion (mostly from agricultural lands; sedimentation from forests is actually considered negligible) in the United States, nearly half gets into streams, and half of that makes it to the ocean. The rest of it fills in ditches, lakes, and harbors, alters the navigable course of rivers, and causes the early demise of reservoirs. Turbid water can severely damage public water supplies forcing municipalities to issue "boil" warnings since chlorine treatment is not very effective in sediment-loaded water. Excessive sedimentation also changes the ecology of streams and rivers by increasing water temperatures and decreasing oxygen supply. When soil gets into streams at the wrong time of year, it can kill insects and other organisms and can blanket newly laid fish spawn, causing eggs to suffocate. A muddy stream that looks "too thick to drink, too thin to plow," is a stream in trouble but a situation that is easily avoided.

On forest access routes, water is the culprit of erosion and soil is the victim. But when soil suspended in water reaches streams, roles are reversed: soil is the culprit and water quality the victim. Although stream sedimentation from timber extraction is a minor source of pollution, according to most regulatory officials, when people see a muddy brook in the forest, it is not difficult to discover the cause.

On a geologic timetable, logging activities, even those as careless as could possibly be, hurry the inevitable to an insignificant degree. Soil, after all, is "particles of rock on their way to the ocean," and without erosive forces of wind and rain, temperature extremes and moving water, there would be no soil (Foth et al. 1978). One could easily argue there is not a process on earth more natural and inevitable than erosion. This argument notwithstanding, when soil washes away from forest ecosystems at an accelerated rate, it can downgrade water quality, harm fish habitat (where fish are most susceptible to harm, which are the small woodland streams where they spawn), lower stand productivity, and destroy access routes. Excessive erosion also has a negative impact on the ability of forests to provide periodic benefits such as timber. When soils erode from carelessly placed skid trails, haul roads, and landings, it is the investment equivalent of losing capital and wealth.

The Clean Water Act of 1977 (reauthorized in 1987) empowered the federal Environmental Protection Agency (EPA) to establish rules for reducing nonpoint pollution from agricultural activities, including forestry. The term *nonpoint* refers to pollution sources that can not be traced back to a single source, such as a discharge pipe from a factory. The EPA developed guidelines for states to promulgate their own water quality statutes. Those guidelines are called *best management practices* (BMPs), and included in them are many excellent, common-sense ways to protect soils and water quality from logging.

The current debate in forestry centers on measures of monitoring pollution control known as *total daily maximum loads* of sediment (TDMLs). The gist of TDMLs is this: If soil movement from timber extraction exceeds the guideline limits, a permit is necessary. EPA requires a TDML standard for silvicultural activities, a restriction many forestry officials disagree with since most states rate timber extraction activities as a minor source of sedimentation, especially when compared to soil lost from agricultural fields and nonpaved roads. Furthermore, the cost of TDML monitoring and of issuing permits to virtually every timber harvest falls on the states. Fortunately, protecting water quality during logging is mostly intuitive, and practices are easy to install, inexpensive, and serve the dual purpose of dissipating the energy of moving water and filtering out sediments before they cause damage in streams.

All states now have statutes that govern water quality and—directly or indirectly—logging practices, and some laws are more stringent than others. In Vermont, for instance, forestry-related water quality rules specify voluntary use of *acceptable management practices* (AMPs), a very clever twist on the federal government's concept of *best*. The term is attributable to the late Mollie Beattie who, while commissioner of the state Department of Forests, Parks, and Recreation, was of a mind that the best logging road is paved— clearly a ridiculous notion. People who disturb soil in forests should, however, act responsibly and have the necessary skills to apply reasonable practices that fit the circumstances. The most interesting aspect of AMPs in Vermont is that they are optional. If a logger employs the AMPs and there is a discharge of soil into streams, there are no fines, provided the situation is corrected. If there are no AMPs in place, the landowner is subject to onerous daily fines if problems are not corrected immediately. Enforcement is delegated to teams composed of local loggers, foresters, and regulatory officials. They visit the site with the offending parties and recommend mitigating practices. So long as the practices are installed, at least to the minimum standards of the AMPs and within a reasonable time frame, there are no fines.

Since 1986, when the AMPs were introduced in Vermont, there have been remarkably few incidents where fines were levied, and water quality is measurably improved. Most other states have similar laws. But unlike Vermont, the use of practices to protect soil during logging is not optional. Whether called AMPs or BMPs, the practices are very similar. The best thing about them is that they are obvious solutions, generally inexpensive and—when properly installed—they can improve safety, harvesting productivity, and cause less wear and tear on machines.

The most important erosion-control technique is implemented before logging equipment shows up on the site—planning. With good planning, a manager can reduce disturbed soil area by up to half. All log landings, haul roads, primary skid trails, and stream crossings are mapped first on topographic sheets or aerial photos and then laid out with plastic flagging in the field. The nice thing about flagging is that it can be moved, whereas planning from the seat of a bulldozer or skidder is often final.

During layout, the locations of water-control structures are identified and a preliminary estimate of culvert pipe, gravel, geotextiles, and other materials such as seed and hay mulch are completed. Geotextiles are fabrics used as underlayment on sections of haul roads or landings that are difficult to drain or that tend to be soggy. In any application where gravel disappears after a few years of service, geofabrics work well to support traffic and conserve gravel without seriously affecting drainage. The fabrics are water permeable, allowing water to move freely in both directions, but prevent the infusion of fine particles into coarse gravel (fig. 5.1).

There are many variations in the composition and weave of road underlayment fabrics each suited to different soil textures. One of the most common and cost-effective fabrics is the slit-tape weave, a single layer of thin nylon tape woven in perpendicular directions. A cheap substitute is the tarp material used to protect lumber during shipment to local retail lumber yards. It is usually discarded, but store owners are often willing to give it away for the asking. Generally, consulting foresters and loggers are very familiar with geotextiles, sources, and applications.

Prospective timber buyers need to know before submitting a bid the amount of road work required. Loggers are more receptive to a manager's demands regarding the condition of roads and trails during and after the sale if they know in advance what is expected of them.

Minimizing erosion from trails and roads is simply a matter of diverting water from exposed mineral soils as quickly as possible. The ability of water to carry sediment increases as the fifth power of velocity, and the maximum particle size water can move (known as *competence*), increases as the

FIGURE 5.1 Geofabrics or geotextiles, usually woven from nylon, are used as underlayment on poorly drained soils.

sixth power of velocity. For example, when the speed of water running down a roadbed doubles, it can carry thirty-two times as much sediment and move particles that are sixty-two times the size of what it could carry before velocity doubled. Look at any streambed and note the change in particle size from the edge of the stream to middle of the current. Particles range from very fine silt to stones of varying size. In fact, the average stone size in the middle of a stream is a good indicator of the maximum stream velocity at peak flow. A tame and sedate brook meandering around toaster-size boulders or larger is a good indication of a stream that turns into a torrent when conditions cause maximum runoff.

Slope gives moving water its energy, and even an angle undetectable to the eye can move soil particles. Undisturbed forest soils are usually able to absorb even the most torrential rain, except when slopes are steep. On compacted soils, water absorption rates decrease, especially when the soil texture is clay or silt. Water that is not absorbed follows the path of least resistance—downhill—gaining speed and energy. In any circumstance in which the rate of water supply is greater than the rate of absorption, the result is *overland flow*. Since the relationship of flow to energy is exponential, even a slight incline on exposed soils can cause an unbelievable amount of soil movement in a very short time. Undisturbed forest soils, even on steep slopes, are protected by the top layers of organic debris. But when organic layers are removed, mineral particles are easily picked up by overland flow.

Slope incline is usually measured as the percentage of vertical rise over horizontal run. Under most circumstances, the incline of forest roads and skid trails should not exceed 15 percent. In other words, a point on a road at eye level uphill from an observer of average height should be at least 40 feet away. Less than this distance (except for tall people) represents a grade in excess of 15 percent. Although trail and road grades can exceed this guideline for short sections, generally the less grade overall, the less potential for erosion. The ideal trail has a slight (3–5 percent) grade to facilitate surface drainage and allow soils to dry as quickly as possible.

Waterbars are probably the most common method of slowing and diverting water from woods roads and trails (fig. 5.2). A waterbar looks like a speed bump in a parking lot, but it is angled to the downhill side of the road and its purpose is diversion—getting water off the roadbed before it picks up speed and energy. Spacing between waterbars is critical: the

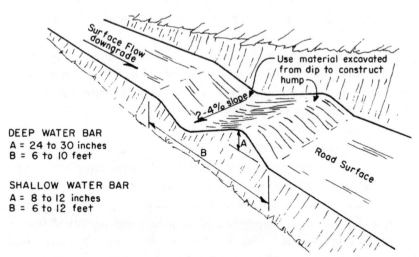

FIGURE 5.2 Waterbars are intended to slow moving water and divert it from exposed soil surfaces. Illustration courtesy of Wiest 1998.

TABLE 5.1

Recommended distances between waterbars as
a function of grade

Road Grade (%)	Distance between Waterbars (ft.)
2	250
5	130
10	80
15	60
20	40
30	30

Source: Vermont Department of Forests, Parks, and Recreation.
2002.

steeper the road, the closer the spacing (table 5.1). Those who exceed these spacing guidelines may as well have never installed a single waterbar, because overland flow will have accumulated enough energy to overrun and breach anything in its path that even approximates a waterbar. On fine-textured soils, consider using closer spacings than indicated in table 5.1.

Most forestry professionals use plastic flagging to locate the tops of waterbars and the outflows before road construction. Installation is as simple as carving into the road surface with a dozer blade or the back blade of a skidder, creating a slight downhill angle, and using soil from the gash to create a berm. On active trails, waterbars need to be refreshed daily because travel tends to flatten them out. Before leaving the site at day's end, all waterbars are checked and reconstructed if necessary. Vigilance is essential because a heavy downpour can destroy a roadbed in minutes if waterbars fail, depositing tons of soil in streams and rivers. In fact, timber sale contracts should require waterbars correctly placed and functional at all times. As mentioned earlier, water quality statutes in most states hold the forest owner liable for violations.

Even after harvesting is completed, waterbars need maintenance. When sediment-laden water encounters a waterbar, it slows, depositing soil on the uphill side. Eventually, it fills in and no longer serves its intended purpose. Well-constructed waterbars on active roads need cleaning once or twice a year—or more—depending on frequency and severity of storms. Some years ago, I visited a woodland owner who stores old shovels near major waterbars so that he can clean them out when in the area. Sure enough, we stopped that morning at a half-dozen waterbars that he quickly cleaned out; one, with nothing more than the stub of shovel.

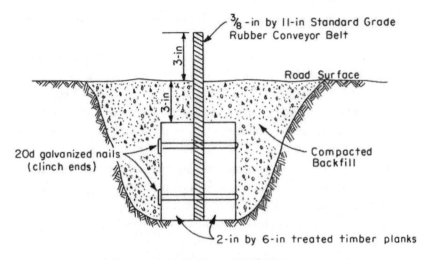

TYPICAL CROSS SECTION

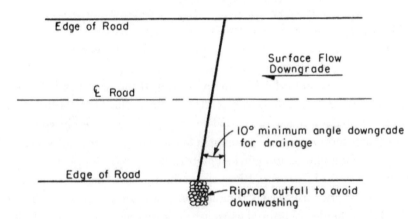

TYPICAL PLAN VIEW

FIGURE 5.3 The conveyor belt water bar. Illustration courtesy of Wiest 1998.

An interesting alternative to the traditional waterbar described to me by a logging contractor in Vermont involves the use of a worn-out snow-machine drive-belt (or a length of conveyor belt works just as well) (fig. 5.3). Most of the belt is buried in a trench dug at an angle to the downhill side (as with the waterbar, but with a slightly greater angle) leaving at least 6 inches of the belt above ground. The aboveground portion is stiff enough to divert moving water but flexible enough that vehicles can easily drive over it. Although this is not the sort of structure one would install on an active skid road, it is suitable for use on *haul roads* (road surfaces over which loaded trucks can pass) or on primary skid trails that have been put to bed until the next scheduled harvest. The U.S. Forest Service has also published a design for a conveyor belt water bar (Wiest 1998). A listing of sources for recycled conveyor belt is included in appendix A.

An expanded variation of the waterbar is known as a *broad-based dip*. It is three to four times wider than a waterbar (from front to back) and a little more difficult to construct, but it is easier to maintain and much less susceptible to damage from traffic. Broad-based dips are more commonly used on haul roads or on primary trails than on skid trails. The trick to constructing a successful broad-based dip is providing adequate drainage at the bottom of the dip. A really wide broad-based dip is also know as *reversing grade*, which is another trick for slowing runoff and keeping road surfaces dry.

It is virtually impossible to harvest timber tracts of any size without crossing a brook or stream. Depending on its size and potential for storm flow, crossing alternatives include a bridge (temporary or permanent), a culvert pipe, or fording. State laws vary on stream crossings; some do not allow fording under any circumstances, so check with the proper authorities before crossing perennial streams.

Locating a good ford is like finding money. It the easiest and cheapest way to cross streams, but the special circumstances that make fording practical—gradual approach and a shallow, rocky bottom—are not common. Also, since fording requires equipment to travel through streams, there is a potential for pollution from fuel and lubricants. In most forest areas, especially east of the Mississippi River, all good fords have been discovered, so evidence of prior use is a good indication that fording may be an alternative. Fords should not be used when fish are spawning—in spring and fall—since even slight turbidity can suffocate eggs. Skidpans on equipment should be completely free of oil before fording for the first time. If logging equipment has oil leaks that can't be stanched, the manager should propose other means of crossing a stream (and require all leaks repaired before logging commences).

Culverts can carry small streams under a roadbed or allow runoff in ditches to drain under the road. Installations are temporary or permanent, although most forestry professionals will recommend permanent installations. Locating and sizing culverts is an exacting task, and installation is an art. Pipe size for cross-drains under roadbeds is not as crucial as for stream culverts, but they are usually no smaller than 12 inches in diameter.

TABLE 5.2

Culvert diameter as a function of drainage area and
soil permeability

Watershed area (acres)		
Well-drained (sandy) soils	Poorly drained (clay) or shallow soils	Minimum culvert diameter (inches)
16	4	15
64	16	18
150	45	36
260	80	48
400	150	60

Source: Vermont Department of Forests, Parks, and Recreation. 2002.

The size of a stream culvert depends on the watershed, both its area and permeability of soils (table 5.2). One of the two most common mistakes in culvert installations is undersizing the pipe; the other is placing it too high relative to the streambed. Undersized culverts eventually wash out, usually following a severe, short-duration storm that develops flows exceeding pipe capacity by two or three times. Although it is impossible to predict unusually high storm flows, most road engineers prefer to err on the side of oversizing than of undersizing. Culverts placed too high relative to the streambed act as an impediment to fish.

One of the easiest and most environmentally friendly methods of crossing streams is with a temporary bridge. There are as many variations on these structures as there are people who make and deploy them. For example, I know a logger who uses the discarded frame of a flatbed truck as a temporary bridge. It is not very pretty, but it works like a charm. He uses a cable and winch to pull the frame across a section of the stream where there is adequate deflection above the water and sound footing on either end. When the crew is done, they simply pull it out and stabilize the banks where soil has been disturbed.

Others construct what amounts to the same thing using poles and thick planks that are easily and quickly assembled on site (fig. 5.4). A listing of online publications that describe construction methods for portable skidder bridges is included in appendix A.

Filter strips are a very common tool in forestry to filter sediment-laden runoff over undisturbed forest floor before it reaches streams. Steeper

FIGURE 5.4   Cable skidder crossing a portable bridge. Reproduced by permission from Gary Sabourin.

grades require wider strips (table 5.3). Another important function of filter strips along streams is to maintain shade over water surfaces, keeping temperature low and oxygen content high, both essential habitat requirements for trout.

When skidders and dozers have finished timber extraction, then landings, skid trails, and haul roads—especially areas near streams—are seeded with local cover grasses. Conservation Mix is usually available but should be avoided since most mixes include exotic species that are potentially invasive, a subject discussed in greater detail later. A successful planting will require a minimum of 10–15 pounds of seed per acre of exposed soil (or double this amount if mulch is not used) applied mid- to late spring, or in early fall. Often the difference between success and failure is mulch, which is applied at a rate of forty bales per acre (use only local hay that is as free of weed seed as possible). Mulch retains moisture and protects seed, and its importance increases with slope and exposure. Despite the fact that many forest trail and road re-seeding guides recommend using fertilizers with

TABLE 5.3

Width of filter strip as
a function of grade

Slope (%)	Width (ft)
0–10	70
11–20	90
21–30	100
31–40	120
41–50	150

Source: Vermont Department of
Forests, Parks, and Recreation.
2002.

cover grasses, fertilization is necessary only on the poorest soils, applied after seed has germinated. Fertilizer applied at the time of planting is often
wasted, and excessive amounts getting into streams can cause pollution.

After trails and roads have been put to bed, the best way to keep trespassers out is to put up a gate and post the area off limits without permission. Another low-tech alternative is to install a tank trap, which is like a tall
(4–6 feet), very narrow waterbar. The idea is to create an impassible breach
for four-wheelers—not to punish them—so the best place to install a tank
trap is in a section of the road that must be negotiated slowly, so trespassers
do not injure themselves. And, it is always prudent to warn trespassers of
tank traps, just in case someone does try to drive over one at 30 miles per
hour. Woodland owners have a duty of care even to trespassers.

Safe and Productive Tree-Felling Techniques

Soren Eriksson revolutionized logging practices in the United States. As
founder and principal of the Game of Logging, Eriksson began his career
in Sweden in the 1960s, serving as an industry consultant on logging safety and productivity. In the mid-1980s, he came to the United States and
brought with him nothing less than revolutionary ideas about safe and productive tree felling. Those ideas, along with early financial support from
Scott Paper Company, evolved into a world-renowned training curriculum
known as the Game of Logging (GOL).

Gaming is built into the GOL training concept because to gain proficiency loggers must practice the techniques that are taught over the course of four day-long workshops, which are usually spaced a few weeks apart. Competition helps loggers perfect the new techniques. According to GOL instructor David Birdsall of Tinmouth, Vermont, "complete novices pick up the concepts almost instantly, but it takes seasoned loggers a little longer. Generally, the more experienced a logger, the longer it takes for GOL concepts to sink in. Old habits are hard to break." Birdsall goes on to say, "GOL is a cookbook that demonstrates the safest and most productive way to get trees on the ground. But teaching it is akin to showing someone how to, say, pedal a bicycle in reverse. It's essentially the same skill, but backward. Once a logger gets comfortable with the practices, productivity goes up, safety improves dramatically, and profits follow. Some of our biggest critics going in to the first day of training come out the other end born-again advocates of GOL methods."

So what makes the Game of Logging concepts so special? First of all, the GOL mantra is "safety, safety, safety." Certified instructors, of which there are about twelve in the United States, use mnemonics to help loggers recall ideas taught in the course. For instance, loggers are taught to recall the "five points of learning" by looking at the gloved fingers of one of their hands. Each finger represents an important concept. "Thumbs-up," for example, means "hazards above." Since most logging deaths are the result of blunt traumas from above, loggers should always check for overhead hazards. The "death zone" is within 12 feet of the stump and statistics show that 85 percent of all logging injuries occur within this zone. The other fingers, from index to pinky, help loggers recall additional steps of the tree-felling process until the new ideas become habits. Ask any logger who has been through GOL to recite the "five points of learning," and his conditioned response is to immediately look at the palm of his hand, thumbs up.

In addition to safety, the course focuses on reactive forces of a chainsaw and the physics of wood fibers in standing trees. The "pull" from a working chain riding along the bottom of the bar is countered by the "push" of the chain on the top when the saw is cutting. The transition area, where the pulling force of a working chain is converted into push, is at the tip of the bar. The top side of the tip is a danger zone where a chain at working speed will cause the saw to kick back if something comes in contact with this area. Almost everyone who has used a saw knows the feel of this instantaneous push known as *kickback*. When a kickback occurs with the saw-bar outside of the kerf, the reaction is so explosive, it is impossible to control. The chainbrake feature on modern saws is intended to stop a moving chain before it hits the operator, usually in the face or upper body. No person alive is fast enough to control kickback. Anyone who has survived a kickback unscathed should chalk it up to luck, not skill.

On the bottom quarter of the bar tip, just after the moving chain leaves the kickback zone, the operator can use chain pull to gradually pivot the saw, plunging it tip first into the stem. Perfecting the *plunge cut*, as it is known by GOL devotees, is the key to safer felling techniques. It is the primary method users have to manipulate the mechanics of wood fibers in a tree, which is the second major element of GOL training: understanding the forces on wood fibers as a tree begins to fall. The felling techniques associated with plunge cutting are probably the most revolutionary ideas of GOL training. Loggers who learn these techniques experience an epiphany, and for the christened, there is no other safe and efficient way to get a tree on the ground regardless of condition, size, or lean.

The felling process begins in a semiconventional way, but students are taught to pay much more attention to tree lean and any unsafe limbs that might jar loose during the felling process ("thumbs up, hazards above"). GOL instructors advocate an *open-face notch*, where both the top cut and the bottom cut angle into one another (fig. 5.5). The top and bottom cuts are exactly perpendicular to the expected line of fall. The reason for the open face is to allow the hinge to control fall of the tree until it hits the ground.

Another GOL rule is this: the length of the hinge should be about 80 percent of the tree's dbh, and the thickness of the hinge is about 10 percent of dbh. These are golden rules, and anything more or less will result in deductions when students are scored on their skills during the competitive phase of workshops.

Hinge size and shape is absolutely crucial to accurate felling. Once a tree begins to fall, control resides in the hinge. GOL teaches that a logger should not have to shape the hinge while a tree is falling. Herein lies another innovation of GOL concepts: the notion of a shaped, strong-side-weak-side hinge to control the fall of a tree is out the window. Once a tree begins to fall, the logger should be exiting the area via a preplanned escape route, not following the stem by shaping the hinge as the tree falls. Remember, anywhere within 12 feet of the stump is the death zone. GOL teaches loggers to exit the zone as soon as the tree begins to fall. How to accomplish this feat is another innovation.

FIGURE 5.5 Open-face notch.

Once the face cut is complete, the logger uses a plunge cut that is even with, and the correct distance behind, the throat of the open-face notch (remember the 80/10 rule described above). If the tree is 30 inches dbh, the plunge cut is 3 inches behind the throat of the notch, leaving a 3-inch hinge. The feller carefully pivots the bottom tip of the working chain into the stem until the entire tip is safely past the kickback zone (fig. 5.6). The bar is then plunged parallel to the throat of the notch completely through the tree or to the extent of the bar. If stump diameter exceeds bar length, the feller initiates a plunge cut on the other side so that the cuts match.

FIGURE 5.6   Use the bottom quadrant of the tip of a working saw chain to start the plunge cut, and then pivot the saw into the cut once the top quadrant (the kickback zone) of the saw chain is fully plunged into the cut.

When the plunge cut is complete, the logger cuts horizontally—in the opposite direction of the face cut—toward the back side of the tree, using felling wedges if necessary to prevent the stem from settling on to the bar. The plunge cut is completed a few inches from the back side of the tree, leaving two points of connection between the trunk and stump: the hinge, and the *release wood*. On larger stems, and in situations where the intended falling direction is opposing lean, some of the tree weight is taken up by plastic felling-wedges. The final felling cut is initiated in traditional fashion but requires the feller to sever only the last few inches of fiber, the release wood. The tree then falls in the direction the hinge allows while the feller is safely back from the falling tree, well outside of the death zone.

A variation of the procedure described above for use in species like ash and spruce with sapwood that will experience fiber pull in the hinge area is to use *wing cuts* on either side of the hinge, going in no further than the depth of sapwood. The wing cuts will conserve log value in the butt log, the most valuable part of the tree.

In addition to safe felling techniques, the GOL curriculum also teaches loggers how to deal with dangerous situations such as springpoles. Again, the emphasis is on safety and the physics of wood fibers under stress. "Springpoles should be released gradually by shaving the fibers that are compressed (on the underside of the springpole where fibers are compressed the most) until the energy is released," according to GOL materials. The curriculum goes on to say that when done properly, the stem gradually collapses until all the energy is expended. The exact same physics apply to limbing and bucking: students are taught to assess the situation and to deal with kinetic energy in a controlled fashion.

Since 1985, GOL training has been offered in more than thirty states, mostly east of the Mississippi River, and some sources say that more than thirty thousand individuals have completed one or more of the four levels. Graduates include novices to highly seasoned loggers, arborists, and weekend warriors. Instructors tailor the curriculum to meet the needs of a broad clientele, but the basic concepts are the same in each course. A single instructor can handle from eight to ten students per workshop, since the sessions are very hands-on. Participants are usually asked to bring their own saws, and the course also covers basic saw maintenance, including proper filing techniques, maintaining safety features like chainbrakes, and carburetor adjustments. Soren Eriksson certifies instructors, allowing them access to curriculum materials and the well-known Game of Logging imprimatur, in exchange for an annual franchise fee. Only those instructors who maintain their franchise are allowed to use the GOL logo and materials.

As is the case with most good ideas, there are variations on the Game of Logging theme that are mostly differences in business models. But all variations teach essentially the same concepts—the ones Soren Eriksson brought with him from Sweden. What is so remarkable about the concepts is that almost everyone who is exposed to the ideas adopt them, which is highly unusual for any innovation.

According to one certified instructor, "a logger who does not use the techniques taught in the Game of Logging is playing the odds. It is not a question of if the logger will sustain an injury from extracting timber, but when. With GOL skills in hand, the odds are substantially in favor of the logger." See appendix A for more information about the Game of Logging.

Alternative Timber Harvesting and Extraction Systems

Few of the extractive industries have seen as much innovation as forestry. Since the cost of harvesting and transporting timber to processing facilities used to far exceed the value of timber itself, early innovations focused on production efficiencies. With a product as heavy and bulky as timber, increasing production meant faster equipment capable of handling larger loads, and so extraction equipment got bigger, heavier, and more powerful. Because the negative impacts of weight on soils and root systems tend to increase with size, early harvesting innovations were not very soil or site friendly, especially at times when soils are prone to compaction and roots are vulnerable. Fortunately, innovations in recent years have tended to focus on creating efficiencies with electronics and improved hydraulics, increasing maneuverability, and offering sites more protection. Today there are many different equipment configurations, making it nearly impossible to describe advantages and disadvantages of each.

Ask any consulting forester, "What is the most important factor a woodland owner should consider in selecting an alternative timber harvesting and extraction system?" and the answer will be "the attitude, demeanor, and skills of the person operating the equipment, not the equipment itself." A poorly trained logger, or a careless one, extracting timber with equipment that is perfectly suited to the circumstances can do more harm than a highly skilled logger using equipment that is less suitable. Virtually all site and stand damage from logging is caused by machine operators and poor timing, not equipment.

Problem contractors view machines as extensions of themselves; others see them simply as tools. The former is aroused by size and power that—combined—are the perfect disguise for a lack of skill; to this person, a roadless area is nothing more than an invitation to create one. The latter is aroused by a machine's technology, gladly substituting a superior design for power. This person is challenged by the intellectual puzzle of extracting timber efficiently while causing as little residual stand damage as possible.

The logger who fixates on size and power tends to drive over and through obstacles, while others go around them. The movements of a skilled logger are balletic, while those of an unskilled operator are pathetic. One is capable of using almost any equipment configuration to effect positive impact forestry; the other says, "Why bother?"

Forest owners who want to employ positive impact forestry practices should place far more emphasis on the attitudes and skills of woods workers than on equipment. Yes, some of the newer extraction systems are designed to cause fewer negative impacts on sites; but a careful logger can achieve the same effect with older equipment. Also, contractors with well-maintained older equipment are less likely to carry high debt loads, reducing the pressure to make equipment pay for itself, which is often the proximate cause of poor logging practices. Young, silver-tongued loggers with spanking new, state-of-the-art equipment are more apt to make promises they can't keep, especially as the end of the month draws near.

Adequate preplanning is an absolutely necessary prerequisite of any activities that involve harvesting and extraction of timber. In fact, the degree to which a prospective contractor focuses on the need for planning is an excellent indicator of the person's ability to use positive impact forestry practices. Experienced forestry professionals look upon the timber harvest as a four-stage process: (1) tree felling, (2) prebunching products from stumps to a primary extraction trail, (3) moving products from trail to landing and (4) further processing on the landing or sorting and truck loading.

Most tree felling in North America is done by small crews using manual-harvesting methods that employ chainsaws. As described earlier, felling is a highly dangerous one-person task the goal of which is to sever a tree from its stump so that it falls in a direction that facilitates extraction, but without hanging it in the crowns of surrounding trees or causing damage to residual stems. It sounds easy, but there is nothing easy about good tree-felling practices. There are many different ways to fell trees using the chainsaw, but only one correct method: the open face and plunge cut techniques taught in the Game of Logging, described earlier in this chapter. Loggers who ignore these new practices do so at their peril.

Positive impact forestry requires the use of GOL felling techniques when manual harvesting methods are employed. The risks of other felling methods, both in terms of causing injury to the feller and in terms of damage to residual stems, is too great to advocate their use. Woodland owners should insist loggers use GOL methods, and if there are no contractors who have had the training, implore local cooperative extension specialists and state foresters (listed in appendix C) to host workshops. The GOL contacts found in appendix A can supply names of certified instructors, most of whom are willing to travel if necessary to teach a course.

Stumps should be kept as low as possible to maximize value in the butt log. Extra inches at the stump are so valuable, old-timers used to say: "An inch in the butt is worth a foot in the tip." The feller must also ensure that the stem of a harvest tree is not damaged when it falls. A tree that hits the ground the wrong way can easily split, ruining log values. Further processing of felled timber at the stump depends on the extraction system: *whole-tree systems* require no further processing, *tree-length* systems necessitate the removal of all branches and unmerchantable portions of the stem, and *log-length* systems process the entire tree into logs before they reach the landing.

Generally, the shorter the product at the stump (when using intermediate treatments, or uneven-aged methods), the easier it is to extract products and the less potential for damage to the residual stand. Shorter products at the stump, however, require more trips, increasing extraction costs and the potential for soil and root damage. It is also absolutely essential that the felling stage is carefully synchronized with the person or persons engaged in the second stage. For example, if the feller(s) gets too far ahead of the extraction process, it easy for valuable logs to get lost in the woods.

As discussed earlier, whole-tree harvesting is not a positive impact practice because nutrient removals are excessive. Nevertheless, in situations where whole trees are removed for sanitation purposes during regeneration (usually clearcutting followed by planting) it is a valid method. In most other situations, a high probability of excessive stem damage, coupled with excessive nutrient removals, makes whole-tree harvesting unsuitable for intermediate treatments and for uneven-aged methods.

Tree-length systems leave foliage nutrients on the site, but extracting long products without causing damage to residual stems is next to impossible. For this reason, tree-length systems are only suitable for even-aged, low-density regeneration methods such as clearcutting, or in mountainous terrain where products are to be extracted via cable-yarding methods. The potential for residual stand damage when using tree-length systems for timber stand improvement or for uneven-aged reproduction methods is too great to warrant their use on most sites, but there are exceptions.

Very commonly, contractors will combine stages two and three into one operation so that products are handled only once between the stump and the landing. For example, in the many variations of cable-yarding systems—used mostly for even-aged regeneration treatments in mountainous areas in the western United States and, to a lesser extent, in the same type of terrain in the east—tree-lengths are extracted from the stump to a *header*, or landing, where stems are further processed into logs (fig. 5.7). The high cost of rigging some cable-yarding systems, coupled with the cost of creating access suitable for loaded log trucks, relegates these methods to relatively high-value stands with limited access alternatives. Cable yarding is commonly employed in stands that are being regenerated using even-aged methods, especially on sites that are to be replanted after harvest. It is probably the most common method of timber extraction in mountainous regions of western United States, even though the methods of extracting timber via cable were first employed in the cedar swamps of northern Michigan.

The web address of an excellent compendium of illustrations showing the wide diversity of cable-yarding systems is listed in appendix A. The

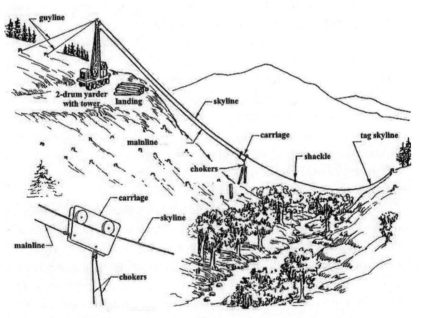

FIGURE 5.7 One of many versions of a high-lead cable-yarding system, used mostly in western timber types. Courtesy of Virginia Tech. *http://www.cnr.vt.edu/ visser/cable_logging/*

site, hosted by the Occupational Safety and Hazard Agency (OSHA), also includes a summary of safety- and health-related rules that apply to logging contractors.

Possibly one of the most common methods of timber extraction in the United States is by cable or grapple skidder (fig. 5.8). Machines come in varying sizes (usually matching local timber types), are fully articulated in the middle to improve maneuverability, and employ four rubber-tire drive wheels. The operator sits in a protective cage, just behind a diesel power plant. In back, configurations vary: one has a winch-driven cable spool with a main cable and four to six log chokers; the other has a grapple at the end of an extendable arm. Both models also come with a small, dozerlike blade on the front that serves many functions but is most commonly used for dislodging hung trees and for pushing logs into piles. The blade is also capable of constructing waterbars.

Cable skidders are usually driven close to stumps where the operator, or another person called a *choker setter*, pulls enough of the main cable to allow safe setting of as many chokers on logs as possible, but usually not

FIGURE 5.8   A rubber-tired grapple skidder, with a cable skidder inset. See fig. 5.4 for a closer look at a cable skidder. Reproduced by permission of John Deere Inc.

more than five or six at a time. The choker functions like a noose around the end of log (preferably the butt end). When chokers are set, the operator carefully spools in the main cable until log ends are lifted off the ground and are just touching a bumper plate in the back. When the load is secure, the operator drives off with the far ends of logs dragging behind. Grapple skidders use a claw to pick up prebunched piles of logs. It is not usually necessary for the operator to leave the cab of a grapple skidder, and log loading and unloading requires a fraction of the time necessary to set and retrieve chokers. The grapple does, however, require prebunching of logs and this necessitates an extra piece of equipment to bring logs from the stump to a main skid trail, or one of many variations of a machine called a *feller-buncher*.

The feller-buncher combines stages 1 and 2. Machines employ tracks or rubber tires, a diesel power plant, and an extendable arm with a grapple that holds the tree above a shear or saw that severs the stem from the stump (fig. 5.9). What happens after that depends on the sophistication of the machine. Some will accumulate a few trees and then lay them down in a pile along the primary trail for the grapple skidder to pick up; others handle only one stem at a time. Sophisticated tree harvesters will sever a tree and

FIGURE 5.9   A feller-buncher working in a stand of white pine. Reproduced by permission of David Kittredge.

then, by means of electronic sensors controlled by a central processing unit, employ a cut-off saw to process the stem into logs. Some machines (feller-forwarders) also have the capability of loading logs into a bunk on the back.

The all-in-one machines are collectively known as *mechanized harvesting*. Most of the designs originated in northern Europe, and they are perfectly suited to thinning and harvesting in uniform stand and terrain conditions such as plantations. But sophistication comes with limitations, both in terms of size and type of timber machines can handle and in the terrain over which they can operate. Mechanized harvesting systems require fewer people, but the faster pace can spawn more accidents. Nevertheless, a mechanized system is capable of processing ten times more timber than a nonmechanized operation. Even with innovations that increase production capacities tenfold, harvesting and extraction costs are still high relative to standing timber values in most stands.

A machine that has become increasingly associated with low-impact logging methods in recent years, especially in the eastern United States, is the *forwarder* (fig. 5.10). It combines stages 2 and 3, and when used on frozen soils there are virtually no machine impacts. Because the load is secured in a bunk, no log ends are dragging behind, which obviates the need for bumper trees along trails. Another advantage of the forwarder is that it requires little or no road building, and that means no exposed soil surfaces, no erosion, and no sedimentation. Landings are smaller, too, since logs can be transferred directly from the forwarder's bunk to the log truck (although the forwarder usually piles logs in a convenient location for truck loading). Mills are always pleased to take products handled by forwarders because logs are clean of mineral particles that dull saws.

The greatest potential for soil and root damage is during the second stage of extraction: moving timber from stump to primary skid trail. Scheduling logging during frozen-ground conditions can eliminate site risks. But at other times of the year, or in areas where soils do not freeze, low-tech prebunching methods include horses, farm tractors, and small bulldozers (generally light equipment that has a high weight displacement). High-tech methods include stationary prebunching winches that either use tracks to move from place to place or are set up to winch themselves to a new set point. Some prebunchers operate by radio control; others are manual.

In forests where soils do not freeze, harvests should be scheduled during dry soil conditions, prebunching logs using the methods described

FIGURE 5.10 A forwarder, with power plant in the front and a bunk for carrying logs in back, articulated in the middle for manuverability. Reproduced by permission of John Deere Inc.

above, or with a forwarder capable of moving logs from stump to landing. The goal is to avoid soil compaction and damage to root systems. In northern locations, forest owners should always take advantage of frozen ground conditions, even when logs are to be prebunched or when a forwarder is used. The only possible exception is on coarse, sandy soils, but only when stands are dormant.

Moving prebunched timber to a landing (stage 3) almost always causes serious soil disturbances, root damage, and stem injuries along primary skid trails, except when soils are frozen, or when a forwarder is used. Good preplanning and careful trail layout, including the requisite water diversion methods discussed earlier in this chapter, can keep damage to a minimum. For example, where primary trails curve, a loaded skidder—even when soils are frozen—will need a bumper on the inside of the curve to turn the logs with the machine. The bumper is usually a tree the base of which is se-

FIGURE 5.11   Bumper trees along skid trails retain the effects of injuries for the life of the tree. Illustration by David M. Carroll. Reproduced by permission from Shigo 1979.

verely injured after bumping even a few log loads (fig. 5.11). Good planning and trail layout relegates cull trees to serve as bumpers. On trails that are not apt to be used again for many years, the bumpers are felled on the way out (leaving a high stump, just in case an earlier entry is necessary). On active trails, bumpers are left in place unless the owner finds them offensive, in which case they are removed, again leaving a stump high enough to bumper future loads (and also crowned so that water drains off, slowing decay). In situations where the only bumper is a crop tree, it is possible to protect the stem with an apron of medium-gage galvanized steel, attached with cable or wire, and removed after the harvest and stored until it is needed again. A 4-by-6-foot sheet of 20-gage galvanized steel weighs about 40 lbs; weight and thickness are inversely related to gage.

Landings are usually located so that skidding distances are a half-a mile or less, close to public roads to minimize the distance trucks must travel over unpaved surfaces but not so close as to risk offending the sensibilities of local people who may object to logging. Equipment left on landings hidden from public view is far safer from vandalism and "monkeywrenching" than on exposed landings.

Landing size is a function of extraction methods, and the size and maneuverability of log trucks. The more log making taking place near the stump, the smaller the landing. For example, a forwarder can get by with a "hot landing," which is nothing more than a roadside pile of logs where the shoulder is wide enough to allow traffic to pass while the trucker loads logs. Landings that service skidders need more space, and should be laid out, if possible, so equipment moves in a circuit. In other words, a skidder can drop its load and drive right back onto the trail without having to back up. The same goes for log trucks. When equipment is always following the same path, landings are much safer and far more efficient. Finally, with good planning, landings and primary trails can serve more than one treatment and more than one stand, so long as erosion control measures are installed, and the landing is cleared of pollutants and trash following each use.

CHAPTER 6

Managing Forests for Wildlife and Nontimber Products

Most forestry practices are not necessarily bad for wildlife. In fact, there is absolutely no reason to sacrifice wildlife opportunities even when income from timber production is the most important value to an owner. With a little extra planning and, occasionally, some sacrifice, even the most timber-oriented prescription can improve conditions for wildlife. The trick is to be ever mindful of the impacts harvesting will have on habitat and to plan the harvest with an eye to creating, maintaining, or protecting good habitat for species in the surrounding landscape.

Habitat defines the conditions where a plant or animal can live and maintain itself. This is a broad definition, but it says something important about the concept as it applies to wildlife that use forests. Almost any set of circumstances will provide adequate habitat for some species, or complement of species. When forests change—in composition or structure—habitats change and the species that frequent a particular area will change as well. Habitat is not a static concept, and change is not always bad.

Most people who oppose timber harvesting on the grounds that it destroys wildlife habitat do not realize forest changes that might prove negative for one species are usually positive for another. Even the outcome of poor silviculture can prove extremely positive for some wildlife species, but not all.

The three primary elements of habitat are food, water, and cover. A biologist will evaluate habitat for a particular species in the context of these elements. Most forest stands provide one or two elements, but rarely all three. And, generally, the larger a species, or the higher it is on the food chain, the farther it must travel to obtain all elements. Bears, for example, have home ranges that can cover many square miles, whereas a ruffed grouse can live its entire life on a 20-acre parcel.

The area over which an animal must travel to locate all the critical elements of habitat is known as its *range*. In human terms, it is the equivalent of the area a person travels on a regular basis for work, shopping, and other reasons. Mammals and avian species tend to have ranges extending over areas that are much wider than a single forest stand, or even a single property. For this reason, woodland owners who want to manage lands for wildlife species need to view their land within the context of the surrounding landscape. Knowledge of the conditions on neighboring lands will guide decisions of owners looking to improve local conditions for wildlife. The boundaries that are significant to wildlife relate exclusively to resources a surrounding ecosystem can provide, not fence lines or political boundaries.

With knowledge of the habitat requirements for a species an owner wants to favor, treatment prescriptions tend to focus on supplying the missing (or limiting) habitat element(s) within the range of that featured species. For example, if a forest owner—surrounded by miles of closed canopy—wants to improve habitat for ruffed grouse, he or she might consider opening the canopy with small, clearcut patches to favor reproduction of early-successional poplar species (food) and to create a dense, shrubby cover that protects young hatchlings as they forage behind mom for insects (cover). Food and cover are most often limiting in forest habitats while water is abundant, although not always. Where water is in short supply or available only seasonally, it is a limiting factor for wildlife.

Another important wildlife habitat concept is that of *edge*. This is the transition from one cover type to another, between a hay field and a woodlot, for example. A *hard edge* is an abrupt transition, while a *soft edge* is more gradual. Of the two, soft edges are more valuable for a wider array of species than hard edges because the transition is usually a dense, shrubby cover. A mother partridge, for example, can lead her hatchlings out into the field to glean for insects, but if trouble appears overhead in the form of a hawk, she can quickly move her young back into the protective cover of a soft edge. In this example, the value of edge goes both ways: a tree canopy that overlooks a field ripe with mice and baby partridge provides an excellent perch for hawks and other avian predators. Habitat that attracts prey is also attractive to predators.

To create a soft edge between mowed fields and forest, leave a strip between the woodlot and the open field that is at least as wide as surrounding trees are tall. Let half of this zone grow back into forest; mow the other half on the field side about every three or four years, but delay the mowing until later in the summer to let grass-nesting birds raise their young.

Not too many years ago, creation of edge was considered one of the most important things a forest owner could do for wildlife. It still is, despite concerns in some areas that it is favorable to parasitic bird species, like the cow bird, that will steal nests from other species. In this case, it is creating "edge" in the wrong place that can cause problems. In other words, location is important.

Today, the emphasis for improving woodland habitats for wildlife has shifted from installation of specific practices to a concept known as *juxtaposition*, which is simply the location of critical habitat elements relative to one another. For example, a mature beech stand may provide a reliable source of nuts, but if it is not near a travel corridor (or if there is not other evidence of prior use by bears), the stand is probably not a valuable food source. In other words, the juxtaposition of food and travel routes is not favorable. Although bears may one day discover this wonderful stash of nuts, they are creatures of habit and tend to frequent areas visited in the past. A northern hardwood stand that shows bear sign (such as claw marks on trees and bear "nests" in the canopy—a bear nest being a tangle of broken branches in a beech crown where a bear sat and pulled seed-laden branches in for feeding) is probably near a travel corridor. If this is true, a positive impact practice would be to schedule treatments when bears are not feeding or to leave the stand alone. A northern hardwood stand with mature beech in it near a travel corridor is probably located on a marginal soil only just capable of providing a sustainable source of wood. If soils are good and there is evidence of bear use, treatments can favor both bear trees and other hardwoods. In these types of circumstances, it is always a good idea to seek advice from a local wildlife biologist, especially before cutting in areas where wildlife species are known to congregate or in areas that are suspected travel corridors.

Deer—both white-tailed deer ("whitetail") in the East and mule deer in the West—are perfectly suited to forest habitats, but in northern reaches, winters are a primary limiting factor for the whitetail. Low temperatures coupled with excessive snow depths are the second highest cause of mortality behind hunting. Deer will congregate in dense softwood stands, also known as *deer yards*, for at least a few weeks each winter to take advantage of lower snow depths and the insulating effect of the canopy. But without nearby opportunities to browse during these hard times, many animals can not survive harsh winters. Just like bears and beech stands, deer yards are used historically. That is to say, not all softwood stands are deer yards. Active yards are identified by deer signs, and following an especially harsh winter the remains of animals that did not make it are easily discovered. Clearcutting in hardwood stands surrounding an "active" yard will juxtapose a food source with cover that can make a significant difference in winter survival. Depending on exposure, treatment areas can be from 0.5 acre to 2 acres in size.

Deer yards need to be regenerated periodically but only under the guidance of a local wildlife biologist. The modifications a biologist will suggest to a timber-oriented harvest plan are minor. In fact, if the yard is in a red spruce–balsam fir type, the silvicultural prescription to regenerate the stand (clearcutting strips in widths that are equal to 1.5 times the height of surrounding trees, orienting strips perpendicular to known storm winds) is exactly the same prescription a wildlife biologist would suggest to begin regenerating the stand without destroying its integrity as a yard.

Forests of the United States are used by a number of different migratory species, especially songbirds that come here to raise their young. These species spend most of their lives in tropical or subtropical areas of Latin America and the Caribbean. They fly north every year for a few weeks each summer to use our forests as nurseries. Habitat requirements vary within this group of migrants, also know as Neotropical songbirds, but most prefer the more mature hardwood forests with closed canopies. Good nesting cover is essential to the survival of these birds. Although there are no published guidelines on how to manage for Neotropical songbirds, one safe guideline is this: avoid treatments in mature hardwood stands from the middle of May until the middle of June, or until nesting is completed. The United States has no control over habitats in tropical forests, but positive impact practices here can ensure these species are able to reproduce, and sacrifice of other values is minimal.

Some other practices that are easily incorporated into a timber harvest plan and are generally good for woodland wildlife include the following:

- Leave at least five to ten snags per acre for cavity-nesting bird species (table 6.1). *Snags* are standing dead trees and are fairly common in mature stands. If the snags are mostly early-successional species, like aspen or birch that rot relatively quickly, leave more.

TABLE 6.1

Common cavity-nesting birds in the United States

Species	NE	SE	MW	NW	SW
			Region		
Ash-throated flycatcher				X	X
Black-capped chickadee	X		X	X	
Brown-headed nuthatch		X			
Carolina chickadee		X			
Carolina wren		X	X		
Chestnut-backed chickadee				X	
Eastern bluebird	X		X		
Eastern and western screech-owls	X	X	X	X	X
Great crested flycatcher	X		X		
Mountain bluebird				X	X
Mountain chickadee				X	X
Northern flicker	X	X	X	X	X
Prothonotary warbler		X	X		
Purple martin	X	X	X	X	X
Red-breasted nuthatch	X		X	X	X
Tree swallow	X		X	X	X
Tufted titmouse	X	X	X		
Violet-green swallow				X	X
Western bluebird				X	X
White-breasted nuthatch	X	X	X	X	X
Wood duck	X	X	X	X	

Source: Assembled from information from the Cornell bird lab

- Specify lopping logging slash only near trails and areas that are aesthetically sensitive in order to exploit its positive benefits. *Logging slash* from tree tops is usually lopped as close to the ground as possible, primarily to improve aesthetics. But slash can provide escape cover for many wildlife species, and it can also protect young saplings from deer browse which is a troublesome regeneration problem in some areas of the country.
- Widen skid roads, a practice also known as *daylighting*, which not only helps road surfaces dry out following wet weather, but also promotes the growth of berries and shrubs, a source of food and cover for many species.
- Request that log landings and primary skid trails are seeded with an appropriate mix of local grasses and forbs following the harvest (but

not the local "conservation mix," for reasons discussed in chapter 5). Not only does this help to stabilize soils, but—with the proper combinations of local species—it can also supply a source of food. Using a hay mulch over the top of seed will greatly increase germination, but make sure that the hay is from local pastures that are free of exotic, invasive plants discussed later in this chapter.

Finally, woodland owners who have an interest in managing forests for wildlife should contact local public service forestry agencies for information about Coverts programs (described in the section below) in their home states. The purpose of this education program for woodland owners is to spread the word about managing woodlands for wildlife. Coverts cooperators help coordinate habitat improvements by bringing neighboring woodland owners together.

Good Wildlife Management Is Good Forestry: Twenty Years of the Coverts Program

Since the early 1980s, an educational project for private nonindustrial woodland owners has been having a positive effect on forests, mostly east of the Mississippi River but in some western states as well. Known as *Coverts*—a word from Old English that means a sheltering cover for wildlife—the goal of the project is to get people to manage forest lands for wildlife and other benefits and to tell neighbors how they did it. Managing woodlands for wildlife is an attractive alternative to owners who want to manage forests but fear having their lands devastated by loggers. One of the strengths of Coverts is the network of woodland owners who can promote loggers who do good work and keep tabs on those who do not.

Coverts got started in Vermont, and Connecticut quickly joined suit. The effort was developed in cooperation with state forest and wildlife agencies and was principally funded with grants from the Ruffed Grouse Society, a conservation organization whose primary interest is habitat for the bird that is its namesake. The overall purpose of the project has been to improve wildlife habitat through good forest management practices. Moreover, woodland owners who implement practices on their lands are also the principal educators in their communities, encouraging neighbors to do the same—not just for wildlife and timber but for other resources as well.

Why such a project? Because the greatest opportunities to improve forest management on private lands are through educational efforts that address the goals and objectives of those who own land, not through public incentive programs to increase timber production. It sounds antithetical, but many studies from the 1970s and 1980s showed that people own lands for a number of reasons other than timber production. In Vermont, for example, woodland owners say that even though enhancing timber values is important, creating, improving, or maintaining habitat for wildlife is often more important. For some owners, everything is subordinate to wildlife, but not necessarily to the exclusion of timber and other benefits.

Private forest owners across the United States have been led to believe that forest management means timber management. Indeed, our public agencies with a mandate to provide services and information to woodland owners must use tangible production units—thousands of board feet, cords, and tons—as measures of program accomplishment. But ask woodland owners why they own land and inevitably they identify reasons—for investment, for recreation, or simply because it is part of their residence—that are completely different from those for which public agencies offer assistance.

In the mid-1980s, wood production from private woodlands was estimated by the U.S. Forest Service to be at less than half its potential. It is not clear why, but it is quite likely due to a misconception on the part of millions of forest owners that harvesting timber for the sake of wood production is not compatible with their interests in other less tangible values, such as using forests to help provide for wildlife. This, coupled with the fact that most woodland owners do not depend on forests as a principal source of income, underscores the need for the more holistic, objective-oriented approach to forest management that Coverts teaches. Foresters, both public and private, have oversold the need for timber production and in doing so have missed opportunities to manage forests for other benefits.

The main purpose of Coverts, which is now hosted by fourteen states, mostly in the Northeast and Midwest, is to encourage woodland owners to manage their forests, not to ignore or exploit them. The project was founded on the premise that forest management decisions should be based on two things: the owner's goals and objectives for the land, and the ability of the land to provide a mix of benefits to meet those objectives. Since wildlife habitat interests are high among most woodland owners, Coverts focuses on multiple-purpose management that includes wildlife, particularly grouse, woodcock, turkey, and deer, but also for nongame species as well.

In the beginning Coverts developed demonstration sites on private lands to show the mix of practices it advocated. The sites demonstrate a manifestation of an owner's objectives, not necessarily the practices themselves. Coverts wanted owners to look at the big picture rather than argue the virtues of one practice over another. The innovation of Coverts is its emphasis on holism as the concept applies to forest ecosystems and as it applies to the efforts of like-minded neighbors who have realized the synergy of working together to provide for wildlife.

After nearly twenty years in existence, Coverts has shown that only minimal timber production trade-offs exist on properties where the principal objective is promoting wildlife. By advocating forest management for values other than timber, Coverts anticipates long-term gains in forest productivity (defined here as the land's inherent ability to supply sustained benefits, not just wood products). Thousands of private forest owners who have refused to harvest timber from their lands for the sake of timber production now do so to benefit wildlife, and the "Coverts effect" is growing.

States that host Coverts projects have developed a variety of criteria for selecting participants, but generally a *cooperator* is someone who owns forest land, has had prior management experiences, and lives in the community where his or her forests are located. Prospective cooperators, or *volunteers,* as they are known in some states, must also have the ability to articulate well-informed opinions, and they must have time to contribute to the program. Time commitments vary between states, but it is usually adds up to a couple of hours per week, for one year. Some states also require cooperators to sign agreements that specify the amount of time they will contribute to the project.

The initiation workshops are usually three-day, total-immersion experiences that run from eight o'clock in the morning until nine o'clock at night. Curricula vary but mostly follow three themes: (1) integration of the concepts on which the project was founded—forest ecology, management, and use; (2) communication and leadership skills, because cooperators must function as active voices in their communities; and (3) review of important contemporary issues that affect the way forests are managed locally. Although cooperators are not expected to become experts in forest management, by the end of the third day they know enough to help other woodland owners understand basic ecosystem functions.

The cooperator selection processes have yielded a diverse cross section of community members, from retired diplomats and executives to consulting foresters, farmers, and teachers. And, so far successes have hinged mostly on the ability to select good candidates. Desirable qualities in a Coverts cooperator include someone who is committed to the ideas of holism in forestry and someone who understands local residents and how to reach out to them. Neighbors are much more likely to act on information from someone whom they view as most like themselves rather than on information from someone they perceive to be an expert, so it's essential that cooperators act more like neighbors than experts.

The activities of Coverts cooperators are as varied as the participants. Some like to write articles for local papers, while others prefer to host woodland tours. One fellow even developed a series of lay sermons about managing woodlands for wildlife that he delivered to his church community over the course of a few Sunday mornings. In Vermont, some cooperators have moved on to important leadership positions; a few have served in the legislature; and one of the earliest cooperators now serves as president of a fairly large philanthropic foundation. Another early cooperator bequeathed a sizable gift to the Vermont Coverts to further the cause of its activities. About one-third of those involved with Coverts stay involved after their year of service is up.

In states where Coverts has become a success, the cooperators, as sort of quasi-extension agents, are a unique part of the web of public and private resources available to woodland owners. And, there are many hundreds—if not thousands—of woodland owners who got started managing their woodlands through the efforts of local Coverts cooperators, who may not have known the answer to a question, but knew how to find it. A web address with listings of active Coverts or Coverts-related projects can be found in Appendix A.

Nontimber Forest Products

Although human use of forests for products other than timber predates managed uses, *nontimber forest products* (NTFP) is a relatively new term in the lexicon of forestry. It originated in the late 1980s with the Food and Agriculture Organization of the United Nations, and it is intended to encompass "five broad product categories: food, such as mushrooms, nuts, berries and other fruits; medicinal plants and fungi; floral greenery and horticultural stocks; fiber and dye plants, lichens and fungi; and oils, resins and other chemical extracts from plants, lichens and fungi" (Jones et al. 2002). The list of species, too long to include here, contains hundreds of organisms used as NTFPs in the United States, most of them green plants or fungi. For example, in the western forests of North America, researchers have identified at least five hundred plants that were used by aboriginal cultures, many of which are still used today (Emery and McLain 2001).

Nontimber forest products include all historically useful plants and other organisms that grow in forests (or that come from trees, such as sap), rather than encompassing all values of forests exclusive of timber. Despite an ecologically friendly sounding term with deep roots in the traditions of indigenous people, NTFPs are a significant enterprise in some areas, more so for those who broker products than those who gather them, especially in the case of rare, but highly prized, mushrooms. For example, in much of the western forest, particularly in old-growth forests of the Pacific Northwest, NTFPs have a commercial connotation driven by high prices that attract more gatherers, creating an intense competition for a relatively small supply of products that grow on a limited land base. In the context of positive impact forestry and as the term is used here, NTFPs refer to naturally occurring plants and other organisms from forests. It does not refer to agroforestry in any sense, either by cultivating NTFP crops by any means other than traditional gathering practices or the establishment of crops in the understory with native or nonnative species (cultivating shiitake mushrooms, for example).

Once again, scarcity, in the same context that brought European forestry methods to the United States (i.e., excessive demand for a shrinking supply fueling exploitive practices) spawned the arrival of new ideas to help sustain harvesting of resources that probably first connected humans with forests. Until relatively recently, NTFPs were of interest only to those who learned the oral traditions of indigenous people. The accumulated knowledge of countless generations of forest-dwelling ancestors became the basis of NTFPs. As knowledge of traditions spread, more and more gatherers learned of these modest resources, harvesting them mostly to supplement a subsistence lifestyle. But with more gatherers came conflict and the evolution of commercial markets. This a gross oversimplification of the issues surrounding NTFPs, and is further complicated by the fact that most gatherers do not own forest land. The formal study of NTFPs evolved both as an ethnobotanical inquiry and to discover sensible practices and policies for managing NTPF harvests on public lands. Nevertheless, strategies for managing NTFPs are nascent (Chamberlain, et al. 2002).

Permits are required to harvest from public lands, and gatherers tend to respect permit systems. But they also go where target organisms are apt to reside, including private lands. In some areas where NTFPs fetch high prices, territorial disputes are common and some have lead to violence. Excessive demand, more than any other factor, raises questions about sustainability. Many of the high-value NTFPs—especially the mushrooms, most of which also form mycorrhizal relationships with tree roots (the importance of which were discussed earlier)—have exacting site requirements. Reproduction is unpredictable and too little is known about the ecology of some organisms to develop reliable harvesting guidelines. Even with guidelines, an unscrupulous gatherer can decimate a site in minutes, extirpating a population that may have taken a lifetime to establish and destroying the prospects for future harvests.

The only way to protect and manage NTFPs using positive impact forestry guidelines is to put stewardship in the hands of those who gather. When individuals lack an ownership interest, there is little incentive to use good practices. The way to create an ownership interest is through a lease of gathering rights. It sounds like the perfect solution, but leasing exclusive harvest rights is not without risks. Many gatherers claim rights by tenure, and these rights supersede claims of those who come later, even of someone who buys the land. It is a concept analogous to maritime salvage rights; the person who finds a shipwreck has rights that supersede even those of an owner. On large tracts, the owner is often not aware that unauthorized harvesting is taking place; or he or she knows it is occurring but does not know the identity of gatherers. The point is this: a lease with one person excludes all others, and this could prove to be a serious mistake for the owner.

Forest owners who are concerned about NTFPs—because they have identified an opportunity, or because they have discovered bad practices— may want to attempt to locate the gatherers who are using the property. Generally, a lease is first offered to the person who has tenure unless that person is using bad practices. Gatherers who are concerned with good practices are often very willing to accept a lease as a way to protect a claim. If the person refuses the lease, then it is the owner's right to award it to someone else. An owner may want to first extend gathering rights for a limited probational period of one or two seasons to ensure the person uses good practices and is reliable. After that, consider offering a nontransferable lease for a period of five to ten years, with the following conditions:

- Gathering rights extend only to listed species or products unless the lease is amended in writing. No other NTFPs located by the gatherer are included unless permission is first obtained from the owner.
- The gatherer accepts that an NTFP lease is subordinate to other management objectives of the owner. Nevertheless, an owner who leases NTFP harvest rights has an obligation to the gatherer to use practices that will protect an NTFP as much as possible during silvicultural operations.
- The gatherer is required to obtain information from credible sources on currently acceptable, sustainable harvesting practices for each NTFP and deliver copies of this information to the owner. It is the owner's prerogative to follow published guidelines or reduce harvest levels for any reason and the gatherer agrees to comply.
- A gatherer is required to map the coordinates of an NTFP population using a handheld GPS unit and to estimate the size or extent of a population or resource for the purposes of establishing a base line. These data are jointly owned by the gatherer and owner, both of whom agree to hold information confidential, excepting an authorized agent of the owner (i.e., a consulting forester).
- The owner will supply the gatherer with descriptions of known exotic invasive species, including insect and disease organisms harmful to timber that may or may not be invasive, and a set of guidelines on how to remove a plant, and/or map and report infestations.
- The gatherer is required to annually report on the condition and extent of each mapped NTFP and on any other aspects of the forest that are significant (i.e., a broken fence line, timber trespass, animal signs, windthrow, erosion, etc.).
- Rights do not entitle the gatherer to propagate other NTFPs, or to cultivate or apply amendments and chemicals, or to use practices—other than those listed in the lease—to increase the rate of growth, production, or any other qualities of an NTFP. The gatherer only has the right to harvest products during listed seasons, using procedures described in the lease.
- The owner reserves the right to cancel a lease at any time, for any

reason, or to alter harvest methods as new information becomes available. If the owner discovers that any aspect of the lease has been violated, it is terminated.

Finally, an owner may want to require a performance bond to ensure a gatherer follows lease conditions. This may prove a financial hardship for the person since many gatherers live at subsistence levels. It is, however, possible to obtain a reasonable bond from a bonding authority for a percentage of the bond's face value. After a few years, the owner may decide to suspend the bond requirement. But until the motivations and practices of the gatherer are known, a bond is the only way to protect an owner's interests.

Payments for lease rights are completely negotiable, from a one-dollar-per-year arrangement, because of services a gatherer is providing by monitoring the property, to an amount that is a reasonable percentage of income from brokers who buy NTFPs. If the lessee is the person who has claimed harvest rights by tenure, an owner may stand to gain more by acknowledging those rights and extracting a stewardship promise worth far more than money.

The Threat of Invasive Exotic Species

The presence of nonnative, aggressive, and often pernicious species is either the first or second most important threat to biological diversity of ecosystems, before or after that of habitat loss, depending on the source. Regardless, the impacts of exotic organisms on forests are significant. Despite annual expenditures on the order of hundreds of millions of dollars to eradicate or control the spread of invasive species in this country alone, it is still a growing problem. The U.S. Congressional Office of Technology Assessment estimates that of the 4,500 plants introduced to North America since colonists first arrived, "675 are considered harmful."

From around the time forestry arrived in this country until 1991, approximately eighty invasive and pernicious species have been responsible for nearly $100 billion in loses, mostly to agricultural crops. And the prognosis is not good. Of the nearly seven thousand plants recognized as weeds worldwide, about two thousand currently reside in the United States. This leaves five thousand noxious plants that have yet to cross our borders. Some may have already arrived, but conditions here are such they will not become invasive and harmful. Or their populations are building to the point at which they will eventually become problems. A state is considered fortunate if only one in ten plants is considered invasive. But in states such as California, New York, Pennsylvania, and Hawaii, half or more plants are perniciously invasive. Favorable climates, diverse agriculture, extensive site disturbances, international ports of call, and local policies that interfere with control strategies favor these states over others.

Noxious plants are not the only threat. Potentially damaging species can include animals, fungi, insects, bacteria, viruses, and viruslike particles. Any nonnative organism, often arriving without its natural enemies, with an ability to tolerate a wide range of environmental conditions, is a threat. Invasives are usually sexually precocious, prolific, and they possess a highly effective dispersal mechanism. It is their ability to outcompete native species, sometimes displacing them, that results in ecosystem changes for which long-term impacts are unknown. For example, of the forest insects in the United States that are known to damage trees, only a handful are exotics. But these few are responsible for a disproportional amount of damage, more than half.

How did they get here? The arrival of some, such as the gypsy moth described in chapter 2, can be attributed to ignorance (the "naturalist" looking for a better way to produce silk). Others slip through as a result of lax commerce practices. For instance, wood-boring insects hitch rides on the thousands of wooden crates that arrive here each year, of which only an ineffective few have been inspected for such unintended guests. Some species arrive in the suitcases of travelers or in dried soil trapped in the lugs of their sneakers. Most travelers assume that it is highly improbable they are carrying potentially invasive exotics and so they ignore rules. But the facts are that no one knows how many species arrive in the United States due to the careless acts of travelers. The declarations process is based on an honor system, and if someone gets caught, they can easily claim ignorance about the matter. Thus, the problem is too widespread to rely on enforcement. The only way to stop importation of items that may harbor invasive species is through education, assuming people care about the ecological and economic impacts of invasive exotic species. Most Americans have no idea that there is a problem.

Nevertheless, too many importations have been well-intentioned mistakes, such as Dutch elm disease, American chestnut blight, white pine blister rust, and the gypsy moth. In 1906, a nameless person in southern

Florida imported a tree, called melaleuca, from the coast of northern Australia for use as a fast-growing landscape plant. Coincidentally, the nearby Everglades were being drained for agricultural expansion and its wet soils proved the perfect habitat for this prolific and aggressive species. Now, thousands of acres in south Florida are covered with dense stands of melaleuca, seriously threatening the Everglades ecosystem, and its range is expanding at a phenomenal rate of 50 acres per day.

Kudzu—the infamous "plant that ate the South," which seems more real as the plot to a science fiction story than fact—was introduced to the United States by a Japanese delegation to the 1876 Centennial Exposition in Philadelphia. Fragrant purple blooms and a dense, climbing form made it perfect for arbors. Soon after the exposition, U.S. Department of Agriculture scientists explored the forage value of kudzu. Its fast growth and aggressiveness were seen as positive traits. During agricultural land abandonment in the South at the time of the Great Depression, thousands of men planted thousands of acres with kudzu. After that initial planting and for the next twenty years, the Department of Agriculture continued to advocate kudzu as a cover crop, but not before it had established virtually impenetrable mats of vines on more than 7 million acres (fig. 6.1). Forest industry has spent millions to reclaim kudzu lands for pine, often to no avail, and in 1978 it was officially declared a weed.

FIGURE 6.1 Kudzu is an aggressive and pernicious vine that can completely cover a tree in a single season. Photograph by Kerry Britton, USDA-Forest Service 2002. Reproduced by permission of ForestryImages.org.

Other noxious invaders include plants like mile-a-minute, which is believed to have arrived from Asia late in the nineteenth century in ballast water expelled from of a ship harboring in Portland, Oregon. True to its name, it spread quickly in Oregon, mostly along woodland margins. It has since arrived in eastern states—virtually all of which host international ports—probably by similar means, that is in ballast water originating in Asia. Another species, zebra mussel, is believed to have arrived in the Great Lakes from ballast water expelled there in the 1980s. It is a phenomenally prolific freshwater bivalve (a mollusk with a shell that has two halves) that develops into barnacle-like encrustations that plug intake pipes of public water facilities and power plants, costing billions of dollars since it was first discovered in 1988. In less than twenty years, it had spread throughout the Great Lakes and adjacent waters, the largest source of fresh water in the world.

Some invasive species were imported and promoted by the Department of Agriculture. Autumn olive is a woodland shrub that the Department once encouraged eastern forest owners to plant for wildlife until its highly aggressive nature and tendency to interfere with natural regeneration of valuable forest species became apparent. Multiflora rose, Japanese honeysuckle, barberry, lespedeza, and privet are other examples of invasive plants that forest owners and managers were encouraged to plant by state and federal agencies, usually as food sources for wildlife.

Buckthorn, wisteria, chinaberry, tallowtree, and mimosa are species that escaped from landscape plantings. Generally, escaped landscape species are more common in tropical climates where developers use exotic plants to accentuate architecture. Little thought is given to the reproductive habits of species or of the prospects of plants escaping to become a nuisance. Invasive plants tend to grow fast and mature quickly, producing large quantities of easily dispersed seed. Some are also allelopathic, which limits competition from native species. When invasive species with these characteristics become established in forest stands, it is almost impossible to reproduce stands using natural methods without first incurring the expense of eliminating or controlling invasive species.

The list of exotic invasive organisms that are threats to forests is too long to include here. Nevertheless, it is impossible to practice positive impact forestry without understanding the circumstances under which exotic organisms become threats, what to do when a known threat is present, and how to avoid introductions of invasive species. First, contact either the state forester or the cooperative extension specialist (listed by state in appendix C) to obtain current information on invasive organisms that are threatening local forest ecosystems. Use the materials they send to identify signs and symptoms of insects and diseases, and also learn to identify invasive plants. Many of these materials are easily located on the Internet using a keyword search that combines the state's name with the word *invasives*.

The most effect methods of dealing with invasive organisms is early detection and eradication, and individual forest owners are the first line of defense when a new threat arrives. Practices that forest owners can use to prevent or minimize invasive organisms, such as correctly timing of silvicultural treatments, sanitizing equipment, and planting seedlings and cover crops, and what to do if an invasive species is found, are discussed below.

Timing of Treatments

Trees are more susceptible to insect and disease depredations during or immediately following environmental stresses such as excessively dry or wet conditions, or following silvicultural treatments. If risks from invasive insects or diseases are pending, an owner may want to consider postponing treatments. If risks are subsequent to a treatment, keep an eye on those areas where work has already been done.

Schedule disturbances during the dormant season when there are low levels of inoculum from disease-causing organisms. Soil disturbances at this time are also less apt to serve as a seed bed for invasive plants before areas are reseeded with local grasses and forbs. Also, do not use the locally advertised conservation mix seed mixes for stabilizing forest soils, because these mixes usually contain more exotic than local species.

In stands that are infested with invasive plants, delay all silvicultural disturbances until the invasives have been controlled. Since invasive plants usually thrive on disturbed soils, if immediate control is impractical, leave stands alone until a practical control method is discovered. Fire has proven an effective tool in some eastern forests so long as it kills invasives without damaging native species. However, fire *is not a safe tool* in western forests due to fire-exclusion policies of the past century that have led to a build-up of fuels in highly flammable coniferous forests. Formerly minor ground fires now jump quickly into the canopy because of the ever-increasing accumulation of ladder fuels. When fire reaches a coniferous canopy, it is nearly impossible to extinguish without favorable weather.

Equipment Sanitation

Ted Gomes, a friend, forest owner, and manager on the Big Island in Hawaii—a state that has suffered more forest depredations from exotic organisms than any other—recommends pressure cleaning logging equipment en route from one logging job to the next. Although the practice is primarily intended to remove any "hitchhikers," it also cleans surfaces of potentially toxic fluids and lubricants and allows the contractor to spot leaks before they become problems. The same goes for pickup trucks that might harbor noxious seed. Human activity is the most important dispersal mechanism for invasive species.

In forest areas with known problems involving invasive species, forestry professionals and logging contractors should clean and change field clothing, especially cleaning around the cuffs of pants and the mud between lugs on boot soles. Any equipment or clothing that is apt to harbor noxious seed needs to be checked and cleaned.

Planting Seedlings and Cover Crops

Although positive impact forestry practices emphasize methods that can encourage natural regeneration, sometimes planting is necessary. As a general rule, forest owners should plant with species that occur naturally on the site, using seedlings with provenances that are as geographically close to the site as possible. If outplanting is a regular activity, owners may want to plant locally purchased seedlings in a *transplant bed* on the property, allowing them to grow for a season or two before outplanting. If the stock is infected or infested with invasive organisms, it is far easier to control in a transplant bed than in the field. To establish a transplant bed on a nonforest soil, cultivate the area in the same fashion as a garden (using a 6-by-6-inch spacing for seedlings) and apply at least one shovelful of soil from the forest area that is to be outplanted per 100 square feet of bed. The soil inoculates the transplant bed with favorable fungi and bacteria that the seedlings will encounter when outplanted.

Nonnative species should never be introduced to natural forests, and local communities in forest areas and homeowners should be encouraged to plant only native species in landscapes. Educate people who own homes in forest areas about the dangers of planting nonnative species. Most owners have no idea that their landscaping practices can be detrimental to surrounding forest ecosystems, and given such information they will usually comply.

When reseeding skid trails and landings, use only native grasses and forbs, preferably from local sources to reduce the chances of introducing exotics that are mixed in with seed. Mulch seeded areas with mulch hay, preferably from local sources that are known to be free of exotic species. If manure is used as a combination mulch and nutrient source, make sure it comes from clean pastures. Horse manure may have a higher viable seed content than that of cattle, so it is more apt to contain noxious seeds (although horses tend to avoid feeding on noxious plants). Keep this last point in mind if horses are allowed to use trails on the property.

A forest owner who wants to experiment with bioengineered trees should not transplant these organisms into forests unless they are completely incapable of reproducing. Experiments of this nature are best initiated in old pastures and other areas that have not supported forests for many years, and then only when trees are sterile. The risk of incorporating exotic DNA into natural populations is too great.

How to Cope with Invasive Organisms

Any insect or disease damage that is not immediately recognizable should be reported to the state forester's office. Before you call, however, make detailed notes that describe the insect, injuries or symptoms, and the location. With a good description, a specialist can usually diagnose a potentially invasive organism over the phone. If it is an invasive, someone will probably ask to visit as soon as possible. Any samples of diseased tissue, insects, plants, or any other living tissue should be collected using a ziplock plastic bag and stored in a refrigerated location. Never carry lives sample from place to place outside of an airtight plastic bag or container, and never send unsealed samples by common carrier.

Invasive plants favor disturbed soils, such as landings, skid trails, and other areas where mineral soil has been exposed. Learn to identify locally invasive plants in the field. Those gathered for positive identification at home should be put into ziplock plastic bags with carefully noted locations. A handheld global positioning system (GPS) will come in handy if a location is off the trail.

A single specimen of a known invasive plant is eradicated by digging and lifting the entire plant, root and all. Use care because even a small portion of root left behind is enough for many invasive species to propagate asexually. Another way to kill single plants is with a trick Christmas tree growers use: a concentrated application of a nitrogenous fertilizer; urea

(46-0-0) or ammonium nitrate (34-0-0). These are not herbicides, but an application of 1–2 ounces over the top of a noxious weed (preferably when surfaces are wet) will kill most plants. Ammonium nitrate is an oxidant commonly used as an explosive. Despite the fact it is an excellent fertilizer and can kill weeds, purchases are now controlled. In fact, under the USA Patriot Act, if you ask a fertilizer dealer about obtaining ammonium nitrate, don't be surprised to receive a visit from the FBI, which is reason enough to use urea.

Keep in mind as well that where there is one plant, there are probably more, and thus finding even one invasive plant is cause for concern. If any silvicultural treatments are scheduled on the property, consider postponing until after invasives are under control. Remember, soil disturbances favor the spread of most invasive plants.

An infestation of invasive plants is more difficult to deal with. In some circumstances, prescribed fire is a possibility (in the East), and there are effective biological controls for some species. Large woody trees and shrubs may require the use of a brush saw or chainsaw and an aggressive three- to four-year campaign to remove sprouts until all clones are dead. Shrubs are easily lifted from the soil using a tool called a weed wrench that grabs the plant at its base and levers the root system out of the ground. For more information, on the weed wrench see Appendix B.

Composting invasives is out of the question as is disposing of them at a local landfill. The best tactic is to dry plants (but first make sure there is no chance seed will mature and disperse during the process) and then burn them (after obtaining a permit to do so). If burning is infeasible, bury. Also, make accurate notes of the locations where invasives have been lifted (or treated with nitrogen), so the site can be easily visited early in the next growing season. Invasive species are tough and sometimes it takes more than one season to get rid of a single individual.

Generally, woodland owners should avoid herbicide applications in all circumstances because of risks to ecosystems and to human health. The only exception is to control an infestation of invasive woody plants that are a greater overall threat to ecosystem integrity than the potential negative effects of a biodegradable chemical applied directly to cut surfaces. There are systemic herbicides that bind with organic compounds on the forest floor and break down into nontoxic by-products within a few weeks to a few months. Check with your state forester to discover which compounds work best. The Nature Conservancy advocates the use of an easy-to-construct wand with a sponge-tip applicator that allows the user to apply chemical just to a cut surface. The wand applicator design is available on The Nature Conservancy's Web site listed in Appendix B.

Positive impact forestry is predicated on being able to craft disturbances in forests that mimic natural disturbances and provide benefits. When invasive species take advantage of disturbances and compete for resources with native species, effecting successful silvicultural practices is much more difficult, if not impossible. Opportunities for benefits are less when invasives reach infestation levels and forest ecosystems change in unpredictable—but probably far less favorable—ways. For example, invasive exotic organisms are a threat to biodiversity. According to one source, 42 percent of all threatened and endangered species in the United States have experienced declines caused by exotic species. And at least three of twenty-four known extinctions of species listed under the Endangered Species Act resulted from hybridizations of native species with closely related exotics (Schmitz and Simberloff 1997).

"Extinction by habitat destruction is like death in an automobile accident: easy to see and assess," according to E. O. Wilson. "Extinction by the invasion of exotic species is like death by disease: gradual, insidious, requiring scientific methods to diagnose."

CHAPTER 7

The Future of Forests
and Forest Products

When presettlement forests were logged for the first time, capitalism was still experimental and forest industry was an unorganized collection of mostly family-owned, vertically integrated companies that owned the land, the trees, and the means to process them into useable products. Timberlands were obtained through federal and state grants, leased concessions from the railroads (Congress granted enormous tracts of land to railroads, ostensibly for fuel and ties but also as incentives to expand transport routes westward), or by outright purchase. Timber was the only recognized value of forests, to feed mills whose principal products were boards of varying widths and lengths, all 1-inch thick (timber was processed into other dimensions, but boards were the principal product) .

As discussed earlier, cutover lands were a liability, so companies disposed of them as quickly as possible, even before the first property taxes were due. Forests were held only for as long as it took to strip them of timber, and the less-than-reputable methods used to dispose of cutover lands—even as formerly pristine streams and rivers were choking with logging slash and sediment—has left a legacy of inaccurate property boundaries and faulty land titles in the eastern United States.

When forestry came to North America in the waning years of the nineteenth century, timber-using companies had only just arrived in the West, leaving too little time to strip the more inaccessible sites of their timber before President Theodore Roosevelt convinced Congress to impose controls. Many highly inaccessible lands at the time were organized into a federal system of national forests (including cutover forests in the East, mostly in mountainous areas), while more accessible western lands ended up in the hands of timber-using companies. Despite mergers, acquisitions, and transformations, some of these companies survived, evolving into the big-name forest product companies of our time.

A common public perception—one many executives would rather all of us accept as fact—is that forest product companies manage lands from seedling to sawtimber. For most wood-using companies, such is not the case. In fact, some of the largest companies associated with forests—by name and by reputation—now raise more revenue selling office furniture and business supplies than lumber and paper. And for those companies that still raise revenue processing timber, many hold forest lands solely as a source of supply to fill the gap when timber is not readily available from other lands, both public and private. There are plenty of exceptions to this. But, generally, wood-using companies—especially publicly held corporations—prefer to obtain timber supplies from lands other than their own.

Securities statutes require publicly traded corporations to manage resources so as to conserve asset value and maximize profitability. Thus, companies have a fiduciary responsibility to shareholders, and it is this principle—more often than not—that precipitates shortsighted decisions and careless practices, especially when the principal assets are forests. Why? Because the value of woodlands for purposes other than timber production in recent years far exceed the capitalized value of periodic timber crops. For a vertically integrated, publicly held company, valuations of this nature are an invitation for hostile takeover, especially when stock prices are low. The sum of the parts of a marginally profitable wood-using company that owns developable land is far greater than the whole. Companies that are required to protect shareholder assets "divest" their interests in land, a phenomenon that has plagued forests of the northeastern United States since the 1980s, signaling a trend that is apt to continue throughout North America.

Marginal returns on timber investments are due, in part, to the fact that forest assets are an aggressive investor's nightmare: relatively high front-end costs (site preparation, access, planting costs, etc.), excessively expensive carrying charges on the facility (mostly in the form of property taxes), the very real and highly probable threat of regulation (discussed below in the "Forest Regulation" section) that will further increase production costs, risks of loss during a rotation, and long investment periods (remember the power of compounding, discussed in chapter 3). It is no wonder that wood-using companies are disposing of their forests. But divestitures bring large blocks of forest land onto the market, attracting speculators with cash. Tract sizes and market value of lands often exceed the capacity of land trusts. And large, contiguous blocks of forest (usually cutover lands) are sold to the highest bidder, causing parcelization of forests and fragmentation of purpose.

It is easy to blame forest industry for these trends. But the forces that control decision making in a fair market economy are the proximate cause of divestiture, not necessarily the behavior of companies that must play by the rules. Adam Smith's "invisible hand" guiding allocation of resources to build capital, coupled with the long-standing principle of laissez-faire, tends to ignore nonmarket elements of forests. Nevertheless, based on what we have learned about forest ecosystems since the time of Adam Smith, there is good reason to rethink the accepted tenets of free markets as they apply to forests. A positive impact approach places value on whole ecosystems and not necessarily on any one benefit, despite the difficulty of assessing ecosystem values in terms of dollars.

A healthy forest products industry is essential to maintaining a forest landscape. But when wood-using companies go out of business, the primary purpose of land shifts from forests to residential housing or some other use that has nothing to do with healthy forest ecosystems. It is ironic that people who want to protect forests in the name of environmentalism usually excoriate the companies that make forests a viable alternative. Even so, forest industry is consolidating in the United States. Where there were three hundred mills ten years ago, there are two hundred today, and there may be only a handful within the next twenty years. Consolidation in some areas is contributing to an excess capacity in the logging sector. Fewer mills mean less demand for logs and too many loggers chasing an inadequate supply of profitable timber. Many local primary wood processors are small, private, mostly family-owned operations. They are not publicly traded companies and so do not have to answer to shareholders. But they do need to be profitable, at least sufficiently enough to compel them to stay in business.

Since logging is not an especially profitable business to begin with, stumpage buyers usually want to harvest the most valuable trees despite the fact that under positive impact guidelines the most valuable trees are the ones growing in value at an increasing rate. The very trees loggers need to harvest to stay in business are the ones forest owners should keep, allowing them to continue growing in value for another generation or two, especially on good soils. But expensive logging equipment and high labor costs—including payroll and worker's compensation insurance that every logger should carry—coupled with cutthroat competition for a limited supply of good timber, makes it more difficult—if not impossible—for people to stay in business.

Unfortunately, loggers who were seduced into buying new equipment with loans carrying finance charges that exceed all other costs combined now find themselves making decisions solely on the basis of money. Every month they are confronted with bills that completely obviate good practices, making it impossible for them to advocate positive impact forestry *and* stay in business. The result: loggers are enslaved by their equipment, forced to do whatever is necessary to make payments. Often, it is the financial pressure of staying in business that spawns poor practices, not a lack of knowledge or skills.

Perhaps one day a forward-thinking administration will take office and realize that forest lands are abused because it is economically expedient to do so, and a forestry-equivalent of the federal dairy buyout program might relieve some of the pressure. In other words, public revenue will buy out a contractor, completely relieving a logger of debt and the means of production. Participants would receive education, training, and employment counseling—and possibly a year or two of internship-oriented employment—introducing them to a realm of services they can offer to forest owners that are not dependent on stumpage sales. In exchange, loggers agree to stop buying stumpage (and local mills agree to not accept logs from participants) for at least ten years.

For those owners who are willing to accept the conditions of local statutes that allow lands to be taxed at current-use values as opposed to fair market value for more developed uses, forests are a reasonable investment—but only for patient people. Witness the surge of woodland investments on the part of insurance companies, like Prudential, John Hancock, and others who are more concerned with conservation of equity over the long haul than short-term gain. Aggressive investors looking for quick profits are often disappointed with timber investments, or when they succeed, the impacts on ecosystems are devastating. Not surprisingly, interest in woodland investments is inversely proportional to economic growth. When the economy is growing, investors put money in the stock market. When the economy slows—or when it feels like it is about to slow—investors look for ways to conserve capital and woodlands fit the bill.

Economic conditions have an effect on stumpage prices, but it is almost never acute nor very drastic. This "stumpage cushion" is due to the fact that timber is one of the most highly brokered commodities in North America, changing hands many times between stump and store, and there are also many stages of production. Good timber is especially scarce, so much so that the effect of an economic downturn is greater on the profit margin of the final product than it is on stumpage. In other words, sawmills, shops, wholesalers, and retailers face the brunt of a poor economy while timber owners are relatively unaffected. This is not to say a slow economy does not influence stumpage prices. Rather, the effects are much less than expected. Another factor in favor of private forest owners is this: timber scarcity is exacerbated by current and projected decreases in timber supplies from public lands. Public timber sources have for years competed with privately held timber, and the overall effect has been artificially low stumpage prices. With less and less timber coming from public lands, stumpage buyers will bid up the price of private timber due to supply limitations. Sawtimber will finally appreciate at rates that exceed inflation with the greatest rates of appreciation in large sawtimber and veneer-quality trees of now commercially desirable species.

Forest Regulation

One certainty in the future for forests is more regulation. Since most of the forces that drive decision making are based on maximizing economic values, and it is largely these forces that have been the proximate cause of poor practices, the only way to protect nonmarket values of forest ecosystems is to place controls on when and how people use them. This despite the fact that control is antithetical to what most owners assume are the rights associated with private property. Those rights—guaranteed in the Constitution—allow owners to enjoy full control over property so long as it does not impinge on the rights of others.

The premise of regulating forests is complicated and by no means widely accepted, especially among those who own forests and those who depend on income from services and products. It is based on a theory that has always been an inherent aspect of real property but has only recently become more widely known and accepted: the notion that society shares an interest in forest ecosystems with those who own the land. Within the context of this theory, society has rights and obligations to exercise control over practices that may impinge on ecosystem functions, for example, practices that result in significant wildlife habitat alterations, or construction and maintenance of access routes that can potentially cause soil erosion and sedimentation in public waters. The public has a vested interest in any practices that might have long-term effects over areas wider than the property on which the practices are installed.

Families that have owned forests for many years tend to interpret society's interests more narrowly, and rightly so. The expense of owning forests on most sites far exceed a sustainable rate of return, and until society is willing to acknowledge and compensate owners for the positive externalities of forests—clean air, carbon sequestration, wildlife habitat, watersheds, pleasing vistas, recreational opportunities, and all the intrinsic values of healthy, sustainable ecosystems—owners will have little incentive to practice positive impact forestry. Without market-based incentives to manage forests sustainably, there are few alternatives but more regulation.

Although forest owners might disagree on the extent of society's interests in their forests, virtually all say that ad valorem property taxes on forest lands are too high. Forest lands should be taxed only on the net financial benefits that accrue to the owner, not on fair market values of land converted to other uses. When lands are taxed based on the economic value of conversion, it becomes a self-fulfilling prophecy.

Regulation of activities on privately owned forests are difficult to carry out. Generally, regulations are promulgated at state and local levels, often in the cause of protecting water quality. The Clean Water Act empowered the Environmental Protection Agency to make states accountable for water quality. Most states have exempted silvicultural activities from permitting requirements provided owners use best management practices (see discussion in chapter 5). Most states have avoided enacting statutes that directly control practices owners can use, or they have disguised controls in the form of statutes that require "notification of intent." A notification of intent law requires owners to file activity plans with a proper authority if activities are expected to exceed an established threshold. The thresholds are commonly tied to the extent of a treatment (e.g., how many acres are to be affected?), or to the degree of disturbance (e.g., what is the extent of canopy removal?). Generally, notification of intent statutes appear more onerous than is the case, and they are the least invasive form of regulation. If a practice is clearly silvicultural in nature (as opposed to creating landscapes for housing), and the owner agrees to use accepted silvicultural techniques, it is doubtful a permit will be declined. It is often the process that causes owners and managers to bristle, not the outcome if the intent is to practice silviculture.

Despite the fact that many owners and forestry professionals would argue that regulation of forestry practices is already excessive and generally bad, we should all expect more regulation in the future, not less. Here is a sampling of what to expect:

- Harvesting will be disallowed at times of the year when forest ecosystems are most vulnerable. For example, the spring "mud season," when frost leaves the ground in northern states, soils are saturated, and heavy equipment can compact soils and injure roots; when migrant birds are breeding in certain forest types; following widespread defoliations or other stressful events such as drought; or at times when transportation of timber may cause the spread of disease.
- Stronger "notification of intent" statutes will be enacted that effectively prevent speculators from disguising development intentions with silviculture by requiring an owner to "maintain" a practice for an extended period.
- States will require licensing and bonding of logging contractors, forestry consultants, and others that provide services to forest owners, requiring education programs even more rigorous than those described in chapter 4.
- States may require that forest owners have credentials before allowing them to harvest timber from their lands. Even owners that work with forestry professionals must demonstrate they have a basic understanding of forest ecosystems and that they are fully aware of the impacts of their activities on long-term health and integrity of forests.

A governing authority's rights to enact statutes is the equivalent of enacting the will of a collective public conscience. When it is unreasonable to assume forest owners and forestry professionals will always use practices that protect nonmarket ecosystem values, lacking incentives or disincentives to do so, there is no other alternative but to control behaviors through legislation. Antiquated taxation policies, coupled with a long-standing view of forests as nothing more than assets—for timber or for development—sets the stage for more regulation of forestry practice, not less.

Climate-Induced Changes in Forests

The Intergovernmental Panel on Climate Change, established by the United Nations in 1988 and charged with preparing periodic assessments of world climate, has arrived at an irrefutable conclusion that the earth's atmosphere is warming. Even since its first report in 1991 there have been measurable temperature increases in both the atmosphere and the ocean. But what is really startling is that warming has now been directly linked to human activities. As little as ten years ago, one could attempt to refute human connections to climate change, but now the evidence is too overwhelming (McCarthy et al. 2001). The developed world's thirst for carbon-based fuels is catching up, and it is now painfully clear that the cause of most global warming is anthropogenic.

Why carbon? There is a direct relationship between the amount of atmospheric carbon dioxide (CO_2) and temperature. Although scientists are not sure which is the driving factor—CO_2 concentrations or atmospheric temperatures—the long-term trends move in the same direction. Ice cores extracted from polar glaciers provide evidence that the two factors have moved in tandem for hundreds of thousands of years: high levels of atmospheric CO_2 coincide with warming, and low levels of atmospheric CO_2 coincide with cooling. During times when glaciers advanced, CO_2 was mostly dissolved in oceans and in ice. But when oceans warm, CO_2 goes out of solution and into the atmosphere causing more warming. The difference in atmospheric temperature between an "ice age" and an interglacial period, such as we are in the midst of today, is about an 11 degrees Fahrenheit.

Before the twentieth century, the interglacial trend was a gradual cooling, until about fifty years ago. Just after the end of World War II the trend reversed, beginning a dramatic warming at a rate much faster than at any other time during the past ten thousand years. Scientists have been attempting to demonstrate this abrupt warming trend was coincidental to an explosion in the use of fossil fuels, and now the jury is in.

Carbon dioxide is a greenhouse gas, which means that, although it is colorless and odorless, it tends to blanket the earth, trapping atmospheric heat by reflecting infrared radiation back to earth. CO_2 concentrations and atmospheric temperature trends are self-perpetuating: a warmer atmosphere means a warmer ocean forcing more CO_2 into the atmosphere, causing more warming.

When carbon is not in the atmosphere, it is "sequestered" in plants and animals, in fossil fuels (formerly living plants and animals in the form of coal and oil), and in water and ice. Ever since the earth developed a climate, there has been a natural flux in carbon—atmospheric levels are high during interglacial periods, and low during glacial periods. In 1900, data from ice cores indicated that atmospheric concentrations of CO_2 were about 290 parts per million (ppm). Direct measurements today indicate that atmospheric CO_2 is about 370 ppm and climbing, far beyond the range of natural variability at other times in the past. Scientists estimate earth's climate will continue to warm until 2100, even if we were to use far less carbon. The most conservative projection is an atmospheric increase of 2.5 degrees Fahrenheit. The most dire prediction—which assumes no major changes in the way we use fossil fuels (also considering that there is no more than a fifty-year supply of oil and natural gas left in the earth after which we are back to using coal)—is 10.5 degrees Fahrenheit.

A warmer earth means a warmer ocean, which takes up more volume. Most people conjure images of the movie *Waterworld* due to melting of the polar ice caps. But the facts are there is not nearly enough water to inundate continents, and most of the rise in sea level will result from temperature-induced expansion of water, not melting ice caps. Under the direst predictions, 10–20 percent of the earth's land area will inundate over the next one hundred years due to global warming.

During the twentieth century, warming caused sea level to rise by 4–8 inches. Scientists predict it will rise an additional 4–36 inches by the end of the twenty-first century. Barrier islands that have been popular for vacation and retirement homes will cease to exist and the ski industry, already suffering from changing demographics (snowboarder populations are growing at a phenomenal rate, but boarders are perfectly willing to hike back to the top of a "half-pipe," obviating the cost of a lift ticket, and generally seem unwilling to purchase expensive slopeside condos, the real source of revenue in the ski industry) is now faced with erratic winter weather and environmentally driven controls on snowmaking. Snowpacks are expected to become so inconsistent that the industry as we know it will most likely disappear by 2100.

Although global warming is expected to decimate coral reefs by 2050, the impacts on agriculture and forestry (in the northern hemisphere, anyway) are likely to be positive. A warmer climate means longer growing seasons in the subpolar regions and this may translate into higher levels of production. There is also a chance that green plants and trees will benefit from increased levels of atmospheric CO_2, an essential raw material of photosynthesis. Although it is not clear if this effect will really pan out, greenhouse studies of "CO_2 fertilization" have shown impressive growth responses of 20–35 percent in cotton plants. The ability of trees to take advantage of higher atmospheric CO_2 levels is debated among scientists, mostly on the grounds that trees will not have had time to adapt to higher concentrations. But some reputable sources suggest that net primary production in forests may increase by as much as 14–20 percent. These highly optimistic estimates are based on the combined effects of longer growing seasons, CO_2 fertilization, and the increased deposition of nitrogen (in the form of nitric oxides, one of the culprits of acid deposition in the Northeast)—one of the only mineral nutrients to which trees consistently respond. Nevertheless, increasing acidity may reverse some of these positive trends and may even prove devastating to beneficial soil organisms.

Over the next one hundred years, forest types will begin poleward migrations, even though it will most likely take hundreds of years for migrations to become obvious after the earth's temperature reaches equilibrium, sometime after 2100. We may begin to see positive impacts of global warming on forest growth within the next century, but it is doubtful that the natural ranges of species as we know them today will have changed much by 2100. Eventually, tree populations will shift to the north (it is their DNA that is migrating, not the trees themselves), but it will take a long time for this to happen. Species with wide environmental tolerances, like northern red oak in the East, or Douglas-fir in the West, will most likely not disappear with even drastic global warming. But species that are now distinctly boreal will head north from their current native ranges, even at high elevations.

The one unknown about global warming is its effects on rainfall patterns. During the warming phase, we can expect to see more turbulence in the atmosphere, and more turbulence means more storms. Warmer temperatures will also increase evaporation rates and transpiration from plants. More water in the form of vapor means more clouds. Increased cloud cover may actually promote atmospheric cooling, but it will also cause more rainfall. The question is, where will rain fall and are future patterns apt to be substantially different from patterns we see today? Predicting rainfall is especially difficult, but the climate models suggest that most of the northern hemisphere will be in good shape. Tropical regions may experience drastically different rainfall patterns, so much so that many third-world populations will suffer from pending climate changes. One of the cruel ironies of the calculus of climate change is that the principal beneficiaries of earth warming are the developed nations in the northern hemisphere that have largely caused the problem. Poor countries have contributed little to the problem but are apt to suffer the most.

There are no forest management guidelines that factor in the potential effects of climate change, probably because most observers expect the effects to be insidious. There are, however, a few things to keep in mind. In northern regions, warmer winters will most likely cause trees to break dormancy more than once. This can prove stressful, and the effects of stress—discussed earlier—must be factored in to management decisions.

Another thing to watch for in northern regions is an increased incidence of ice accumulations in tree crowns. Winters of the future will likely consist of dramatic swings in temperature, and precipitation that used to fall as snow may end up as rain or freezing rain. Where this is apt to happen, managers may want to maintain higher stocking, thinning stands less frequently and favoring trees with balanced crowns (so weight accumulations are evenly distributed around the central stem).

Finally, changing conditions are often favorable to the establishment of exotic species many of which tend to be opportunistic, as discussed in chapter 6. Climatic changes may favor already highly aggressive exotic plants, and managers may want to contemplate control measures before bad situations get worse.

Green Certification of Forest Practices and Products

Every time a consumer buys a product it is the equivalent of casting a vote. The purchase is a proxy in the marketplace that tells the producer to increase or decrease production, or to raise or lower price. Translation of consumer trends at the production level is an exacting science: producing too much will force lower prices; produce too little and demand outstrips supply at any price.

So what does this have to do with forests and green certification? Recent consumer trends suggest that people may demand and pay more for earth friendly products. An earth friendly product is one that has been manufactured without exploiting people or the earth. In other words, there is evidence to suggest consumers are sending a message to corporate America: value is important, but not if it means destruction of the planet or exploitation of people in third-world countries. Witness all the products that tout "made from recycled materials." Recycling, rare not that long ago, is so common now that people risk shunning from neighbors if they do not put a recycling bin out with the trash. It is a very green thing to do, and for most it has also become routine.

The green certification movement emerged in the late 1980s in response to excessive and careless logging in tropical forests, particularly by large companies felling extensive swaths of rainforest for wood production and land clearing. Unfortunately, even recently enacted laws have not successfully prevented such practices in some third-world countries. The developed world's taste for exotic woods still feeds markets for tropical hardwoods despite the fact that most American and European consumers have no idea that picture frames, moldings, fine furniture, and other such products they buy are supporting devastating practices far from home. For example, felling and extracting a single tree in rainforests—possibly the only representative of its species in an area of 20 acres or more—can take a small crew a week to accomplish. In rainforests, many plant and animal species live in the canopy, 100 or more feet above the forest floor. A single tree can host dozens of species of fauna and flora, including vines that take down anything in their path as the crop tree falls. Harvesting such trees—even illegally—promises monetary rewards that far outweigh risks.

When conservation groups began to protest these destructive practices, market inertia was already so great, it seemed that the cutting would stop only after all valuable trees had been harvested. Change was slow—too slow—for those who witnessed the effects of crude and careless extraction practices, not to mention the devastating effects on already threatened habitats. Governments of third-world countries were fairly quick to react but were powerless to control the steady stream of now-illegal exports. It is impossible to stem the flow of wood without stanching demand, and this is where the concept of product certification was born: Educate consumers about the perils of buying tropical woods, they stop buying them, and eventually demand subsides.

Further down the supply chain, incentive to deliver tropical hardwoods at all costs was eventually lost, and manufacturers began to demand wood certified as having been harvested in a sustainable fashion. The best thing about green certification is that it is driven by consumer choices—capitalism at its best. When word of rainforest deforestation got out, it was easy to convince people to avoid tropical hardwoods or to look for woods that had been harvested in an acceptable way. Green certification was borne of a need to assure consumers that in purchasing a product they are not contributing to destructive practices in other parts of the world.

The principles of green certification arrived in the United States in the early 1990s. Although the United States does not have the same forest utilization problems as in tropical regions, there is still much room for improvement. The problems are different but the principles behind good practices that define sustainable forests are exactly the same: use the best methods to harvest and extract timber while protecting forest soils and habitats. A certified forest is one that above all else maintains the integrity of forest ecosystems; human use is secondary, which is exactly in line with positive impact forestry.

There is only one worldwide forest and forest product certification organization, the Forest Stewardship Council (FSC). Based in Bonn, Germany, but with offices around the world, FSC has ten principles to which a woodland owner or manufacturer must adhere to receive and maintain certification. The principles require an ecosystem approach to management and a commitment to sustainable practices that protect plant and animal diversity, wildlife habitats, forest streams, and scenic landscapes.

FSC contracts with third-party "auditors," usually foresters but also wildlife biologists, economists, and others. Their job is to visit candidate woodlands and wood-products businesses to determine if its practices meet FSC standards. Producers that meet and adhere to FSC principles can market wood with the FSC logo. Retailers can advertise the earth-friendliness of products, helping consumers make informed decisions. The idea is similar to a grade stamp on lumber except that it has nothing to do with wood quality or value but rather with how it was produced. Since certified wood is in short supply, buyers will (theoretically) offer a premium for wood that can be sold to consumers as "green-certified."

Since its establishment, the Forest Stewardship Council has certified more than twenty million acres in the United States and nearly five times this amount worldwide. The key to FSC's program is its system of third-party certification. It ensures, through independent audit, that harvesting and utilization practices follow FSC guidelines and that the entire supply chain—from forest to finished product—is certified to deliver products that meet or exceed FSC standards.

When many mainstream U.S. forest product companies first heard about FSC, they assumed it would fail, if not worldwide, then at least domestically. After all, how could practices that amount to regulation, conceived and promulgated by environmentalists, replace traditional silvicultural methods that forest product companies had been selling hard to American woodland owners and consumers? The American Forest and Paper Association (AF&PA), representative of wood-using industries and sponsor of the popular Tree Farm program (through its American Forest Foundation), decided to ignore FSC until it became apparent that retailers were ready to put green-certified products on their shelves and that U.S. consumers were "voting with their wallets." Less than two years after FSC announced its worldwide forest certification program, AF&PA came up with its own version called the Sustainable Forestry Initiative (SFI, which is a registered trademark of the American Forest and Paper Association).

Although most observers assumed that SFI was more marketing campaign than innovation—some even accused it of attempting to nip the concept of third-party certification in the bud—it was an honest attempt by forest industry to effect change from the top down. By requiring its members to accept and adhere to a broad set of principles, AF&PA allows companies to retain membership status and to use the SFI logo for its products and programs. In execution, SFI was looking a lot like FSC's program but with two major differences: (1) The SFI program utilizes an AF&PA internal auditing procedure to monitor its members that resembles a third-party audit but is not—companies that adhere to SFI practices can maintain their membership while those that do not are expelled; and (2) SFI extends only to AF&PA's sphere of influence, mostly in the United States and to a lesser extent in Canada. With the onset of globalization, this weakness may prove far more significant than self-controlled audits.

To its credit, however, AF&PA through the Sustainable Forestry Initiative has changed the way mainstream forest industry does business in the United States, especially concerning its timber extraction practices. For example, International Paper Company—a member of AF&PA and a significant primary wood user in the United States—on its own initiative instituted a policy of not accepting logs at its mills during the height of spring mud season. It is a disincentive to keep loggers out of forests when soils and tree roots are highly susceptible to damage, and it is a policy the company has stuck with during good times and bad.

One of SFI's most notable requirements of companies is that they purchase logs only from contractors that can prove their crews have completed a logger education curriculum, such as Logger Education to Advance Professionalism (LEAP) described in chapter 4. Log suppliers are also required to maintain their credentials. This one far-reaching requirement may prove to have a greater long-term positive impact on forests than anything else. It also distinguishes the Sustainable Forestry Initiative from the Forest Stewardship Council, which does not require loggers to hold credentials.

Responsibility and accountability are often intended benefits of logger education programs, and many newly established programs remind participants that with education comes responsibility. "I didn't know," is no longer an adequate excuse for poor logging practices from those contractors who now hold credentials.

A third forest certification alternative has emerged as a middle-ground between FSC and SFI. Known as 'Green Tag Forestry,' it is touted by its sponsors—the National Woodland Owner's Association and the National Forestry Association—as a moderate-cost alternative to owners of smaller woodlands who are seeking third-party certification. The program is available in all 50 states and parts of Canada, and certified tracts display the 'Green Tag Forest' sign. For more information see: www.greentag.org.

Forest industry in the United States has a love-hate relationship with product certification, and there is no middle ground or fence-sitting. Those who embrace it see new marketing opportunities and an emerging consumer that wants more from products than just service. Those who hate it decry another layer of bureaucracy that spreads profits thinner and unnecessarily increases production costs. But, as with most things, the truth lies somewhere between the extremes: Yes, it costs more to produce a certified product, but manufactures who produce green products believe that consumers will increasingly demand them and profitability will follow.

Is forest product certification here to stay? Or is it a fad that will disappear with rising housing costs or recession? It is looking more and more as though it is not a fad. According to some experts, there is plenty of unmet demand for certified wood; the problem is matching supply with demand. Product certification has already survived one violent swing in the business cycle, from the boom of the late 1990s to the bust that arrived with the millennium.

Retailers like Home Depot and Lowes are attempting to expand their green-certified offerings, probably for public relations more than to steer consumers toward green products. It is still unknown if consumers will create enough demand to make a major market shift worthwhile. Keeping green-certified products separate from other inventory is costly for retailers. In theory, the eventual groundswell of demand for certified wood will mostly displace demand for uncertified wood, and everybody wins. So far, this has not proven to be the case, but changing consumer habits takes time and there is a lot of forest industry money betting that green products will catch hold in a big way.

Given the successful establishment of green certification in the United States, how should private woodland owners position themselves to take best advantage of this new market? First, the positive impact forestry practices outlined in this book far exceed the certification requirements of FSC or SFI, so owners who embrace these concepts are capable of supplying certifiable products. Second, it is essential to understand the importance of credibility among consumers who must perceive that extra costs for building materials or other wood products are supporting sustainable practices that protect forest ecosystems. A true third-party auditing procedure, carried out by qualified professionals who have no stake in the outcome, is the only way to achieve credibility among consumers. Until AF&PA proposes an alternative to its current procedures under SFI, it is doubtful that consumers will pay more for its products. Unfortunately, this one failing alone may thwart the entire cause of product certification, because a confused consumer will always choose the cheaper of two products. Nevertheless, those forest owners who want to supply green-certified forest products from their lands have no choice but to seek certification under FSC guidelines. Posting an AF&PA "Tree Farm" sign is not the equivalent of third-party certification unless state-hosted Tree Farm committees, which are managed by volunteers, take drastic and expensive measures to change their certification procedures.

Even those who employ positive impact forestry methods must pay the cost of an FSC third-party audit to qualify as a source of green-certified timber. But audits are expensive—at least three to five times the cost of a forest management plan. As the program matures, audit costs will come down, so it may pay to wait. Consider, too, the possibility of having a prospective timber buyer pay FSC audit costs. Recognizing that high audit costs were dissuading many qualified forest owners from seeking certification, FSC has instituted a program to certify consulting foresters and, by association, the lands of their clients. For this reason, locating an FSC-certified manager may be the most cost-effective strategy.

So far, there is little evidence in U.S. markets to suggest that green certification of woodlands is immediately profitable. If consumer trends continue, however, the future value of timber from certified lands will far exceed certification costs over the next ten years. Even so, woodland owners may want to hold out until audit costs come down.

To find out more about the Forest Stewardship Council and its certification program in the United States, visit: http://www.fscus.org.

Forest Prologue

Since the end of World War II, almost every attempt to predict the future of forests has been unsuccessful. For example, economists have been predicting shortfalls of timber since the late 1950s, but they never materialized. Another example: companies that moved from the West Coast to the southeastern United States based on growth projections for genetically improved southern pine forests discovered that projections overestimated actual yields. In other words, trees are not growing as fast as predicted, causing excess capacity for some mills and forcing others to contemplate moving elsewhere, this time, experts say, to the hardwood forests of the Northeast. And who could have predicted the meteoric rise of environmentalism that has so effectively questioned the motivations of traditional forestry?

So much has happened in less time than it takes a forest to grow from seedling to sawtimber that the only constant anymore is change. What used to be a staid, comfortably predictable but sometimes boring field is now at the center of many debates, and no one has a crystal ball, or at least no one is willing to say where they think forestry is headed.

The future evolves as a single path from a virtually infinite array of opportunities. But divining that path is anybody's guess. Sure, "past is prologue," and circumstances of the present affect the chances of any given future. But the connection between the here-and-now and next year, or two hundred years from now, ends there. In a sense, the future only exists as we know it in the present, and this is why few of us are ever prepared for what's next. But there are some indicators worth thinking about to help divine alternative futures for forests in the United States.

The mantra of the next economic expansion in the United States is globalism. Whether we had intended it or not, our fate is now tied to the rest of world, and we are fast approaching a single, worldwide economy that floats (or sinks) all ships. The United States is poised to lead this expansion, but doing business in this "brave new world" will be far different than in the past. We will likely gain in areas of high technology and investment, but at the expense of labor. There are just too many emerging economies, such as China, which recently joined the World Trade Organization, and India, that have unbelievably cheap labor. For many third-world countries, exploitation of low-cost labor is the only way to grow their economies, and the United States—and other wealthy nations around the world—must be willing to help. This is not good news for a labor-intensive industry like forest products, but it may be good news for forest ecosystems.

Soon, timber owners in the United States will be able to communicate with a manufacturing facility in China, through a simultaneous translation function over the World Wide Web (in other words, language barriers are no longer a problem), effecting a transaction almost as easily as selling logs to a mill in a neighboring state. It will be cheaper to export timber for processing in China and import the finished product than to manufacture it at home. The American economy is no longer insulated, and it will become less so in the future. Our economic well-being will increasingly depend on the successes and failures of our trading partners. This, too, is not good news for forest products industries unless they position themselves to take advantage of changes.

As discussed earlier, forest ownership is changing. The generation that lived through "multiple-use," "green gold," "wood is renewable," and other clichés is passing its woodlands on to its heirs or to younger buyers. These new owners are even more distant from the land than their predecessors and so are less likely to manage lands for traditional forest values. Among new owners who recently acquired land, the most commonly stated reason as to why they obtained forest is: "it came with the house or home site." Of course there is a chance that these new owners will take over the management efforts of those who came before them, provided there are no regulations that prevent them from doing so. But state and local regulation of harvesting practices, and of forest use, will increase in the future, making harvest and extraction of timber a much more involved process than it is today. For many of these new owners, the hassle—not to mention what many of them have been led to believe is environmental degradation—of harvesting will not be worth the income, unless stumpage is a lot more valuable than it is today, which is a distinct possibility.

An increase in demand for nontimber values from public forests will likely compel Congress to change the U.S. Forest Service charter to substantially alter or remove the "timber production" element from its mission. When this happens, Forest Service lands will no longer serve as local timbersheds, and many unprepared, timber-dependent communities will suffer. The argument raised by those who champion a hands-off policy is this: public lands are too important for watershed protection, critical habitats for threatened species, wilderness (a designation only Congress has the right to grant), recreation, and to demonstrate ecosystem approaches to managing private lands. But different sentiments are held by an increasing majority of Americans: leave our public lands alone, especially if private forests are capable of meeting demand. The future of public lands—federal and state—will most likely be that of ecological reserves, and extractive uses of these lands will be the exception rather than the rule. But the good news is, less wood supply from public lands means more demand from private forests and higher stumpage prices.

At some point in the future, trees—or at least trees growing in forest ecosystems—could be replaced as a principal source of fiber. Is it quite likely that in the not-too-distant future we will discover a bioengineered process to grow wood fibers without forest-grown trees. As farfetched and fanciful as this may seem, such a process would completely displace the need to harvest trees for paper and lumber if it proved to be cheaper than growing fiber in forests and the products were just as serviceable as wood from trees. An extruded two-by-six from these bioengineered fibers would, in time, completely replace the same product sawn from trees if the specifications were similar and the extruded product substantially cheaper. Although some characteristics of wood are impossible to duplicate, cost is always a primary factor.

Heavy-handed regulation, the Internet, globalism, and wood growing in vats—perhaps all of this is nothing more than science fiction applied to forests and none of it will come to pass. But who would have predicted one hundred years ago—less than a single rotation for many timber species—humans traveling in airplanes, or interplanetary exploration? In the 1970s, the idea of a computer on every desk was ridiculed by those who designed room-sized, mainframe computer systems. In the 1980s, a facsimile machine seemed nothing less than magical, but now they are in every office and in most homes. Video cassette recorders, and now DVDs, have brought big-screen entertainment to television. In the early 1990s, no one had heard of the World Wide Web. Yet its astronomical growth fueled a business cycle the likes of which this country has never seen. Technological developments and economic change have bred resiliency into the U.S. economy, and there is very high probability technology will one day change the way we use forests.

Regardless of what the future holds for alternative methods of growing wood fiber, there will always be a demand for natural wood with a beauty and texture that will prove impossible to duplicate. Within a time less than the equivalent of two hardwood rotations (three hundred to four hundred years under positive impact forestry guidelines), wood may have become so valuable that relatively small pieces of lumber will be used for decorative purposes. Imagine people hanging veneer wood panels on walls for aesthetic purposes in the same way we enjoy fine paintings, photography, and other artistic objects. Yes, these are fanciful—but not unreasonable—predictions given technological innovations in other areas such as aviation, electronics, and information. Any serious contemplation of future forest policy must consider the impacts of emerging technologies that can drastically change the way we use forest ecosystems. Even remote possibility of a future such as described above is reason enough to embrace the concepts of positive impact forestry.

Parcelization of Forests and Fragmentation of Purpose

One of most insidious problems facing forest areas is parcelization of land: the division of larger tracts into smaller ones (Harris 1984). According to one source, about three million acres are converted every couple of years into parcels that are less than 100 acres in size, and during the same time frame about 2.5 million acres of forests are "developed" into other uses (DeCoster 2000). Forest-land conversion and diseconomies created by parcelization cause erosion of the forest land base; and less woodland means less timber and higher stumpage prices. So serious is forest parcelization that it makes the sum of every other economic threat to forest utilization pale in comparison (with the possible exception of economic impacts from pernicious invasive species, discussed in chapter 6). Moreover, it is impossible to lay blame for the effects of parcelization; there are no environmental groups to excoriate, no federal programs to criticize, no laws to condemn. Forest owners, or prospective forest owners, are the cause of parcelization and there is almost nothing short of major policy changes that will turn things around.

But how did it get to this? Why has parcelization been allowed to proceed unabated with no regard for the future of forests or agriculture? It is a long story, but one worth telling.

Private property law in the United States is mostly based on English common law, the first codification of which was known as *feudal law*. Under feudal law the king owned everything, but his lands were managed by lords who were responsible for keeping the peace among vassals and for collecting taxes. A lord could pass within his family the privilege of managing the king's lands, but to only one heir: usually his firstborn son.

Eventually the king realized that, with a system of taxation, he did not need to own land to extract its wealth. Thus, feudal law evolved into the allodial system, which is the precursor of common law in most of North America. A lord owned land in the allodial system (provided he paid his taxes), but his ability to divide the estate was limited. Upon his demise, the lord's entire estate passed to only one heir: his first-born son, or to the closest consanguine male (father, brother, uncle, cousin, and so on). Known as *primogeniture*, it was not uncommon for an eldest daughter to see her father's lands inherited by a late-born, five-year-old brother, or—if her father never sired any sons—the land might go to her uncle. If the uncle predeceased her father, the estate might end up in the hands of a male cousin. It is primarily for this reason that kings and other nobility were so hung up about fathering sons. Since determination of a child's sex resides with the male's chromosomes—a fact that was not known to science until much later—it is ironic that the wife was blamed for being barren of sons, when in fact it was her husband who was responsible. It is quite likely that primogeniture would have never developed if nobility had been aware of this, and women would have enjoyed a higher social status much earlier in the human experience than proved to be the case.

Primogeniture evolved in feudal times as a way for the king's lands to pass within families of nobility, but since the king was under no obligation to share his interests, the lords had no rights to divide the estates entrusted to them. Primogeniture survived evolution to the allodial system because it prevented fragmentation of productive lands and also maintained a relatively easy method of gathering taxes.

With a growing population of noble-born second sons, the king was faced with the question of what to do with these disinherited whose choices were few. Colonialism was a result of primogeniture and the Americas were settled mostly by sons who were expatriated to the colonies. For this reason, primogeniture was one of the first concepts abandoned by the separatists and in doing so, the Continental Congress added rights to the bundle of private property rights: the right to divide and the right to bequeath. Little did they know it would lead to a quiet crisis of epic proportions in less than three hundred years. One can only wonder what the founding fathers would think of the situation today. Although it is doubtful they would have embraced primogeniture as a way of keeping lands intact, conversion of productive lands to idle or unproductive uses would have been unacceptable. "Highest and best use" in an economic sense was for agricultural purposes when the Constitution was drafted, not residential housing or retail space as is the case today. Who could have foretold that productive land would be worth more for housing than for timber and crops? Anyone suggesting a future such as this in the late eighteenth century would have been branded a heretic and a fool.

Under our current system, land is a capital asset that has the same status as any other form of capital except that it cannot be moved from place to place. Land ownership is defined by rights in exactly the same context as originally claimed by the king. One can easily argue that the state has taken the king's place under our current interpretation of real property rights. The state reserves the same rights as those reserved by the king: the right to tax, the right to eminent domain, the right to escheat (to claim land when an owner dies intestate and without legal heirs), even the rights to wildlife. But the one deviation from the old English allodial system is the right to divide land however the current title holder sees fit. It is this deviation from a course that was obvious to the king of England hundreds of years ago, when the only true wealth was measured in land, that makes parcelization one of the most difficult issues of our time.

Families who measure a substantial portion of their wealth in forest land face a major dilemma: How to pass wealth from generation to generation without dividing up the forest? Fortunately there are many alternatives to keep land intact. The bad news is, parcelization is proceeding at a rate that exceeds the ability of alternatives to make even a small dent in the urbanizing of America's forests. With the median age of forest owners still increasing, most parcelization and conversion will take place over the next twenty to thirty years as lands are passed to heirs, many of whom want nothing to do with managing forests. When a surviving parent dies, heirs are concerned not with land, but with how quickly the estate is settled. In the near term, liquidation of forest assets can result in a windfall for local primary wood-using companies. But as conversion to other uses proceeds, or as forested parcels are subdivided, there is less timber available and the cost of doing business increases.

What does the effect of parcelization hold for the future of forests? Less harvesting on public lands has already led to increasing reliance on private lands. This trend will continue, especially as more public lands are taken out of production. Some local wood-using companies will profit from probate of family forests, but where there is one owner now, expect to see five, ten, or more owners in the future. These new owners will have almost no connections to the land and they will be less willing to manage lands for periodic timber production. Those who do agree to harvest will expect high stumpage rates and impeccable extraction methods.

Wood-using companies that rely on local timber supplies need to develop ways to thwart the impacts of parcelization within their procurement areas. Forestry professionals need to have candid conversations with clients about the long-term disposition of woodlands. And they must also be prepared to suggest estate-planning alternatives, discussed in chapter 8, that keep forest lands intact. Other ideas to prevent parcelization include the following:

- States, using federal grants, can offer local taxing authorities "payments in lieu of taxes" for forest lands owned by families that have agreed to effect a long-term easement (three hundred years or longer) that passes down forest lands within the family or to heirs that agree to maintain practices for the requisite period. In exchange, forest lands would be exempt from all forms of taxation, including property, estate, and even income tax. The latter exemption would be "scaled," so that the longer timber is held, the lower the tax on income from its sale.
- Owners who agree to establish ecological reserves by means of long-term (200–300 years) easements are also exempt from taxation (under the same concept described above). As a condition of benefits, owners must allow qualified research projects on the property. And, if an owner (now or in the distant future) violates the easement, title is forfeit and monetary penalties are levied.
- Local communities in forest areas wanting to expand opportunities for

commerce may offer packages of incentives to forest owners who agree to supply raw material for processing facilities that provide local employment opportunities. The same incentives would be available to owners who agree to protect viewsheds that support tourism, a method that at long last would share tourism wealth with those who provide the view.

- Generally, wood-using businesses have been wary of land trusts because of the misperception that trusts take forests out of production. Mills may want to consider establishing long-term relationships with local land trusts to help woodland owners sell or give development rights that maintain traditional forest uses. Working with a land trust may seem like a foreign concept to some mill owners, but the key to keeping productive lands intact lies with separating the bundle of rights and disallowing the possibility of future development.

- And, lastly, an idea that has less to do with parcelization than with ending a long-standing practice of liquidating timber assets when an owner feels too old or otherwise unable to continue holding forests and the children or heirs have no interest in managing them: A federal banking authority (or a state banking authority using federal grants) buys stumpage, or the rights to stumpage through an easement, and manages the timber and other ecosystem values—using positive impact practices—by paying the family an annual lease, possibly equal to the value of annual increments, property tax liabilities, or by some other measure. Such a program can end the nonsustainable practice of cutting over woodlands before selling them while allowing families who cannot afford to wait for social change, to cash in on their equity. The result: timber is left to grow in volume and value, and forest ecosystems are protected, providing a complement of public services and benefits that society expects of forests but for which it has yet to discover a way to reimburse woodland owners.

CHAPTER 8

Intergenerational Planning Methods for Forests

One of the most tragic failings of traditional forestry is an unreasonable emphasis on profitability. Although woodlands are capable of producing a sustained flow of products, the shorter the planning horizon of any particular owner, the less sustainable woodlands become (Landsberg and Gower 1997). The root of this unreasonable emphasis is a ridiculously antiquated system of property taxation based on "highest and best economic use." It is hard enough for a woodland owner to keep up with property taxes in areas where the highest and best use is for forestry purposes. Near urbanizing areas, forests are assessed—by law—at highest and best use for development.

Property taxes and other expenses of owning forest land force the hands of many owners to cut timber more frequently than is prudent or to liquidate timber at a fraction of its maximum value. But the situation is dire in forest ecosystems located within a few hundred miles of cities. In these areas, "highest and best economic use" is defined not in terms of ecosystem values—for both private and public benefits that forests provide—but for the number of housing units land is capable of supporting. Where taxes are onerous and there is little incentive for owners to manage and protect forest ecosystems, owners are forced to harvest all merchantable timber using nonsustainable practices before lands are sold for development. The calamity of property tax policies is in their failure to account for the enormous public benefits forests provide: clean water; buffering of storm runoff that if not for forests would cause flooding and serious loss of property downstream; scenic vistas that support tourism in many forest areas; habitat for wildlife that is owned by the state; natural filtering systems that remove pollution and sequesters carbon from autos, home heating systems, and manufacturing facilities; and recreational opportunities for millions of people who do not own the forests they enjoy.

Framers of the Constitution intended to allow local governments to use the property tax as an inviolate source of revenue for local services, especially education. To this day, it is the principal means of paying for services that local citizens understand and use, but it is based on an indicator of wealth that no longer applies. Not too long ago—the equivalent of a millisecond in "forest time"—land ownership was a good indicator of wealth and means. But this is no longer the case. Socioeconomic patterns shifted during the first half of the twentieth century (probably coincidental with the Great Depression) placing wealth in the hands of those closer to consumers. A widely dispersed agricultural economy gave way to a more centralized industrial one, obviating wealth on which local communities depend. It is quite likely that one day the destructive effects of property taxes on parcelization of farm and forest lands—causing fragmentation of habitat and other forest values—will become enough of an issue to effect changes. But until then, no woodland-owning family should have to liquidate timber or land to pay property or estate taxes. All states offer programs to owners that tax lands based on "current use" or on actual "yields" from forests that can substantially reduce the property tax burden. Unless fair market values are low in a community, it is virtually impossible for owners to practice positive impact forestry without some form of property tax relief.

Some owners avoid these special valuation programs out of mistrust or because of penalties associated with converting forests to other uses. Local officials tend to disfavor current-use taxation out of a mistaken belief that it severely limits a community's ability to raise revenue, reasoning that developed lands bring in more taxes. Numerous studies, have demonstrated however, that increased tax revenues fall far short of the eventual costs of development, while forests require few municipal services and do not send children to school.

There are a number of alternatives available to woodland owners who intend to keep forests intact and pass them on to succeeding generations. Each, however, comes with two requirements: (1) long-range planning must extend far beyond the ten- to twenty-year planning horizon of most traditional forest management plans, and (2) forest owners and their families must accept the fact that truly sustainable forests are measured in terms of centuries, not decades. Families that subscribe to the concepts of positive impact forestry are willing to forego current income opportunities to create a legacy for the future.

Estate Planning for Forests

Good planning to maintain land through many generations requires a long view extending far beyond an individual's life span. This is so for all land but is especially true for forests, because managed woodlands change slowly. A conscientious forest manager realizes that the fruits of his or her labor will ripen for subsequent generations, not his or her own. And yet, alarmingly, few forest owners have planned for the disposition of land in their estates—probably fewer than 10 percent and possibly as few as 5 percent. Some refuse to confront their own mortality; others simply leave the problem for their heirs to solve. Unfortunately, the forest and the family both suffer when siblings are left to fight over an estate that must be divided and for which federal and state estate taxes may be due. The result: forest ecosystems are abused and timber is sold before it reaches maximum value, or the land is sold to the highest bidder, often to be developed. To top it off, a federal tax may be due on the fair market value of the decedent's estate, and the children—held together only by the ties of parents now gone—never talk again after the estate is settled.

There are many reasons why individuals put off estate planning, but high among them is an unwillingness in families to communicate. Children are reluctant to bring up the subject for fear parents will think them greedy and wish them dead, and parents don't discuss it because the subject is uncomfortable. Notwithstanding, if spouses do not resolve matters involving forests between them and make their intentions clear to their children, chances are slim that important issues will ever be resolved. Other reasons for delay include mixed feelings about children, an unstable marriage, or a mistaken belief that the estate is too small to worry about.

Good planning requires open and candid conversations between spouses. Even if one spouse has been the principal decision maker, both must share in long-range estate planning, because one spouse will likely predecease the other. An easy way to initiate such conversations is by making lists of things about the land that are important to both spouses. A list can include forest values such as: a quiet knoll where wind whispers through trees, even on a calm day; a young stand of timber on rich soils that has veneer potential 150 to 200 years from now; a favorite trail, a scenic vista, or a special habitat. Couples should view this exercise as a chance to leave a living memory of the combined efforts of both partners. The goal is to ensure that future decisions are made with the land in mind. It is remarkably easy to do so without hamstringing future generations. Any practices that are detrimental to forests or decisions that are predicated solely on quick financial gain are disallowed.

When spouses have established priorities, it is time for a candid conversation about heirs. Who among them is best suited to ensuring that ideas, concerns, and objectives for the land are fulfilled and passed on to future generations? This is often more difficult than it sounds, particularly when the couple discovers that none of their closest relatives meets the test. Choosing a son or daughter to assume responsibility for managing forest ecosystems should not be a process of picking the lesser of evils. If none of the prospective heirs is suitable, other options are available. It is, however, essential that children understand and accept the wishes of parents. Communication is paramount.

Prospective heirs need to be made aware of and thoroughly understand their parent's long-term goals for the forest, although it is not essential that they agree with these goals. By understanding their parents wishes, children are less apt to dispute the provisions of the estate plan when it goes into effect, realizing that their control over the forest land may be limited. If necessary, there are also "disincentives" that parents can declare that make it risky for an heir to actively dispute the estate when parents have passed.

After details are resolved between spouses and with the rest of the family, it is time to locate a qualified estate planner. This person is apt to be a lawyer, but not just any lawyer will do. Estate planning is still a relatively new area of law, except among the very rich, who have been planning their affairs to avoid taxation ever since the estate tax was levied. In fact, many forest owners never think of estate planning, because of its association with the wealthy. Most attorneys will offer estate-planning services if a client requests it, but locating a qualified estate planner for forests is another matter and may require some shopping around.

A general guideline is to seek an attorney who has experience with forests and devotes at least one-third of his or her practice to estate planning, working with three to five families or more, preferably woodland owners, each month. Also look for someone who develops his or her own forms for easements, wills, trusts, and other documents rather than using standard documents—also known as *boilerplate*—with fill-in-the-blanks capabilities. A good source of information on attorneys with these qualities is the local land trust.

An estate planner may also be able to suggest opportunities for estate tax savings. The estate tax is due to expire in 2010, but unless Congress votes to continue the repeal, it will be reinstated in 2011.

Keeping Forests in the Family

The sad fact is most children will end up selling the family forest to settle an estate unless parents have set up an alternative that prevents such a sale. Everyone likes to think that their children will not quibble about money after they are gone, but the fact is that it happens, and leaving well-managed forest land to children in the hope that they will carry on the parent's forest management ideals is often a prescription for failure. There are more than a few instances in which the best-laid plans of Mom and Dad were discarded the first time children argued about "their share." Soon after, the woodland is sold to a buyer who is usually thinking about where to put houses rather than how to protect and sustain healthy forest ecosystems.

So what can parents do? Some woodland owners have formed legal "entities" that own the land, and gradually "vest" children into ownership and decision-making positions. Doing so keeps land intact and passes not only the land but the value of good management on to children who will eventually benefit from dad's or grandpa's or great-grandpa's good decisions. There are basically three choices: a family partnership, a closely-held S-corporation, or a limited liability company.

Until just a few years ago only the first two options were available. Family partnerships and S-corporations have served many families that have passed managed forest to heirs. But both strategies have limitations that may kick in years after the founders pass away. For this reason, the newest of the three—the limited liability company (LLC) holds a great deal of promise for woodland owners who are looking for a way to pass forests to children who continue to manage the forests using positive impact practices.

Although the concept of a limited liability company has been in existence for more than one hundred years, first in Germany then throughout Europe, spreading in the twentieth century to Latin America, it has only been in the last few years that every state in the United States has developed a statute that allows this form of organization.

An LLC combines the most favorable aspects of a partnership with the best characteristics of a corporation. In a partnership, decisions are made exclusively by the partners, but the partners are liable for those decisions, jointly and individually. The bottom line is that partners are responsible for each other's mistakes. This liability, or potential liability, far exceeds one of the primary benefits of a partnership: the profits, losses, and credits are passed directly to the individual tax returns of the partners and are taxed only once.

A corporation, on the other hand, is set up as a separate entity—just like another taxpayer. The shareholders, or owners of a corporation, are for this reason protected from liability: if someone errs, the corporation is responsible, not the individuals who own the corporation. Since the corporation is a separate entity, it is taxed as such, and profits paid out to owners are often taxed a second time.

Congress created the S-corporation to allow small businesses and nonprofit organizations to incorporate, providing owners protection from liability while eliminating double taxation. But—as is the case with most things involving the Internal Revenue Service (IRS)—it is not as simple as that. There are many rules that an S-corporation must abide by to maintain its status. For example, an S-corporation can not have more than seventy-five shareholders and it can have only one class of stock. A "closely held" S-corporation can develop rules about who can hold stock (which is one of the reasons it is favored by families that want to pass forest lands), but it can have no more than thirty shareholders. An S-corporation that breaks the rules will end up being viewed by the IRS as a regular corporation, with the threat of back taxes and penalties.

Of the many entities devised to manage family forest land, the simplest to set up and easiest to manage is also the most flexible alternative: the LLC. One of the most useful features of an LLC structure, especially as it relates to long-term management of forests, is that the profit motive is irrelevant. Thus, the family forest LLC can be dedicated to any purpose, including investment, business, conservation or—best of all—a combination of the three. LLCs provide the liability protection of a corporation, pass-through taxation aspects of a partnership, and the essential ability to restrict ownership in the family forest that a closely-held S-corporation provides.

Another benefit crucial to an entity that must add members at the same rate that families grow: there are no limitations on the number of members an LLC can have. The individuals that form the LCC, also known as "founders," have the choice of restricting the number of members (the concept of "members" to an LLC is exactly the same as "shares" to a corporation), allowing fractional membership, forming more than one class of membership, or allowing membership to grow with the family.

Every state in the United States now has an LLC statute, and for reasons mentioned above, it has become a popular way to organize businesses, nonprofits, and other types of organizations in which people come together to make something happen. When that *something* is long-term management of forests, the LLC can allow family members to be the recipients of both tangible and intangible forest benefits but without forcing any one family member to dedicate his or her life to "carrying on Grandpa's legacy." It is this perception that often causes current owners to rethink the wisdom of dedicating one child with the "golden brick," who must then sink or swim while attempting to keep the forest afloat. And when a forest is the principal asset, other children are apt to feel cheated, even though the son or daughter who accepted the responsibility would gladly pass it off. By forming an LLC, the golden brick resides with the "company," leaving the children to enjoy the benefits of forests without the hassles, or to get involved if they are so inclined. It sounds too good to be true, but it is not, so long as the founders give careful thought to language in the LLC's operating agreement.

An LLC is defined by two documents, one of which is public (the *articles of organization*) and the other private (the *operating agreement*). The articles of organization includes such information as the name of the company (which must include the letters "LLC" or "LC" to publicly declare the nature of the company), the state law that governs the few statutory requirements of the LLC, the physical location of its offices, the name and location of the agent of process (the person designated to accept legally served papers on behalf of the LLC), and the LLC's fiscal year.

The articles of organization also include two important questions, the answers to which are especially significant for woodland owning families: (1) "Is it a term LLC, or is it an at-will company?" and (2) "Is the company a member-managed or a manager-managed LLC?" By default, most states will assume an LLC is *at-will* and that it is managed by members. But an LLC established for the purposes of maintaining a forest management legacy and for keeping forest lands intact should probably designate the company a *term LLC* of 100–150 years or more. Although this may sound somewhat drastic, the operating agreement, discussed below, can specify conditions the members can use to shorten the LLC if absolutely necessary, or to establish a new term upon expiration of the old one, or both.

The second question—how is the LLC managed—is initially more difficult to answer because the founders are likely already adequate managers and therefore have no reason to relinquish those responsibilities. Nevertheless, they will want to address the issue of future management in the operating agreement, possibly by designating a trusted consulting forester or property manager to serve as manager after the founders have passed away. As a general rule, it is a good idea to place management decision making in the hands of one person rather than in the hands of a committee, for obvious reasons. But, to avoid the risk of an errant manager, the operating agreement should also provide a series of checks and balances to impeach a manager for cause. Those checks and balances are usually spelled out in the operating agreement, discussed below.

After completing the single-page articles of organization, the founders sign and date it (including their mailing addresses, E-mail addresses, and daytime telephone numbers), and then submit it along with the required filing fees to the secretary of state. Within a few weeks, the founders should receive notification that the LLC is formed. The founders must then draft an operating agreement that explains the purpose of the LLC, the relationship of members to it, and important matters of governance. Once the operating agreement is finalized, or nearly so, the founders can initiate transfer of title in forest lands to the LLC either directly or as a trust of the LLC. The process of title transfers should not be taken lightly, however, and so at this point retaining the services of an attorney who has had experience with LLCs is essential.

The forest land is also appraised at the time of transfer, so the founding members can use IRS tax-exempt gift rules to vest children into ownership interests in the LLC over time. Under current rules, a married couple can give tax-exempt gifts of up to $22,000 per child per year ($11,000 per qualified spouse). And, when the terms of a gift are controlled by a charter, IRS also allows parents to "discount" the gift for its lack of marketability. In other words, parents can give each child $30,000 of an undivided interest in forest land to create a $22,000 gift for tax purposes (by discounting the gift 26.6 percent due to the limitations imposed on the gift by the LLC operating agreement).

The operating agreement is a proprietary document of the LLC, which means that it is private to all except the members and does not need to be filed with the state. There are, however, some necessary requirements implicit to the LLC that the operating agreement can not obviate. For example, members have rights to see the books and records of the company, all members have a duty of loyalty and care to one another and to the purpose of the LLC, and they are obliged to act in good faith and deal fairly. Statutory requirements vary by state, and some allow more freedom than others. For this reason, prospective founders many want to read up on LLCs and choose to organize in a state that offers the best set of conditions for a company whose purpose is to manage forest lands and keep them intact for many years.

When the purpose of an LLC is to pass forest lands within the family and to create a management structure that allows goals and objectives established under the current forest management plan to be maintained until the plan says it is time to act, organization and wording of the operating agreement are crucial to long-term success. Following are suggested elements to include in a family forest operating agreement.

The operating agreement should begin with a strong opening paragraph that clearly describes the purpose of the LLC, which is to pass forest lands within the family, intact, for the LLC's term and longer; to manage long-term timber investment values; to create and maintain wildlife habitats (for named species); to provide opportunity for recreational purposes (either reserved for the family or for local residents by including a clause that allows public access to forest lands for stated recreational purposes, possibly in exchange for an agreement from the town or county to lower property taxes). The opening paragraph sets the tone for the rest of the agreement, and so it is essential that it clearly explain the founders' rationale for setting up the LLC.

The operating agreement should also describe a legislative structure that puts most of the decision-making power into the hands of a relatively few members or a single manager. For example, in the former instance (i.e., a member-managed LLC), children and grandchildren are automatically members of the LLC, but their ability to vote is vested to them as they acquire a financial interest in the company. It is the equivalent of having more than one class of stock. The highest class of stock has voting rights to select a board, the board appoints a set of directors, and the directors make the management decisions.

Another version of a member-managed LLC divides governing members into three categories by function: administrative, resolution of disputes, and interpretation. The administrative arm makes day-to-day management decisions, but for decisions that require drastic measures, such as authorizing a reproduction treatment or the installation of an expensive road, there must be a vote of the entire membership. Discrepancies are sent to the resolution of disputes board charged with making a decision that the members agree to accept. There are many ways to structure a member-managed LLC, but the goal of any structure should be to further the original cause of the family forest while providing necessary checks and balances.

If the operating agreement is amended to put a manager in charge (a consulting forester, for example), the manager is a fiduciary of the LLC, the equivalent of a trustee to a trust. Even with a manager-managed structure, the members should retain the power to impeach a manager, as described above. The operating agreement can spell out conditions for automatic impeachment and should also describe procedures for appointing a new manager.

Generally, the members of an LLC are the owners, and income and expenses are passed directly to them for tax purposes, unless the operating agreement describes a different method. Given the marginal return on forest investments, the agreement may want to specify periodic payouts of profits rather than annual payouts. Income can be distributed to members (or held in trust for children), much as dividends are paid by a corporation. Given a choice, most owners will choose simplicity over almost any alternative, allowing them more time to enjoy forests and less time spent worrying about the business.

The operating agreement should restrict membership to children who are direct descendants of the founders. In fact, prospective spouses should agree to waive any rights to the family LLC as a potential marital asset in the case of divorce. If a future family member wants out of the LLC, the agreement describes how that member's shares are purchased, and whether or not the member's offspring are eligible to buy back in to the LLC. The operating agreement can also grant a nonvoting membership to any direct descendent, but each generation must choose one family member to obtain a voting interest.

At the end of a designated term, the operating agreement should spell out the process that voting members will use to establish a new term or to dissolve the LLC for cause. Because dissolution of the LLC involves land, legal advice in such cases is absolutely essential. The founders may want to think about local conditions 150 years from now that might prompt them to encourage members to dissolve or to create a new term. Finally, the operating agreement should also include a copy of the management plan and should make reference to it in virtually every clause. Future LLC members should never lose sight of the original purpose that caused the founders to take the steps they did to ensure that forests are kept intact and in the family.

Conservation Easements and Land Trusts

Virtually every private forest owner has heard of land trusts, which are becoming increasingly common, especially in rapidly urbanizing forested areas. The unfortunate perception of many owners, however, is that land trusts are the product of a conspiracy to steal private property and pull lands out of production. Critics of land trusts often rely on false threats and rumors to discourage their use by land owners, but owners who know something about how land trusts operate are much more likely to make use of them.

A common goal of land trusts is to keep important lands intact for a variety of purposes, such as to protect significant wildlife habitats, to avoid overdeveloping an area, or to maintain a working landscape. The premise of their existence is that parcelization of land leads to fragmentation of purpose. It is the process by which land trusts are able to protect lands that has created confusion and distrust on the part of many forest owners, a process that is not nearly as obscure as critics make it seem.

A *trust* is a separation of legal and beneficial interests in property that involves three parties: a trustee, who holds the legal interests; the trustor or grantor (also called a *settlor* in some states, although a settlor simply forms a trust without funding it), who provides assets for, or funds, the trust; and the "beneficiary" who, as the name implies, has a beneficial interest in the assets of a trust. When an asset is held in trust, the trustee makes all the decisions, but the benefit of those decisions go to the beneficiary.

Trusts have been a common way for wealthy families to pass assets to children or grandchildren before the children are mature enough to make their own investment decisions. Another common form of trust is known as a *unified credit trust* that a married couple can use to shelter assets from estate taxation. In this type of trust, the three parties mentioned above are all assumed to be the husband and wife: they are at once the trustors, the trustees, and the beneficiaries.

Although the practice of putting land in trust has been known ever since the concept of trusts evolved under English common law, land trusts as we know them today are not that old. In the early 1970s, the steep trajectory of forest parcelization was becoming increasingly apparent, especially in the eastern states. Large tracts of woodland were destined to become smaller, and accessible, usually productive, forests were being converted into non-productive uses at an alarming rate. It was in this climate that the popular concept of land trusts evolved as a way to separate the legal and beneficial interests in real property.

The one aspect of land that makes it different from other forms of capital is that it can not be moved around. A person who acquires land obtains the rights associated with the use of that land, also know as the *bundle of rights*. The most common method of separating the bundle of rights is through *easements*. An easement grants rights to land without actually giving up the land. An "easement for conservation purposes," which almost always includes a transfer of development rights, is arguably the most important tool to keep forest ecosystems intact. More than 6.2 million acres of farm and forest land have been protected from development since lands trusts came on the scene, but this is just a drop in the bucket in comparison to many millions of acres considered at risk.

The process to protect land often begins with the current owner, but sometimes the land trust will contact an owner if there is some significant value the trust wants to protect. The trust will usually ask the owner to "donate" an easement, but in some instances the trust may offer to buy it. A donated easement for conservation purposes constitutes a "gift" under IRS rules, and it can offset income from other sources (up to a limit of 30 percent of adjusted gross income in any one tax year). Any excess gift is carried over for up to five additional years.

The exact nature of an easement depends on the interests of the current owner, and it is usually negotiated with the trust. For example, if a woodland owner wants to spell out the conditions for managing forest stands or protecting special habitats or maintaining vistas, the easement articulates these values and the trust agrees to ensure values are managed or protected after the owner has passed. Land trusts like to keep things as simple as possible, but they are usually also flexible. Nevertheless, the more complicated the easement, the more expensive it is to enforce. Land trusts commonly request an endowment in the form of a cash donation from owners who donate easements. This may sound like an unreasonable request but the trust incurs expenses, initially to prepare the easement and annually thereafter, to make sure the easement is honored in perpetuity. The size and timing of endowments is usually tailored to the financial capacity of each owner. If the woodland owner is cash poor, the trust may request a *remainder gift* from the owner's estate to fund the endowment. A remainder gift is an asset (or cash) that irrevocably passes to the land trust when the gift is made, but the land trust does take possession of the gift until the decedent passes away.

If the owner wants to set aside a portion of the land for future generations to build on, it is usually not a problem so long as the plan does not damage ecosystem values. Arranging set-asides like this is more costly, and the owner is expected to foot the bill. Almost any reasonable conditions are acceptable provided there is an easy and cost-effective way to enforce the condition and the current owner is willing to pay the cost of creating the easement.

Land trusts will usually handle all of the legal paper work, have the land appraised (for tax purposes), and make sure that all documents are properly executed and recorded. When it is done, virtually nothing changes, including property taxes. One would expect taxes to fall since the woodland owner has given up most of the taxable value of land, but such is not the case. Local taxing authorities will still tax the land as though it is being held in inventory for development, and land trusts do not pay property taxes on the easements it owns, for a good reason: it has made promises to protect the easements in perpetuity and these promises represent liabilities, not assets. A future owner of protected land may have more success arguing for a lower appraisal, but conservation of forest and farm lands has so far not had the effect of lowering property taxes based on fair market value. Some communities will assign a "payment in lieu of taxes" to reflect a change in appraised values. And some communities have been known to increase the assessment of lands belonging to abutters of protected land on the grounds that conservation easements increase the value of surrounding lands.

An owner who later decides to sell his or her woodlands instead of leaving them to descendants can easily do so. Most likely, the owner has already agreed to contact the land trust in the event of a sale, and a local land trust enforcement official is one of the first "neighbors" the prospective buyer will meet. In fact, the land trust may even have a buyer.

The land trust will review conditions of the easement with a prospective buyer, most of whom are not intimidated by the conditions. There are even instances in which "protected" land is worth more to a buyer than unprotected land, because the hassle and expense of setting up the easement was borne by a former owner. The trust will also schedule annual or semiannual visits to make sure the new owner is not violating the conditions of the easement.

If an owner wants to implement silvicultural practices, treatments are scheduled and implemented according to the forest management plan. Chances are that the land trust takes a more active role in making silviculture decisions than most private owners would prefer, but not necessarily. It is, however, the trust's prerogative and responsibility to ensure silvicultural practices are sufficient to meet treatment objectives. Virtually all land trusts in forest areas have a qualified forester on staff, or it purchases services from a local consultant.

What happens if the local land trust dissolves? State laws require land trusts to have successor agreements with other land trusts so that if one folds, its responsibilities are picked up by another trust. An owner who decides to work with a local land trust will want to explore the successor agreements to be sure the easements are protected in perpetuity. Woodland owners who protect lands by giving or selling easements to land trusts are less concerned with financial gain than with maintaining and protecting intrinsic values of woodlands and the integrity of forest ecosystems. They are banking on the fact that one day these values will be far more important than money.

Epilogue

In a book intended to have broad public appeal among owners, managers, and users of forests, the risk of omission is exceeded only by that of oversimplification. Nevertheless, I am confident that readers who grasp the concepts presented here are also fully capable of recognizing the limitations and exceptions in a work such as this. I have tried to emphasize the more global concepts of positive impact forestry, ideas that apply to forests irrespective of regions, forest types, and ownership patterns. But to a reader from the ponderosa pine forests in the Black Hills of South Dakota, or to an owner of extensive loblolly pine plantations in Georgia, the author's bias toward hardwood forests is obvious and irrefutable, yet also irrelevant to the premise of positive impact forestry.

I have attempted to convince readers that forests are special not because of trees, although it is the presence of trees that spawned the development of forestry. They are ecosystems, home to many different species and life-forms in a milieu that is both highly organized and unbelievably complex. This, I have emphasized throughout the book, is the context of forests that should define human actions, not merely the presence of trees.

Lest the major kernels of ideas I call "positive impact forestry" get buried in the context of examples readers might consider irrelevant because my illustrations are too far removed from their own circumstances, I have extracted the principle tenets of this thinking and summarized them here as ideas that stand on their own.

On Forests . . .
Knowledge of forests, respect for land, use of good practices, healthy soils, and patience are the essence of positive impact forestry.

231

Forests—for the sake of forests—supercede human benefit, and those of us
who disturb them do so with great caution, humility, and respect.

It is possible to use forest ecosystems without destroying the essential
functions that keep ecosystems intact.

Human benefit is subordinate to ensuring that—above all else—forests
provide for the complements of species that make forests what they are.

On Forestry . . .

Forestry is a science borne of scarcity.

Positive impact forestry recognizes and accepts the attendant risks of managing forests but also underscores a manager's ability to avoid or mitigate potentially negative impacts.

The first concern of positive impact forestry is to protect, maintain, or
even enhance the health and integrity of forest ecosystems over and
above opportunities to generate income or enhance investment.

Virtually all commercially important forests in the United States are capable of providing sustainable timber yields. But if ecosystem health and
integrity take precedence over production—as it should—then timber
production capabilities of many forest sites are less than we expect of
them today.

On Forest Management . . .

An owner who controls forests for the allocation of benefits, regardless of
the nature of benefits—extractive or otherwise—is managing forests.

When the past is used as sole justification for current practices, it is easy
to ignore reasons to change even though failure to change may one day
prove problematic.

The more a management practice focuses on immediate gain—especially
when "gain" is solely the product of one value—the more prone management is to fail over time with respect to that value.

Management practices are a means of achieving desirable futures, but only
for those who see the future as more important than the present.

Untended forests are apt to disappear, gradually converted into other developed uses that are far less beneficial than the complement of values
forest ecosystems are capable of providing.

The difference between activities that merely avoid impacts and those
that craft impacts to optimize ecosystem values while also providing
benefits is the difference between low-impact and positive impact
forestry.

Healthy and sustainable ecosystems, not timber, are the products of positive impact forestry.

Most silviculture encompasses planned disturbances intended to speed up succession, reverse it, or slow it down depending on the owner's objectives. Positive impact forestry attempts to mimic natural disturbances so as to provide benefits.

Positive impact forestry is predicated on the idea that humans are a part of forests and thus have an interest in maintaining them for their intrinsic values and not merely as places for growing and harvesting fiber.

Avoiding the tendency to overmanage woodlands is a fundamental tenet of positive impact forestry.

Long-range planning must embrace ecosystem values that extend far beyond the ten- to twenty-year planning horizon of most traditional forest management plans, and owners should accept the fact that truly sustainable forests are measured in terms of centuries not decades.

On Forest Soils . . .

Forest soils are an unheralded biological and ecological treasure, where communities of bacteria and fungi are to this "hidden forest" what trees are to woodlands in the landscape.

Future forests are more apt to be defined on the basis of the hidden forest of soils than on the presence of trees.

Positive impact forestry practices advocate extracting timber only when soils are least susceptible to physical changes; on frozen, snow-covered soils or—in areas where soils do not freeze—when trees are dormant and soils are dry.

Until more is known about the impacts of periodic harvesting on soil nutrients and cost-effective, ecosystem-safe methods to replace essential nutrients, forest owners should manage timber on nutrient-poor soils extensively—or not at all.

On Timber Management and Logging . . .

Timber harvesting should always be done for silvicultural reasons, to achieve more than one objective, and only within the context of a long-term plan.

The value of periodic thinning to increase diameter growth rates is easily wiped out by root and stem injuries from careless logging.

Positive impact forestry methods can include clearcutting when it is used as a silvicultural tool employed at a reasonable scale to reproduce species adapted to catastrophic disturbances. But when it is used only as an efficient means of converting trees into fiber, clearcutting is not positive impact forestry.

Irrespective of soil conditions, keep timber extraction trails to a minimum.

Generally, whole-tree harvesting systems—which extract leaves, twigs or any tissues smaller than primary-order branches, rich in nutrients—are not positive impact forestry, except when it is necessary to harvest whole trees for sanitation purposes.

On Foresters . . .

The key words to remember when selecting professionals with whom to work are: *credentials, skills, motivation,* and *attitude.*

Just because a person has forestry credentials does not mean he or she subscribes to the concepts of positive impact forestry.

Whenever the word *selective* is used as an adjective in the context of timber harvesting, chances are it has little to do with positive impact forestry and those who use the term should be challenged to explain it.

The best way to avoid a conflict of interest (and the only way a consultant can act as an owner's agent) is if fees for services are not dependent on income from timber sales.

Higher bids offered for consultant-administered timber sales more often than not offset the cost of services by a wide margin.

Many who do not subscribe to the ideas of low-impact logging and positive impact forestry are simply refusing to acknowledge that forestry needs to change.

On Loggers . . .

It is often the financial pressure of staying in business, not a lack of knowledge or skills, that leads to poor logging practices.

The better the logger, the more he or she is in demand and the longer it takes to obtain a commitment for services. Good loggers are always in short supply, so be prepared to wait up to year or more, and be cautious of contractors available "next week."

Responsibility and accountability are often intended benefits of logger education programs, and many newly established programs remind participants that with education comes responsibility.

Attitude, demeanor, and skills of the person operating logging equipment, and not the equipment, are the primary determinants of "good" versus "bad" logging. Virtually all site and stand damage from logging is caused by careless machine operators and poor timing, not equipment.

On Forestry Investments . . .

Time is the bane of forestry investments, when even insignificant costs at the beginning of a rotation grow by Herculean proportions at harvest.

Forest land is a great investment for patient people who are willing to pass wealth on to future generations.

Since good timber is usually scarce, the effect of an economic downturn is often greater on the profit margin of the final product than it is on stumpage.

The better the site, the longer the rotation, almost regardless of species (assuming timber is not allowed to grow larger than processing facilities can handle).

On Plantations, Planting in Forests, and Nontimber Products . . .

Positive impact forestry is not intended to follow the path of modern agriculture, to convert forests into farms, or to remake forests in the image of humans.

Positive impact forestry practices do not necessarily exclude planting as a reproduction alternative, so long as the ecosystem-related risks are addressed and the purpose of planting is to reproduce natural forests and their complement of benefits, both tangible and intangible. Planting solely for timber production (or any single-use purpose) is not positive impact forestry.

As a general rule, forest owners should plant with species that occur naturally on the site, using seedlings with provenances that are as geographically close to the site as possible.

The only way to protect and manage nontimber forest products using positive impact forestry guidelines is to put stewardship in the hands of gatherers.

The most effect methods of dealing with invasive organisms are early detection and eradication, and individual forest owners are the first-line of defense when a new threat arrives.

Nonnative species should never be introduced to natural forests, and homeowners in forest areas should be encouraged to plant only native species.

On the Future of Forests and Forestry . . .

It is highly probable that ingenuity and bioengineering will soon allow us to grow wood fibers in structures other than trees and in places other than forests.

Any serious contemplation of future forest policy must consider the impacts of emerging technologies that can drastically change the way we use forest ecosystems.

Despite the fact that many owners and forestry professionals would argue that regulation of forestry practices is already excessive and generally bad, we should all expect more regulation in the future, not less.

Parcelization of land leads to fragmentation of purpose.

Most children of forest-owning families will end up selling the family forest to settle an estate, unless parents have set up an alternative that prevents such a sale.

A healthy forest products industry is essential to maintaining forest landscapes. When the primary purpose of land shifts from forests to residential housing or to some other use that has nothing to do with healthy ecosystems, forests are converted from vital landscapes to backyards.

Regardless of what the future holds for alternative methods of growing wood fiber, there will always be a demand for natural wood with a beauty and texture that will prove impossible to duplicate.

The one thing that differentiates resource values of forests from their far richer values as ecosystems is time. Humans and forests have different clocks. Two hundred years of forest use in North America has demonstrated the impossibility of managing forests so as to conform to the limitations of time imposed on humans. Truly sustainable forests are a function of forest time and positive impact forestry is a guide on how to reset the clocks.

Online Resources

Sources of Information about Skidder Bridges

Portable timber bridge systems for forest roads:
http://www.eng.auburn.edu/users/staylor/ptbsfr.pdf

University of Massachusetts portable skidder bridge:
http://www.umass.edu/umext/nrec/pdf_files/skidder_bridge.pdf

Sources for Nontoxic Lubricants, Fluids, and Fuel Additives

Bioblend: *http://www.bioblend.com*

Environmental Lubricants Manufacturing Inc.: *http://www.elmusa.com/products*

Green Oil Company: *http://www.greenoil-online.com*

Renewable Lubricants Inc.: *http://www.renewablelube.com*

For more information, contact equipment manufacturers.

Sources of Fuel-, Fluid-, and Lubricant-Spill Kits

Aabaco Industries Inc.: *http://www.aabaco.com/O-skdbs.html*

AbsorbentsOnline.com: *http://www.absorbentsonline.com/spillkits.htm*

Breg International Inc.: *http://www.bregenvironmental.com*

EnviCARE USA: *http://www.envicareusa.com/line_card.html*

ForestryMall.com: *http://www.irl.bc.ca/Safety%20+%20Clothing/spill-kits.htm*

Loyola Enterprises Inc.:
  http://www.loyola.com/environmental/enviro_products.html

For more information, contact individual suppliers of fuels and lubricants.

Warning: Do not apply spill-kit products that employ biological methods directly to forest soils to "digest" petroleum spills. The risks from introduction of exotic species are too great.

Sources of Information about the Game of Logging

Soren Eriksson's Game of Logging: Tel. 800-798-4839;
  http://www.gameoflogging.com

Sources of Used Conveyor Belt for Flexible Water Bars (Chapter 5)

Ashmus Belting Co., 1016 50th Street, Kenosha, WI 53140
  (phone: 262-652-4596) (fax: 262-652-3709)
  Web site: www.ashmus.com

Portland Rubber Co. (c/o Inside Sales), 21 West Commercial St.,
  Portland, Maine 04101 (phone: 800-322-3100) (fax: 207-775-3351)

Information on Cable-Yarding Systems (Chapter 5)

http://www.osha.gov/SLTC/etools/logging/manual/yarding/
  cableyardingsystem.html

Coverts Programs

http://www.ruffedgrousesociety.org/covertsprogram.asp

Woodland Owner Associations

http://www.woodlandowners.org

http://www.nationalforestry.org

Forestry-Related Internet Sites of Interest

Information about wood and wood uses from the U.S. Forest Products Lab:
http://www.fpl.fs.fed.us/pubs.htm

Building woods roads: A Landowners' Guide to Building Forest Access Roads:
http://www.na.fs.fed.us/spfo/pubs/stewardship/accessroads/accessroads.htm

Common log rules: *http://www.ext.vt.edu/pubs/forestry/420-085/420-085.html#L3*

Forest plant species gathered for decorative, food, or medicinal uses:
http://www.ifcae.org/cgibin/ntfp/db/dbsql/db.cgi?db=prod&uid=default&vr=1&
ID=&sb=1&so=ascend*

Available software describing woody plants of North America:
http://www.cnr.vt.edu/dendro/wpina/index.html

Database of invasive plants in North America:
http://invader.dbs.umt.edu/scripts/esrimap.dll?name=map_query&Cmd=Map

Information on controlling invasive plants in forests:
http://tncweeds.ucdavis.edu/products.html

Measuring timber volumes in logs and standing trees:
http://ohioline.osu.edu/for-fact/0035.html and
http://www.ext.vt.edu/pubs/forestry/420-560/420-560.html#tvm

Forestry measurement tools and how to use them:
http://www.agnr.umd.edu/MCE/Publications/PDFs/FS629.pdf

Forestry links offered by the National Association of State Foresters:
http://www.stateforesters.org/NASFlinks.html

Internet forestry resources for the northeastern states:
http://www.na.fs.fed.us/pubs/misc/flg

Information on Weed Wrench (Chapter 6): *http://www.canonbal.org/weed.html*

Wand Applicator for Topical Application of Herbicides (Chapter 6):
http://tncweeds.ucdavis.edu/tools/wand.html

Public Sources of Forestry Assistance

State Foresters in the United States

Alabama
334-240-9304
boycet@forestry.state.al.us

Alaska
907-269-8474
jeff_jahnke@dnr.state.ak.us

American Samoa
011-684-699-1394
ssuemann@yahoo.com

Arizona
602-255-4059
kirkrowdabaugh@
   azstatefire.org

Arkansas
501-296-1941
john.shannon@mail.state.
   ar.us

California
916-653-7772
andrea.tuttle@fire.ca.gov

Colorado
970-491-6303
jhubbard@lamar.colostate.
   edu

Connecticut
860-424-3630
don.smith@po.state.
   ct.us

Delaware
302-698-4548
austin@dda.state.de.us

Florida
850-488-4274
peterse@doacs.state.fl.us

Georgia
478-751-3480
blazenby@gfc.state.ga.us

Guam
671-735-3949
dlimti@mail.gov.gu

Hawaii
808-587-4177
michael_g_buck@exec.
   state.hi.us

Idaho
208-334-0242
wwiggins@idl.state.id.us

Illinois
217-785-8774
thickmann@dnrmail.state.
   il.us

Indiana
317-232-4105
bfischer@dnr.state.
   in.us

Iowa
515-281-8657
mike.brandrup@dnr.state.
   ia.us

Kansas
785-532-3300
raslin@oznet.ksu.edu

Kentucky
502-564-4496
eah.macswords@mail.
   state.ky.us

Louisiana
225-952-8002
paul_f@ldaf.state.la.us

Maine
207-287-2791
alec.giffen@maine.gov

Marshall Islands
011-692-625-3206
agridiv@ntamar.com

Maryland
410-260-8501
skoehn@dnr.state.md.us

Massachusetts
413-442-4963

Michigan
517-373-1056
hubbardb@michigan.gov

Micronesia
011-691-320-6854
fsmagri@mail.fm

Minnesota
651-296-4485
mike.carroll@dnr.state.
mn.us

Mississippi
601-359-1386
jsledge@mfc.state.ms.us

Missouri
573-522-4115
kreppr@mdc.state.mo.us

Montana
406-542-4300
rharrington@state.mt.us

Nebraska
402-472-2944
ghergenrader1@unl.edu

Nevada
775-684-2500
stever@ndf.state.nv.us

New Hampshire
603-271-2214
p_bryce@dred.state.nh.us

New Jersey
609-292-2520

jbarresi@dep.state.nj.us

New Mexico
505-476-3328
ablazer@state.nm.us

New York
518-402-9405
rkdavies@gw.dec.state.
ny.us

North Carolina
919-733-2162
stan.adams@ncmail.net

North Dakota
701-228-5422
larry.kotchman@ndsu.
nodak.edu

North Mariana Islands
670-256-3319
victordlg@gtepacifica.net

Ohio
614-265-6690
john.dorka@dnr.state.
oh.us

Oklahoma
405-521-3864
jburwell@oda.state.ok.us

Oregon
503-945-7211
rwoo@odf.state.or.us

Palau
011-680-488-2504
damr@palaunet.com

Pennsylvania
717-787-2703
jagrace@state.pa.us

Puerto Rico
787-725-9593

Rhode Island
401-647-3367

tdupree@dem.state.ri.us

South Carolina
803-896-8800
bschowalter@forestry.
state.sc.us

South Dakota
605-773-3623
ray.sowers@state.sd.us

Tennessee
615-837-5411
steven.scott@state.tn.us

Texas
979-458-6600
jim-hull@tamu.edu

Utah
801-538-5530
joelfrandsen@utah.gov

Vermont
802-241-3678
ssinclair@fpr.anr.state.
vt.us

Virgin Islands
340-778-0991
vidoa@vitelcom.net

Virginia
434-977-6555
garnerj@dof.state.va.us

Washington
360-902-1603
pat.mcelroy@wadnr.gov

Wisconsin
608-264-0224
paul.delong@dnr.state.
wi.us

West Virginia
304-558-3446
dye@gwmail.state.
wv.us

Wyoming
307-777-5659
dperko@state.wy.usnasf

Extension Forestry Leaders in the United States

Alabama
334-844-1044
mcnabb@forestry.auburn.
edu

Alaska
907-474-6356
ffraw@uaf.edu

Arizona
520-621-7257
cppr@ag.arizona.edu

Arkansas
870-460-1092
whiting@uamont.edu

California
510-642-2360
rrharris@nature.berkeley.
edu

Colorado
970-491-6281
dlamm@vines.colostate.
edu

Connecticut
860-774-9600
sbroderi@canr1.cag.
uconn.edu

Delaware
301-831-2501
pbarber@udel.edu

Florida
352-846-0891

ajl@gnv.ifas.ufl.edu

Georgia
912-681-5653
ddickens@arches.uga.
edu

Hawaii
808-956-7530
elswaify@hawaii.edu

Idaho
208-885-6356
rmahoney@uidaho.edu

Illinois
217-333-2770
g-rolfe@uiuc.edu

Indiana
765-494-3580
billh@fnr.purdue.edu

Iowa
515-294-1168
phw@iastate.edu

Kansas
785-532-1444
cbarden@.oznet.ksu.edu

Kentucky
606-257-7610
dgraves@ca.uky.edu

Louisiana
225-388-4087
bmills@agctr.lsu.edu

Maine
207-581-2885
jphilp@umext.maine.edu

Maryland
301-432-2735
jk87@umail.umd.edu

Massachusetts
413-545-2943
dbk@forwild.umass.edu

Michigan
517-355-0096
koelling@.msu.edu

Minnesota
662-625-1288
baughma@umn.edu

Mississippi
662-566-2201
robertc@ext.msstate.edu

Missouri
573-882-4444

Montana
406-243-2773
efrsl@forestry.umt.edu

Nebraska
402-472-5822
fofw093@unlvm.unl.edu

Nevada
775-784-4039
walker@ers.unr.edu

New Hampshire
603-862-2619
bob.edmonds@unh.edu

New Jersey
732-932-8993
vodak@aesop.rutgers.edu

New Mexico
505-827-8085

New York
607-255-4696
pjs23@cornell.edu

North Carolina
919-515-5574
rick_hamilton@ncsu.edu

North Dakota
701-231-5936
michael.kangas@ndsu.
nodak.edu

Ohio
614-292-9838
heiligmann.1@osu.edu

Oklahoma
405-744-3854

Oregon
541-737-4952
teschs@ccmail.orst.edu

Pennsylvania
814-863-0401
fj4@psu.edu

Puerto Rico
787-832-4040
s_gonzalez@seam.uprem.
edu

Rhode Island
401-874-2912
tom@uriacc.uri.edu

South Carolina
864-656-4866
lnelson@clemson.edu

South Dakota
605-688-4737
john_ball@sdstate.edu

Tennessee
865-974-7988
ghopper@utk.edu

Texas
903-834-6191
eric-taylor@tamu.edu

Utah
435-797-4056
mikek@cnr.usu.edu

Vermont
802-656-2913
tmcevoy@together.net

Virginia
540-231-7679
jej@vt.edu

Washington
509-335-2964
baumgtnr@wsu.edu

West Virginia
304-293-2941
dmcgill@wvu.edu

Wisconsin
715-365-2658
william.klase@ces.uwex.
edu

Wyoming
307-235-9400

Glossary

acre. An area of land containing 43,560 square feet, approximately equal to the playing area of a football field.

advanced reproduction. Well-established young trees that are capable of surviving after a regeneration treatment.

adventitious bud. Meristematic tissue that forms into a bud, usually in response to a disturbance.

allelopathy. The inherent ability of some plants to excrete substances that are toxic to other plants; believed to have developed as a strategy to prevent competition.

aspect. The compass direction a slope faces.

basal area. One measure of tree density. It is determined by estimating the total cross-sectional area of all trees measured at breast height (4.5 feet above ground) and expressed in square feet per acre.

biodiversity. Also called *biological diversity*. The natural diversity of all organisms that occupy a given landscape or ecosystem, including diversity within and between species.

biome. The highest level of organization in plant and forest ecosystems largely determined by broad climatic patterns, such as rainfall, temperature, and the like. See also **forest region.**

biomass. The total green weight of above-ground tree vegetation, including leaves, twigs, bark, and stem, that is usually processed into short bolts or chips for fuel or for further processing into paper.

board foot. A common measure of lumber that is 1 inch thick and has a surface measure equal to 1 square foot, regardless of dimensions.

boilerplate. Standard language in documents such as management plans and contracts.

browse. Leaves, buds, and woody stems used as food by woodland mammals such as deer and moose.

bucking. The process of converting a tree stem into logs.

buffer strip. Any type of protective strip of undisturbed forest that shelters treated areas from view; or, a protective strip of undisturbed forest floor between exposed soil surfaces and streams to allow sediment particles to filter out before overland flows reach a stream.

bull cruise. An estimate of standing timber volumes based upon a walk through an area designated for harvest where the estimate is based solely on the visual observations of the person doing the cruise without the aid of equipment or scientific procedures.

bumper. Also called *bumper tree*. Any tree near the inside curve in a skid trail that is used to pivot a load of logs keeping them behind the machine. Trees used in this manner sustain serious stem injury unless protective measures are used.

cable logging. Any type of timber extraction system that uses cables, but commonly used in reference to "running" cable, of high-lead systems used in the West.

callus. The tissue that forms around a break in the cambium of a woody plant.

cambium. A thin layer of cells between the inner bark and sapwood of a tree where cell divisions take place, forming xylem tissues to inside and phloem and bark to the outside.

canopy. The uppermost layers of a forest encompassing branches, twigs, and leaves.

cleaning. Also called *weeding*. A silvicultural term to describe practices that regulate species composition of a young stand by eliminating some trees (weeds) and encouraging others.

clearcutting. A silvicultural reproduction method that removes all trees from a designated area in one operation usually for the purpose of creating a new, even-aged stand.

climax. An association of plants and animals that will prevail in the absence of disturbance; or, the culmination of a successional cycle.

clones. A collection of stems that have propagated by vegetative (asexual) means from the stump, root collar, or the roots of a single parent.

community. A collection of living organisms functioning together in an organized system through which energy, nutrients, and water cycle.

corridor. A travel route that connects important wildlife habitat elements.

cover type. The designation of a vegetation complex described by dominant species, age, and form.

crop tree. Trees that are selected and favored because they are expected to increase in value until they are ready for harvest.

crotch. The area where the topside of a branch joins the main stem.

crown. The above-ground portion of a tree extending up and out from the first main branches on the stem. When preceded by the word *root*, it is the point when the stem emerges from soil.

crown class. The relative position of the tops of tree crowns in an even-aged forest that is an indicator of competition, consisting of four classes: dominant, codominant, intermediate, and suppressed.

crown closure. The degree to which tree crowns in the main canopy occupy space, preventing a view of open sky; expressed as percentage of closure.

cruise. A survey of forest stands to determine the number, size, volume, and species of trees, as well as the terrain, soil condition, access, and any other factors relevant to forest management planning.

cull. Trees that have no current or potential market value for sawtimber.

culvert. A metal, plastic, or concrete pipe of varying diameters that carries the flow of surface water under roads and trails.

cut. Forestry slang used in reference to a prescription that involves the felling and extraction of wood products.

cutting cycle. The time interval between harvesting operations when uneven-aged methods are employed using group or single-tree selection.

cutting methods. Timber management practices employed to either regenerate a new stand (*regeneration cutting*) or improve the composition and increase the growth rate of residual trees in a stand (*intermediate treatment*).

decay. Alteration of the physical structure of wood so that it is weakened by the action of fungi and bacteria.

deferment cutting. A variation of the shelterwood method where the final removal is delayed at least until the first thinning of the new stand.

defoliation. The loss of leaves or foliage on a plant or tree.

density. The number of trees, basal area, volume, or some other measure, per unit of area.

diameter (dbh). Diameter at breast height, measured at 4.5 feet above average ground level around the base of the tree.

den tree. A living or dead tree with a cavity suitable for birds and mammals to use for shelter, escape, or as a nursery.

dieback. A symptom characterized by the death of single branches, or groups of branches, in the crown of a tree due to conditions other than shading.

discoloration. A change in wood color, often appearing as a stain, caused by the action of bacteria or fungi. Stained wood is structurally sound.

dispersal. The mechanism used by an organism to move beyond the location of its parents. For example, wind is a dispersal mechanism used by many organisms.

disturbance. Any event—natural or human-caused—that disrupts forest processes, disturbs soils, changes microclimate, or alters the structure of vegetation. Silviculture is a planned disturbance in forests to achieve human benefits.

dominant. A tree that is free grown under forest conditions so that at least a portion of its crown extends above those of surrounding trees. See also **crown class.**

duff. The topmost layer of a forest soil composed of partially decomposed organic material beneath a litter of recently fallen twigs, needles, and leaves.

early successional. Any association of plants and animals that are capable of establishing, surviving, and reproducing under harsh, exposed environmental conditions, but (in forests) are incapable of reproducing in their own shade. The first species to occupy an area after a major disturbance. Also called *pioneers.*

ecology. The study of interrelationships between organisms and their environment.

ecosystem. Any community of organisms and the physical environment that surrounds them.

ecosystem management. An approach to managing forests that subordinates human benefits to maintaining the long-term health and functioning of ecosystems.

edaphic. Of or relating to soils, especially relating to the effects of soils on plant communities.

edge. The border between different habitats.

edge effect. A condition in which the presence of edge has an impact (positive or negative) on species that are dependent on habitats adjacent to the edge.

endangered species. An organism that is at risk for extinction.

endemic. A species that is historically native to an ecosystem or landscape.

environment. The ambient conditions surrounding an ecosystem that, singly or combined, often limit the extent of a particular ecosystem.

ephemeral stream. Any stream bed that flows intermittently, such as following a rain or only during the spring. See also **stream.**

erosion. As a natural process, the wearing away of bedrock by the action of water, wind, and ice. As an unnatural process, the movement of soil when protective vegetative layers are removed.

even-aged management. A timber management method that produces a stand composed of trees all about the same age; the difference in age between oldest and youngest trees is usually less than 20 percent of the rotation.

exotic species. Any species that is not historically part of a natural ecosystem.

externality. A positive or negative value that arises as an unintended consequence. Beautiful landscapes are a positive externality of well-managed forests; sedimentation in streams is a negative externality of careless timber extraction.

extirpation. Loss of a species due to changes in habitat or other factors that have driven away or destroyed a breeding population.

extraction. The process of removing timber products from forests.

falling. Also called *felling.* The process of severing trees from stumps.

fallers. Also called *fellers* or *choppers.* Those members of the logging crew whose job is to fall (fell) trees so as to lessen stand damage and make it easy for others on the crew to extract logs.

feeder roots. The very finest portions of a plant's root system, usually within the top few inches of soil, that are primarily responsible for uptake of nutrients and moisture.

felling. See **falling.**

fellers. See **fallers.**

fertilizer. Any natural or manufactured material added to soil in order to supply one or more plant nutrients. Most manufactured mineral nutrients are applied as salts, which can be injurious to roots.

final harvest. Under even-aged methods, the culmination of a current rotation when the overstory of the preceding stand is totally removed.

ford. A place in a stream where equipment can cross without disturbing sediments.

forest floor. The surface from which tree stems emerge, usually covered with leaves and woody debris that has not yet been incorporated into the soil.

forest land. Land that is currently supporting forest ecosystems, whether or not trees are present.

forest management practice. Any activity (usually positive, but not necessarily) that is intended to control and allocate benefits from forest ecosystems.

forestry. The art and science of growing and managing forests and forest lands so as to sustain their ability to provide benefits.

forest health. A somewhat controversial term among foresters, ecologists, and others; as used here, it implies that a healthy forest is one in which essential ecosystem integrity is maintained largely within the limits imposed by nature. The term also implies that careless or excessive human use can lead to a degradation of ecosystem integrity.

forest type. A natural group or association of different species of trees that commonly occur together over a large area. Forest types are defined and named after one or more dominant species of trees in the type, such as the Douglas-fir and the birch-beech-maple types.

forest region. The highest level of organization of forests, or potential forests, defined by broad climatic patterns, such as temperature extremes and moisture availability. See also **biome.**

forwarder. A machine used to extract timber by loading logs into a bunk instead of dragging them.

free-grown. A tree that has grown all of its life in forest conditions without being overtopped by other trees.

geocaching. A sport that involves locating a "cache" of known coordinates using a handheld global positioning system. The cache is usually nothing more than a watertight container with a log book inside so the finder can record name, date, and a short message.

geotextiles. Also called *geofabrics.* A fabric of woven nylon used as an underlayment for roads especially on poorly drained soils.

GPS. An abbreviation for *global positioning system.* An electronic device that uses signals from a net of satellites in geosynchronous orbits to locate any position on earth.

grade. *1.* A measure (usually subjective) of a tree's ability to produce high-quality, defect-free lumber. Grading of logs and lumber is progressively less subjective. *2.* Slope.

ground cover. Local grasses and forbs seeded onto exposed soil surfaces for the purpose of preventing soil movement.

group selection. An uneven-aged regeneration method to remove small groups of trees to favor the reproduction and establishment of late-successional species.

growing stock. All the trees growing in a stand that have, or will have, market potential generally expressed in terms of number of stems, basal area, or volume.

habitat. A place where a plant or animal can live and maintain itself.

hardpan. A hardened or cemented soil layer usually associated with soils on glacial deposits.

harvesting. Felling, extracting, loading, and transporting products from forests.

high grading. An exploitive logging practice that removes only the best, most accessible and marketable trees in the stand, leaving defective and unmarketable trees behind.

high lead. A type of logging that employs an overhead cable used to bring logs or tree-lengths to a landing, where products are loaded onto trucks.

improvement cutting. An intermediate treatment to improve the growth rate and vigor of residual trees. See also **timber stand improvement; TSI.**

increment. The increase in diameter, basal area, height, volume, quality, or value of trees in a stand.

intermediate treatments. In even-aged methods, any removal of trees from a stand between the time of establishment and the final harvest, undertaken to improve residual stand growth and to improve species composition or stand health.

intolerant species. Plant species incapable of surviving in the shade of other trees.

landing. A place where logs are gathered near public roads for further transport. Also called *log deck* or *yard*.

land trust. A nonprofit, usually local organization that will accept easements from families who want to protect land from development and to maintain long-term management strategies. The trust only holds the development rights, not the land.

late-successional. See **climax.**

lateritic soils. A red residual soil in humid tropical regions from which soluble minerals have been leached but that still contains concentrations of iron oxides and iron hydroxides. When organic compounds are removed, the soils become impermeable.

liquidation cutting. When the objective of logging is to remove all merchantable product from the forest with no regard to either stand improvement or regeneration. It often precedes an outright sale of the land.

log deck. See **landing.**

log rule. The convention used to measure the amount of usable lumber in a tree or log based on diameter and length. There are three common log rules used in the United States: the International 1/4-inch rule, the Doyle rule, and the Scribner rule.

mast. Fruits or nuts used as a food source by wildlife. Soft mast includes most fruits with fleshy coverings, such as persimmon, dogwood seed, or black gum seed. Hard mast refers to nuts such as acorns, beech, pecan. and hickory.

maturity. In forest trees it is usually expressed in one of two ways: (1) financial maturity is when a tree has reached the point where it has maximized value growth from the perspective of the marketplace; and (2) biological maturity is when a tree has reached the point where the energy costs of maintaining itself exceeds the energy input from photosynthesis. Most biologically mature trees are much older than the age of financial maturity.

MBF. An abbreviation for *1,000 board feet.*

merchantable. A standing tree that has a net value when processed and delivered to a mill or some other market after all harvesting and transportation costs are considered.

meristem. The cells capable of dividing in plants.

mid-successional. An association of plant and animal species that replace early-successional species but are eventually replaced by climax species in the absence of disturbance.

mixed hardwoods. Timber stands, characterized by a mixture of hardwood tree species, including oaks, basswood, white ash, hickories, soft maple, and others. A mixture of forest types.

mortality. Trees that die before the end of the rotation and are usually not harvested.

mycorrhiza. A mutually beneficial relationship between plant roots and some species of fungi.

nonpoint source pollution. Any source of pollution that does not originate from a pipe or other easily identifiable source.

northern hardwoods. A forest region composed of forest types that include sugar maple, yellow birch, and American beech, and may also include red maple, white ash, black cherry, and softwoods such as red spruce and hemlock.

old growth. A self-perpetuating forest community that has reached a dynamic steady state (i.e., changes occur in the community only when gaps are formed as old trees die out, but the changes do not affect the overall character of the community) in the absence of silvicultural treatments. The dominant vegetation is considered to be climax with all age classes present.

operable. In reference to harvesting, a set of conditions including site access, prescription difficulty, and potential product values that, in total, determine if a site is worth logging.

overmature. A stand of trees that is older than normal rotation age for the type and trees are beginning to decline.

overstory. The topmost canopy of a forest, but usually stated in reference to the largest trees.

partial harvest. An official-sounding term that simply means only a portion of the merchantable stand is to be, or was, removed.

perennial stream. A stream that is always flowing. See also **stream.**

permeability. An indication of the amount of pore space in a soil and the degree to which a soil will drain if there are layers that are impermeable.

pioneers. Shade-intolerant species, such as aspen and paper birch, that are the first trees to invade recently disturbed sites and abandoned fields.

pole timber. A dbh size class representing trees that are larger than saplings but smaller than sawtimber; usually more than 4.0 inches dbh and less than 10.0 inches.

precommercial. A silvicultural treatment not expected to result in net revenue.

prebunch. The process of bringing logs or tree lengths to the side of a main skid trail from where they are extracted to a landing.

preparatory cut. The first phase of a three-cut shelterwood system that removes species that will not be favored in the next stand.

prescription. A course of action to effect change in a forest stand.

productivity. Growth per unit time.

provenance. The precise location where seed was gathered to produce seedlings in a nursery.

reforestation. The natural or artificial restocking of an area with trees; it usually implies the former stand is already gone.

regeneration. The natural or artificial renewal of trees in a stand; it usually implies that the existing stand will be used to help secure regeneration.

regeneration cutting. Trees are removed from the stand to create conditions that will allow the forest to reproduce a new stand of trees. This is accomplished using either even-aged or uneven-aged methods.

release. The freeing of well-established cover trees, usually large seedlings or saplings, from closely surrounding growth. It is usually accomplished by means of a precommercial treatment, often done with brushsaws.

removal cut. The final cut of a shelterwood system that removes the remaining mature trees, releasing the young stand.

residual. Trees that are left to grow in the stand following a silvicultural treatment.

root collar. The point where the main stem of a tree emerges from the ground.

rill erosion. An erosion process in which numerous small channels, only several inches deep, are formed. Occurs mainly on disturbed and exposed soils.

riparian. Pertaining to the banks of a stream, river, or pond.

rotation. The length of time it takes to grow an even-aged stand to the point of financial maturity; the culmination of mean annual increment.

rotation age. The age at which a stand is considered ready for harvest under the adopted plan of management or the culmination of mean annual increment.

runoff. Precipitation that does not percolate into the soil.

salvage cutting. The removal of dead, dying, or damaged trees, usually following a natural calamity, to recover timber before bacteria and fungi cause devaluation.

sanitation cutting. The removal of trees to prevent the spread of infection or infestation.

sapling. Trees that are more than 4.5 feet tall but less than 4.0 inches dbh.

sawlog. A log considered suitable in size and quality for producing lumber. Technically, a sawlog is at least 16 feet long, plus a "trim allowance" of 4 or more inches.

sawtimber. Trees that have obtained a minimum diameter at breast height that can be felled and processed into sawlogs.

scaling logs. The process of estimating log volumes and values.

scarification. Disturbance of upper soil layers in forests to expose mineral soil for the purposes of creating a seed bed for natural or artificial seeding.

seedlings. Trees that are less than 4.5 feet tall.

seed tree. An even-aged reproduction method that removes most of the trees in one cut, leaving a few scattered trees of desired species to serve as a source of seed for the new stand.

selection method. Removing mature timber as scattered individual trees or in small groups over relatively short intervals. Encourages continuous reproduction of shade-tolerant species in uneven-aged stands.

selective logging or harvest. A term often used to imply silviculture but in fact has no silvicultural meaning. The term simply means someone has designated trees for harvest.

shade tolerance. The capacity of a tree to regenerate and grow in the shade of, and in competition with, other trees. Sugar maple is an example of a highly shade-tolerant species.

shelterwood. An even-aged reproduction method that uses a series of two or three treatments to gradually open the stand and stimulate natural reproduction of mid- to highly-tolerant species.

silviculture. The art and science of growing forests for timber and other values.

single-tree selection. The removal of individual trees under uneven-aged regeneration methods.

site index. A measure of the relative productive capacity of an area based on total tree height relative to age.

site preparation. An activity intended to make conditions favorable for planting or for the establishment of natural regeneration.

skidder. A four-wheel drive, tractor-like vehicle, articulated in the middle for maneuverability, with a cable or grapple on the back end for bringing logs from the stump to a landing area.

skid trail. Any path in the woods over which multiple loads of logs have been dragged. A trail that enters a main landing area is called a primary skid trail.

slash. Debris left after logging, including branches, twigs, leaves, and other vegetative debris.

slope. The angle of incline of the terrain usually expressed as a percentage of vertical rise over a horizontal distance. See also **grade.**

snag. A standing dead tree or part of a dead tree.

soil pH. A numerical designation of the acidity or alkalinity of a soil solution. Technically, pH is the common logarithm of the reciprocal of the hydrogen ion concentration of a solution. A pH of 7.0 indicates a neutral solution; higher values indicate increasing alkalinity, and lower values indicate increasing acidity. Most forest soils are slightly to moderately acidic.

stand. A local expression of a forest type (usually one that has been disturbed in the past) occupying a specific area and sufficiently uniform in composition, age, arrangement, and condition as to be distinguishable from adjacent areas.

stem. The above-ground portion of a tree between ground level and the first main branches in the canopy.

stream. A natural flowing of water; an *ephemeral stream* flows only during, and for short periods following, precipitation and flows in low areas that may or may not have a well-defined channel; an *intermittent stream* flows only during wet periods of the year (30 to 90 percent of the time) and flows in a well-defined channel; and a *perennial stream* flows throughout a majority of the year (greater than 90 percent of the time) and flows in a well-defined channel.

stocking. An indication of the number of trees in a stand as compared to the optimum number of trees to achieve some management objective, usually improved growth rates or timber values.

strip cut. A clearcut laid out as a long narrow strip.

structure. The vertical and horizontal arrangement of vegetation in a forest. See also **stocking; density.**

stumpage. The value of timber as it stands in the woods just before harvest (on the stump).

stump sprouts. Dormant buds under the bark of most hardwood species that begin to develop (usually at or just below the stump surface) into new stems when a tree has been cut or the stem is severely damaged.

succession. The orderly and predictable replacement of one plant community by another over time in the absence of disturbance.

suckers. A stem that forms from adventitious buds on the roots of some hardwood species, such as aspen and American beech, that begins to develop when a tree has been cut or the stem and root system has been severely damaged.

sustained yield. An annual or periodic output of products from the forest without impairment of the productivity of the land.

sustainability. The capacity of an ecosystem to provide benefits in perpetuity without substantially compromising ecosystem integrity.

switchback. A 180-degree change in the direction of a trail or road for climbing steep slopes.

TDML. An abbreviation for *total daily maximum load*. See **total daily maximum load.**

tenure. Customary or legal rights that arise from former use of a resource.

thinning. Generally, a reduction in the number of trees in an immature forest stand to reduce tree density and concentrate growth potential on fewer, higher-quality trees.

threatened species. An organism that is at risk of becoming endangered and extinct.

timber stand improvement (TSI). Activities conducted in young stands of timber to improve growth rate and form of the remaining trees.

tolerance. The ability of a tree to regenerate and grow satisfactorily in the shade of, or in competition with, other trees. Trees that are classified as tolerant can survive and grow under continuous shade.

total daily maximum load (TDML). An indicator of sedimentation caused by timber harvesting practices that could be used to regulate logging.

treatment. Any action in forest stands that is controlled by a silvicultural prescription.

TSI. An abbreviation for *timber stand improvement*. See **timber stand improvement.**

understory. In forests, the vegetation that occupies an area between the forest floor and the main canopy of the stand.

uneven-aged management. Also called *all-aged management*. A timber management method that produces a stand composed of a wide range of ages and tree sizes.

veneer. A very thin product obtained from defect-free, high-value logs that are peeled or sliced to obtain sheets as thin as paper.

volume table. A table that utilizes dbh or log diameters and log heights (usually 16 feet) or actual log lengths to estimate board foot volumes according to a set of assumptions (known as the *log rule*) about how the log will be processed into boards.

weeding. See **cleaning.**

wildlife habitat. The sum total of environmental conditions of a specific place occupied by a wildlife species or a combination of such species.

windthrow. A forest tree that has been toppled due to high winds, usually coupled with wet ground conditions. It is a common phenomenon along the margins of strip cuts, forest roads, wide skid trails, and clearcuts.

yard. *1.* Any place where animals congregate for protection from the elements. In northern climates, deer will seek coniferous cover to "yard" during the coldest part of winter. *2.* The process of bringing logs to a landing, or the landing itself.

yield. Total forest growth over a specified period of time, less mortality, unmarketable fiber, and cull.

yield table. A species-specific representation of the amount of useable wood fiber a forest can be expected to produce during a single rotation based upon site index.

Literature Cited

Armson, K. A. 1977. *Forest soils*. Toronto: University of Toronto Press.

Bormann, F. H., and G. E. Likens. 1981. *Pattern and process in a forested ecosystem*. New York: Springer-Verlag.

Brand, S. 1994. *How buildings learn: What happens after they're built*. New York: Viking Press.

Braun, L. E. 1950. *Deciduous forests of eastern North America*. Philadelphia: Blakiston.

Brown, L. R., C. Flavin, H. French, J. Abramovitz, C. Bright, and S. Dunn. 1998. *State of the world 1998: A Worldwatch Institute report on progress toward a sustainable society*. New York: W. W. Norton.

Chamberlain, J. L., R. J. Bush, A. L. Hammett, and P. A. Araman. 2002. Managing for nontimber products. *Journal of Forestry* (January–February): 8–14.

Daniels, T. W., J. A. Helms, and F. S. Baker. 1979. *Principles of silviculture*. 2nd ed. New York: McGraw-Hill.

DeCoster, L., ed. 2000. *Forest fragmentation 2000 Conference*. Sampson Group. Washington, D.C. Conference Proceedings. December 22, 2000. Radisson Hotel, Annapolis, Maryland.

Duerr, W. A., and W. E. Bond. 1952. Optimum stocking of a selection forest. *Journal of Forestry* 50 (1): 12–16.

Eldredge, N. 2001. *The sixth extinction*. http://www.actionbioscience.org/newfrontiers/eldredge2.html.

Emery, M. R., and R. J. McLain, eds. 2001. *Non-timber forest products: Medicinal herbs, fungi, edible fruits and nuts, and other natural products from the forest*. New York: Food Products Press.

Foth, H. D. 1978. *Fundamentals of soil science*. 6th ed. New York: John Wiley & Sons.

Fowells, H. A. 1965. *Silvics of forest trees of the United States*. Washington, D.C.: USDA Forest Service. Agricultural Handbook No. 271.

Grime, J. P. 1979. *Plant strategies and vegetation processes*. New York: John Wiley & Sons.

Haney, H. L., W. Hoover, W. Siegel, J. Greene. 2001. *Forest Landowner's Guide to the Federal Income Tax*. USDA Forest Service. Agriculture Handbook No. 718. http://www.fs.fed.us/publications/2001/01jun19-Forest_Tax_Guide31201.pdf.

Harris, L. D. 1984. *The fragmented forest: Island biogeography theory and the presentation of biotic diversity*. Chicago: University of Chicago Press.

Hartmann, H. T., D. E. Kester, F. T. Davies, Jr. 1990. *Plant propagation: Principles and practices.* 5th ed. Englewood Cliffs, N.J.: Prentice Hall.

Horn, H. S. 1971. *The adaptive geometry of trees.* Princeton, N.J.: Princeton University Press.

Hughes, J. 2003. Personal Communication.

Hutchinson, S. B. 1969. Bringing conservation into the mainstream of American thought. *Natural Resources Journal* 9:518–536.

Ingestad, T. 1974. Towards optimum fertilization. *Ambio* 3:49–54.

Irland, L. C., ed. 1996. *Ethics in forestry.* Portland, Ore: Timber Press.

Jones, E. T., R. J. McLain, J. Weigand, eds. 2002. *Nontimber forest products in the United States.* Lawrence, Kans.: University Press of Kansas.

Kossuth, S. V., and S. D. Ross. 1987. *Hormonal control of tree growth.* Dordrecht, Netherlands: Martinus Nijhoff Publishers.

Kozlowski, T. T., P. J. Kramer, and S. G. Pallardy. 1991. *The physiological ecology of woody plants.* New York: Academic Press.

Landsberg, J. J., and S. T. Gower. 1997. *Applications of physiological ecology to forest management.* New York: Academic Press.

Leak, W., and J. Riddle. 1979. *Why trees grow where they do in New Hampshire forests.* Durham, N.H.: USDA Forest Service, Northeastern Forest Experiment Station. NE-INF-37-79.

Leopold, A. 1933. *Game management.* New York: Charles Scribner's Sons.

———. 1966. *A Sand County almanac: With essays on conservation from Round River.* New York: Oxford University Press.

McCarthy, J. J., O. F. Canziani, N. A. Leary, D. J. Dokken, K. S. White, eds. 2001. *Climate change 2001: Impacts, adaptation and vulnerability.* Cambridge: Cambridge University Press. Available online at http://www.ipcc.ch/pub/reports.htm.

McEvoy, T. J. 1990. *An introduction to the ecology and management of hardwoods in Florida.* Gainsville, Fla.: University of Florida. Cooperative Extension Service Circular 889.

———. 1998. *Legal aspects of owning and managing woodlands.* Washington, D.C.: Island Press.

———. 2000. *Introduction to forest ecology and silviculture.* 2nd ed. NRAES Publication No. 126. Natural Resource, Agriculture, and Engineering Service, Cornell Univ., Ithaca, N.Y.

———. 2002a. The founder of forest science. *Forest Products Equipment* 11, no. 4 (December): 14–16.

———. 2002b. *Using fertilizers in the culture of Christmas trees.* 2nd ed. Bolton Valley, Vt.: Racing Dreams.

———. 2003. A new silviculture. *Forest Products Equipment* 11, no. 5 (January): 29–32.

Miller, S., C. Scharf, M. Miller 2002. Utilizing new crops to grow the biobased market. Pp. 26–28 in *Trends in new crops and new uses.* Janick, J. and A. Whipkey (eds.) Alexandria, Va.: ASHS Press.

Morey, P. R. 1973. *How trees grow.* Southhampton, UK: Camelot Press.

Myers, R. L. 1985. Fire and the dynamic relationship between Florida sandhill and sand pine scrub vegetation. *Bulletin of the Torrey Botanical Club* 112 (3): 241–252.

Myers, R. L., and D. L. White. 1987. Landscape history and changes in sandhill vegetation in north-central and south-central Florida. *Bulletin of the Torrey Botanical Club* 114 (1): 21–32.

Ordway, S. H. 1949. *A conservation handbook.* New York: The Conservation Foundation.

Perkey, A., and C. Smith. 1993. *Crop tree management in eastern hardwoods.* USDA Forest Service Publication NA-TP-19-93. Available in pdf format at http://www.fs.fed.us/na/morgantown/frm/perkey/ctm/ctm_index.html.

Pinchot, G. 1909. *The fight for conservation.* New York: Doubleday.

———. 1914. *The training of a forester.* Philadelphia: J. B. Lippincott.

Pritchett, W. L., and R. F. Fischer. 1987. *Properties and management of forest soils.* 2nd ed. New York: John Wiley & Sons.

Rhee, I. 1994. *Development of biodegradable hydraulic fluids for military applications.* U.S. Army Tank-Automotive Research, Development and Engineering Center. Warren, Mich. http://www.dtic.mil/ndia/pollution/sik.pdf.

Schmitz, D. C., and D. Simberloff. 1997. Biological invasions: A growing threat. *Issues in Science and Technology Online.* http://www.nap.edu/issues/13.4/schmidt.htm.

Schnur, G. L. 1937. *Yield, stand and volume tables for even-aged upland oak forests.* USDA Forest Service, Technical Bulletin No. 560.

Schulze, E., M. Küppers, R. Matyssek. 1986. The roles of carbon balance and branching pattern in the growth of woody species. In *On the economy of plant form and function,* edited by T. J. Givnish. New York: Cambridge University Press.

Schwartz, M. W. 1988. Species diversity patterns in woody flora on three North American peninsulas. *Journal of Biogeography* 15:759–774.

Shane, J. 2003. Personal Communication.

Shigo, A. L. 1979. *Tree decay: An expanded concept.* USDA Forest Service Information Bulletin No. 419. Stock no. 001-000-03937-7. Washington, D.C.: U.S. Government Printing Office.

Smith, D. M. 1997. *The practice of silviculture: Applied forest ecology.* 9th ed. New York: John Wiley & Sons.

Thomas, L. 1974. *The lives of a cell: Notes of a biology watcher.* New York: Viking Press.

Tisdale, S. L., W. L. Nelson, J. D. Beaton, J. L. Havlin. 1993. *Soil fertility and fertilizers.* 5th ed. New York: Macmillan.

Tompkins, P., and C. Bird. 1973. *The secret life of plants.* New York: Harper and Row.

Watts, W. A. 1971. Postglacial and interglacial vegetation history of southern Georgia and central Florida. *Ecology* 52 (4): 676–690.

Wenger, K. F., ed. 1984. *Forestry handbook.* 2nd ed. New York: John Wiley & Sons.

Wiest, R. L. 1998. *A landowner's guide to building forest access roads.* USDA Forest Service, Northeastern Area, State and Private Forestry. Publication No. NA-TP-06-98. Radnor, Penn.

Index